THE FIRST YEAR
OF
ROMAN LAW

BY

FERNAND BERNARD

Docteur en Droit
Professeur Libre de Droit

TRANSLATED BY

CHARLES P. SHERMAN, D. C. L.

Instructor in Roman Law at Yale University;
of the Connecticut and Massachusetts Bars;
of the Bar of the Supreme Court
of the United States

THE LAWBOOK EXCHANGE, LTD.
Clark, New Jersey

ISBN-13: 9781584778868 (hardcover)
ISBN-10: 1584778865 (hardcover)
ISBN-13: 9781616190224 (paperback)
ISBN-10: 1616190221 (paperback)

Lawbook Exchange edition 2009

The quality of this reprint is equivalent to the quality of the original work.

THE LAWBOOK EXCHANGE, LTD.
33 Terminal Avenue
Clark, New Jersey 07066-1321

Please see our website for a selection of our other publications and fine facsimile reprints of classic works of legal history:
www.lawbookexchange.com

Library of Congress Cataloging-in-Publication Data

Bernard, Fernand.
 The first year of Roman law / by Fernand Bernard ; translated by Charles Phineas Sherman.
   p. cm.
 Originally published: New York, Oxford University Press, American Branch, [c1906].
 Includes bibliographical references and index.
 ISBN-13: 978-1-58477-886-8 (cloth : alk. paper)
 ISBN-10: 1-58477-886-5 (cloth : alk. paper)
 1. Roman law. 2. Roman law--History. I. Sherman, Charles Phineas, b. 1874 II. Title.
 KJA147.B45 2008
 340.5'4--dc22   2008003776

Printed in the United States of America on acid-free paper

THE FIRST YEAR
OF
ROMAN LAW

BY

FERNAND BERNARD

Docteur en Droit
Professeur Libre de Droit

TRANSLATED BY

CHARLES P. SHERMAN, D. C. L.

Instructor in Roman Law at Yale University;
of the Connecticut and Massachusetts Bars;
of the Bar of the Supreme Court
of the United States

OXFORD UNIVERSITY PRESS
AMERICAN BRANCH
NEW YORK: 91 AND 93 FIFTH AVENUE
LONDON: HENRY FROWDE

COPYRIGHT 1906
BY
OXFORD UNIVERSITY PRESS
AMERICAN BRANCH

AUTHOR'S PREFACE

THIS small work, in spite of its restricted dimensions, is not a *memento*.[1] I have desired to write a book by which one begins, and not a book by which one finishes. I have dwelt upon fundamental principles and have avoided details which in the most of the brochures designed to be read over by the student the night before examination are furnished in abundance, in the style of a telegram. . . . This is not said to attack *mementos*: there are many excellent ones among them, and these render to law school students unquestionable services, conditioned on being consulted at the right time.

I have made in this summary work no claim to erudition, but I have applied to it great solicitude for exactness and modernness of doctrine.

If I have thought it proper to indicate authorities almost paragraph by paragraph, it is because I had need of preserving myself from any involuntary error. It is also because I have provided for the case where some student should make use of my little book as an index, or as a bibliography easy to consult.

The notes, which, outside of this supposition, may interest students, and should attract their attention, are marked with an asterisk (*).

* I have not tried to embellish my treatise with refer-

[1] That is, a small publication designed to refresh the memory in preparation for an examination in some subject : a sort of short synoptic work or digest. — S.

ence, to foreign Romanists,[1] and with citations which can be multiplied the more easily, as quite often they are produced at second hand.

Thinking I should follow very closely the teachings of the law faculty of Paris, I have laid under contribution only five authors, quite contemporaneous, and whose works are in the hands or at the command of every student: MM. Cuq (*Institutions juridiques des Romains*); Esmein (*Mélanges*); Girard (*Manuel élémentaire de droit romain* and *Textes de droit romain*); Gérardin (Articles in the *Nouvelle Revue historique*); Jobbé-Duval (*Études sur l'histoire de la procedure civile*).

The paging indicated in the notes is that of the last edition of the works cited.

[1] That is, civilians, or authorities on the Roman or civil law. — S.

TRANSLATOR'S INTRODUCTORY NOTE

THE object of this labor of love is to place in the hands of students, and of others who desire an acquaintance, readily obtained, with the Roman law, an English version of a French work, designed for use in the law schools of France, which is remarkable for several excellencies that adapt it to become perhaps the best elementary treatise for commencing the study of Roman law. The volume is brief and summary, its style is clear, succinct, and often terse, and withal the book is interestingly written: all of which qualities, coupled with the exactness of Dr. Bernard, render this work authoritatively reliable on the subject of Roman law, as well as appealing by its charms of style to the reader's interest.

The progress of events and the now changed conditions of our national life should sooner or later lead to a revival in this country of the study of the civil law, if for no other reason than that it directly underlies the common law of most of the colonial dependencies of the United States. To be of any service in aiding this movement even by rendering accessible to the American student a book well fitted by its intrinsic merits and its size to be used as a guide to the beginner or investigator in Roman law, would be a privilege not lightly prized.

This is a suitable opportunity to acknowledge the indebtedness of the translator for many useful suggestions and much helpful advice from the late Professor Albert S. Wheeler of Yale University, a teacher of preëminent ability and of great power, who was profoundly learned in Roman law and kindred subjects. To William Frederic Foster, D. C. L., recently professor at and secretary of the Yale Law School, the thanks of the translator are expressed for his acts of kindness and assistance.

The translator has added an index, there being none in the French edition; and his footnotes are marked "S," or are indicated by the use of brackets "[ ]."

CONTENTS

BOOK I

HISTORY OF THE ROMAN LAW

	SECTIONS
DIVISION	1

TITLE I

FIRST PERIOD — LEGENDARY PERIOD

CHAPTER I. The Patrician City	2–15
CHAPTER II. The Patrician-Plebeian City.	
Section I. The End of the Royal Period . . .	16–21
Section II. The Beginnings of the Republic . .	22–33

TITLE II

SECOND PERIOD — HISTORIC REPUBLICAN PERIOD

CHAPTER I. The Rise of the Plebs	34–51
CHAPTER II. The Decadence of the Republic . . .	52–57
CHAPTER III. Sources of Law during this Period . .	58–67

TITLE III

THIRD PERIOD — THE IMPERIAL DUARCHY .	68–83

TITLE IV

FOURTH PERIOD — THE TRUE MONARCHY .	84–92

TITLE V

FIFTH PERIOD — THE LATER EMPIRE — JUSTINIAN	93–101

CONTENTS

BOOK II

PERSONS

TITLE I

PRELIMINARY CONCEPTIONS . . . 102–106

TITLE II

STATUS LIBERTATIS

CHAPTER I. Freemen and Slaves.
   Section I. Condition of Slaves 107–115
   Section II. Sources of Slavery 116–130
   Section III. Quasi-Slavery 131–139
CHAPTER II. Freeborn and Freed.
   Section I. Manumission 140–157
   Section II. Condition of Freedmen 158–175

TITLE III

STATUS CIVITATIS

DIVISION 176
CHAPTER I. Citizens 177–190
CHAPTER II. Non-citizens.
   Section I. Peregrini properly so-called . . . 191–194
   Section II. Latins 195–205

TITLE IV

STATUS FAMILIAE

CHAPTER I. The Roman Family 206–218
CHAPTER II. The Paternal Power 219–233
CHAPTER III. Sources of the Patria Potestas . . . 234
   Section I. Justae Nuptiae.
     § 1. Marriage and Manus 235–255
     § 2. The Essential Conditions of Marriage . . 256–268
     § 3. Effects of Marriage 269–277
     § 4. Dissolution of Marriage 278–288
     § 5. Second Marriages 289–291

CONTENTS

Section II. Adoption.
  § 1. Adoption in General 292–299
  § 2. Arrogatio 300–314
  § 3. Adoption properly so-called 315–323
Section III. Legitimation 324–329
CHAPTER IV. Dissolution of the Paternal Power . . 330–340
  Appendix to Titles I to III and to Sections I to IV of Title IV of Book II. Capitis deminutiones 341–354
CHAPTER V. Incapacities of Fact.
  Section I. Preliminary Notions 355
  Section II. Tutela.
    § 1. Tutela in General 356
    § 2. Guardianship of Minors 357–392
    § 3. Guardianship of Women (tutela mulierum) 393–397
  Section III. Curatelae
    § 1. Of Curatela in General 398, 399
    § 2. Curatorship of the Furiosus 400–403
    § 3. Curatorship of the Spendthrift (prodigus) 404–407
    § 4. Curatorship of Minors under the Age of Twenty-five Years 408–423

BOOK III

THINGS

TITLE I

DIVISION OF THINGS 424–438

TITLE II

SUMMARY NOTIONS AS TO OBLIGATIONS

CHAPTER I. The Obligatory Right and its Sources 439–444
CHAPTER II. Formalism 445–463

CONTENTS

BOOK IV

ACTIONS

TITLE I

GENERAL AND HISTORICAL NOTIONS— THE COURTS 464–483

TITLE II

SYSTEMS OF PROCEDURE

CHAPTER I. The Legis Actiones 484–502
CHAPTER II. The Formulary Procedure.
  Section I. Fundamental Idea of the System . 503–505
  Section II. Composition of the Formula 506–521
  Section III. Powers and Rôle of the Judex . . 522–534
  Section IV. Duration of Actions and of Proceedings 535–542
  Section V. Classification of Actions 543–548
  Section VI. Sketch of a Lawsuit in the Formulary Era 549–563
CHAPTER III. The Extraordinary Procedure . . . 564–566

BOOK V

OWNERSHIP

TITLE I

ATTRIBUTES AND EVOLUTION OF OWNERSHIP 567–570

TITLE II

POSSESSION

CHAPTER I. Elements, Acquisition, Loss of Possession 571–584
CHAPTER II. Possessory Protection 585–596

CONTENTS

TITLE III

DIFFERENT KINDS OF OWNERSHIP . . 597–602

TITLE IV

SANCTION FOR THE RIGHT OF OWNERSHIP

CHAPTER I. Generalities 603
CHAPTER II. Rei Vindicatio 604–619
CHAPTER III. The Actio Publiciana 620–623
CHAPTER IV. Other Actions protecting Ownership . 624–626

TITLE V

MODES OF ACQUIRING OWNERSHIP

DIVISION 627, 628
CHAPTER I. Modes of the Jus Civile 629–663
CHAPTER II. Modes of the Natural Law 664–672

TITLE VI

EXTINCTION OF THE RIGHT OF OWNERSHIP 673, 674

TITLE VII

CIVIL AND PRAETORIAN DISMEMBERMENTS OF THE RIGHT OF OWNERSHIP

CHAPTER I. Civil Dismemberments of Ownership .   675
  Section I. Praedial Servitudes.
    § 1. Character and Divisions of Praedial Servitudes 676–690
    § 2. Acquisition of Praedial Servitudes . . . 691–700
    § 3. Extinguishment of Praedial Servitudes . 701–704
  Section II. Personal Servitudes   705
    § 1. Usufructus 706–722
    § 2. Usus, Habitatio, Operae 723–726
  Section III. Actions relative to Servitudes . . . 727–734
CHAPTER II. Praetorian Dismemberments of the Right of Ownership 735–746

BOOK VI

SUCCESSIONS

TITLE I

SUCCESSION IN GENERAL — INSTITUTION OF THE HEIR   747–760

TITLE II

CONDITIONS FOR THE VALIDITY OF WILLS

CHAPTER I.   Forms of Wills   761–768
CHAPTER II. Conditions Fundamental to the Validity of Wills (testamenti factio)   769–777
CHAPTER III. Invalidation of Wills   778–782
CHAPTER IV. Freedom to make a Will and its Restrictions   783–790

TITLE III

INTESTATE SUCCESSION   . . .   791–798

TITLE IV

ACCEPTANCE AND DISCLAIMER OF THE INHERITANCE   799–812

TITLE V

FIDEICOMMISSA HEREDITATIS . . .   813–818

TITLE VI

ACTIONS CONCERNING THE HEREDITAS   .   819–823

BOOK VII

DONATIONES INTER VIVOS AND MORTIS CAUSA

DIVISION 824, 825

CONTENTS xiii

TITLE I

DONATIONES INTER VIVOS

CHAPTER I. Gifts Inter Vivos.
   Section I.   Gifts in General 826–837
   Section II. Gifts between Husband and Wife . 838–840
CHAPTER II. Provisions in Favor of Marriage.
   Section I. Dos 841–853
   Section II. Donatio Propter Nuptiae 854

TITLE II

DONATIONES MORTIS CAUSA

CHAPTER I. Gifts Mortis Causa 855–860
CHAPTER II. Legacies and Fideicommissa.
   Section I.   Codicils 861–864
   Section II. Legacies 865–875
   Section III. Singular Fideicommissa 876, 877
   Section IV. Restriction of the Right to make
              Legacies — the lex Falcidia . . . 878–881
   Section V. Effects of Legacies and Fideicom-
              missa 882–900

THE
FIRST YEAR OF ROMAN LAW

BOOK I

HISTORY OF THE ROMAN LAW

DIVISION

1. Periods of the History of the Roman Law: Several divisions have been given, however sufficiently close to each other, of the history of the Roman law. The most widespread and best founded is that which distinguishes: —

(1) *A legendary period* (from the origin of Rome to the law of the XII Tables, 754 B. C.–449 B. C.).

(2) *A historic republican period* (from the law of the XII Tables to the principate of Augustus, 449 B. C.–27 B. C.).

(3) The first period of the principate or *period of duarchy* (from Augustus to Diocletian, 27 B. C.–284 A. D.).

(4) The second period of the principate or *period of true monarchy* (from Diocletian to the fall of the empire of the West, 284–476 A. D.).

(5) The Byzantine period or *period of the Later Empire*, which ends only at the fall of Constantinople into the hands of the Turks in 1453.

TITLE I

FIRST PERIOD — LEGENDARY PERIOD

CHAPTER I

THE PATRICIAN CITY

2. Beginnings of Rome: The Romans celebrate yearly the 19th of April as the anniversary of the founding of their city, which tradition places with precision in the year 754 B. C. This date is purely legendary: what is certain is that a small fortified town of the name of Rome sprang up from the middle of the eighth century before Christ, on the Palatine, and that the founding of it was attributed to a leader of the name of Romulus. The original population of this small town was increased first by a fusion with a neighboring tribe of Sabine race, settled on the Quirinal, then by an immigration of Etruscans led by a *lucumon* or prince of their country. This threefold origin would explain the division of the ancient Romans into three tribes: the *Ramnenses*, companions of Romulus; the *Titienses* (Sabine warriors of Tatius), the *Luceres* (subjects or companions of the Etruscan lucumon).[1] These are the three *ethnic tribes*, which must not be confounded with the *tribus* (quarters of Rome)[2] which

---

[1] Varro, *De Ling. Lat.* 5, 55; Cicero, *De Re Pub.* 2, 8; Festus, *De Verb. Signif. vis Lucerenses et Tatienses.*†

[2] *Tribus*: analogous to the modern *district* or *ward* of a city. See *infra*, § 32, note 1. — S.

will be considered when we study the enacting of laws and the *comitia tributa*.

3. **The Patrician City:** The three tribes were divided each into *curiae*, the curiae into *decuriae*, the decuriae into *gentes*. "Among the Aryans the *gens* is the primitive social unit. It is a natural institution which rests on relationship. It comprises the whole of the persons who are connected with a common ancestor. The word *gens*, as the words *gignere* and *genitor*, implies the idea of procreation." [1]

"The members of the gentes formed the patriciate. According to tradition, Rome numbered at the beginning one hundred families whose heads (*patres*) formed the Senate of Romulus. Every senator was therefore *pater*, every son of a senator, *patricius*."

4. The *patricii*, when the first heads of the gentes died, the very companions of Romulus, became in their turn the heads of more restricted agglomerations, subdivisions of the primitive gens, connected with each other by the common name *gentilicie* and the domestic sacrifices, and called *familiae*.

5. **Quirites:** The name so familiar of *quirites* is applied therefore to the patricii alone. Writers differ on the origin and primitive meaning of this appellation. Varro derives it from the word *quiris*, which denotes, he says, the Sabine spear, but there is nothing more fanciful than the etymologies given by the Roman writers. The word 'quirites' might mean quite simply "members of the curiae." [2]

---

[1] Cuq, *Institutions*, vol. i, pp. 30, 31.
[2] Cuq, *ibid*. p. 102.

6. The Patrician Family: The internal constitution of Roman society shows us the heads of families exercising round about themselves, under different forms, an almost absolute power over all those who surround them, *dominium* over the slaves, *manus* over the wife, *patria potestas* over the children. It is scarcely more than the name which changes; for over each the *paterfamilias* has the power of life and death. Such to us appears, with its patriarchal constitution, the *familia Romana*, stamped from the beginning with the seal of this character of powerful concentration which it will preserve throughout the ages.

7. However, on very serious occasions, the head of the family holds council with his relatives, but is not bound to follow the advice which he has called forth.

8. The Clients (Clientes): On the origin and nature of the *clientela* there is more rhetoric than important proof. Virgil indeed may show us that in Tartarus the same punishment is inflicted on the son who struck his father and on the *patronus* who cheated his client.

"Pulsatusve parens et fraus innexa clienti."

We are from this therefore scarcely better informed. "The clients," says Cuq, "are, from father to son, in a state of dependence upon one or several members of the gens. . . . They are free, but they are not citizens; they participate in the life of the gens without participating in that of the city. For the client the city does not exist: the state is not concerned with him." [1]

9. How is the tie formed which unites the client to his patronus and to the gens of the latter? Very prob-

[1] Cuq, *Institutions*, vol. i, p. 33.

ably in two ways: (1) The client is a freedman or the descendant of a freedman; (2) The conquered to whom liberty was left, and who were carried to Rome were placed under the surveillance, authority, and protection of a head of a patrician family who took relatively to them the title of 'patronus.'[1]

10. Organization of the State — Royalty: the Senate: The State is organized on the model of the family: at the head of the State, the king, *rex:* royalty is not hereditary but for life. On each vacancy of the throne an *interrex* is appointed, and the sovereign is chosen by the assembly of the people (*comitium*) on the proposal of the interrex or perhaps by the interrex himself.[2]

11. In the same way as the paterfamilias assembles, on great occasions, a council of the family, so the king, head of the army, sovereign judge, pontifex maximus, has near him a *Senate* which aids him with its counsels, which he consults, but whose advice he is not obliged to follow.

12. The Comitia Curiata: To these two wheels of government, the king and the Senate, a third must be added, — the *assembly of the patricians* (the comitium). The comitium is composed of the three tribes (Ramnenses, Titienses, Luceres); each tribe is divided into ten curiae, whence thirty curiae in all. When the question is the enacting of a measure, each curia meets separately and the vote of the majority of

---

[1] Cuq, *Institutions*, vol. i, pp. 33, 34.
[2] Sulla, when he wished to raise himself to the dictatorship, revived this old practice ; he caused to be appointed an interrex, Valerius Flaccus, who proposed to the Senate the appointment of a dictator and the choice of Sulla.†

its members determines the suffrage of the curia. By collecting the suffrages of the curiae, the vote of the comitium is obtained.

The clients do not vote in the comitia curiata. The patricians alone constitute those whom we should call to-day "the qualified electorate."

13. But what was enacted in these curiae? Are there in existence any laws passed by the curiae in the royal period? Pomponius cites a certain number of *leges regiae* supposedly enacted by the curiae; those which he cites are religious regulations referring to points as to which it is certain that the curiae were not consulted.[1]

The XII Tables were drawn up only because the people complained of not having written laws; these complaints would not have had any reason to exist, if there had been under royalty other than an unwritten law. The 'leges regiae' seem, therefore, to belong to legend, and the collection known under the name of *Jus Papirianum (Jous Papeisianom*, alleged collection of 'leges regiae') would be but a compilation of apocryphal documents appearing in the last period of the Republic.

14. But, if it is so, of what use were the comitia curiata? They intervened, according to Girard, to pass measures of concrete order, to sanction, for example, adoption or a will, but it does not appear that they ever had to establish by their vote any measure of general order.[2]

15. Cuq admits, nevertheless, the possibility of the existence of laws of the comitia curiata as to criminal

---

[1] Cuq, *Institutions*, vol. i, pp. 56, 57 ; Girard, *Manuel*, p. 15.
[2] Girard, *ibid*. p. 14.

matters, and sees trace of them in the narrative of the proceedings against Horatius in Livy; he supposes also that the *jus quiritium* (*patrician* law according to Cuq) was established by a law of the comitia curiata. That is not irreconcilable with the claims of the complaining *plebs*, before the drawing up of the XII Tables, that they do not have written laws.[1]

CHAPTER II

THE PATRICIAN-PLEBEIAN CITY

SECTION I. — **The End of the Royal Period**

16. The Plebs: The plebeians did not appear until the second century of Rome. The origin of the plebs (πλῆθος, crowd) is quite problematical; it is supposed that they were recruited among the vanquished population not reduced to slavery, or among the clientes who found themselves without a patronus by reason of the death without issue of the patronus whom they had chosen, if they had been reduced to dependence by the conquest of their country, or who had been placed over them by custom, if their dependence dated from the slavery of their ancestor.[2]

17. The Census: The institution which awoke the plebeians, become more and more numerous, to public life is that of the census or enumeration which is attributed to King Servius Tullius. The census had for its object the numbering of the army and of the taxpayers; but as the Romans did not separate the ideas of military

[1] Cuq, *Institutions*, vol. i, p. 60 *et seq.*
[2] Cuq, *ibid.* p. 43 *et seq.*

service and participation in public affairs, it follows that all the population numbered with a view to taxation and military service becomes the qualified electorate represented solely in former times by the patrician gentes: it is the substitution of the *comitia centuriata* for the comitia curiata.

18. The Comitia Centuriata: The plan of voting by centuriae is easy to comprehend; all *citizens*, patricians and plebeians, are enrolled upon the register of the census and divided into five classes, which themselves are subdivided into hundreds (*centuriae*).

The five classes of the population comprised: —

(1) First: individuals having more than 100,000 as.

(2) Second: those who had 75,000 as.

(3) Third: those who had 50,000 as.

(4) Fourth: those who had 25,000 as.

(5) Fifth: those who had 11,000 or 12,500 as; the figure varies according to the historians.

(At all events, if the census dates from Servius Tullius, the basis of classification was changed afterwards, since the reign of Servius Tullius was far prior to the use of money among the Romans.[1])

19. The five classes answered only for the infantry list, and were supplemented by eighteen centuriae of horsemen (*equites*). The classes were subdivided into hundreds (*centuriae*), with a very unequal number to each class. The first numbered by itself alone eighty centuriae.

20. The total number of the centuriae was one hundred and ninety-three.

While the comitia curiata met at the *comitium* (at the

[1] Girard, *Manuel*, p. 16, note 1.

forum), the comitia centuriata were convoked on the Campus Martius. The suffrages were taken by centuriae.

If only the eighteen centuriae of horsemen (equites) should vote with the first class, composed of eighty centuriae (which gives ninety-eight votes), the majority was immediately obtained, for the total number of the centuriae being one hundred and ninety-three, ninety-seven votes are sufficient to turn the scale.

21. The introduction of the comitia centuriata substituted the influence of wealth for that of birth; but the existence of laws enacted by the centuriae before the XII Tables is a problem as difficult as that of laws of the comitia curiata, and raises the same objections.

Section II. — **The Beginnings of the Republic**

22. **Revolution of 510 B. C.:** In 510 b.c. there comes in Roman history a crisis which transforms the constitution. For a head for life (king) are substituted two annual heads (consuls) elected by the people. Here is a change more serious in reality than in appearance. The Senate, appointed by the consuls as it was formerly by the king, continued under the consuls, who had to account to it.

Furthermore, the king was without an equal: there are two consuls, and what one consul has done the other can undo. However, we shall see the power, at first absolute, of the consuls dismembered little by little by means of the creation of new magistrates.[1]

23. **Dictatorship:** In reality there is in republi-

[1] Girard, *Manuel*, pp. 19, 20.

can Rome but one power which can concentrate in itself all functions; this is the *dictatorship (dictatura)*. The dictator has absolute rights; his power suspends all authority, all liberty, but he can be elected only for six months. So this institution is only an accident, an expedient to which there is not recourse save in great crises.

24. Social Crises: the Nexum: The plebeians had lost nothing, whatever may have been said about it, by the expulsion of the kings, but they had gained nothing through it. If the reform of Servius Tullius benefited those among them who had known how to acquire a fortune, it had not changed the condition of the poor plebeians, that is, of the immense majority of the plebeians.

25. The poor plebeians used to borrow money, and the unwritten law of the time was pitiless toward debtors. The contract of loan then was the 'nexum,' which was made in the presence of five witnesses and a *libripens*, carrying the balance by means of which the metal loaned was weighed (money was not introduced at Rome until 268 B. C.); the creditor who was not paid at maturity had the right to arrest his debtor, sell him *trans Tiberim*, and even to kill him.

26. All crises of the first periods of the Republic occurred on account of the condition of misery and the debts of the plebeians. At different times the latter starved out their oppressors by leaving Rome to withdraw to Mt. Aventine (Aventine and Janiculum were, even under the reign of Augustus, outside of the *pomoerium*). It was endeavored to bring them back, for there was need of them.

27. After the withdrawal of 494 B. C. (sixteen years

after the founding of the Republic), they consented to return to Rome only upon the exacting of guarantees, and these guarantees consisted in the creation of the tribunes of the plebs.

28. **The Tribunate:** The tribunes of the plebs were magistrates annually elected by the plebeians; they were inviolable during their magistracy and had the right of *veto*, that is, the right to arrest by their *intercessio* all acts of magistrates done inside of Rome and its outskirts, not excepting legislative acts.

29. The negative power of the tribunes acquired a greater importance by means of the right, not negative like the right of veto, but positive, of convoking the assembly of the plebs (*concilium plebis*) and of causing it to pass resolutions.

30. In principle the concilium plebis had only the force of a *meeting*, and the resolutions which were there voted, of no authority other than that of orders of the day which are, in our time, voted in public assemblies.

Perhaps these resolutions had the force of law with regard to the plebs, without being binding on the patricians. Nevertheless, it seems that quite early this value was exceptionally attributed to them when the tribunes had them approved by the Senate, before the plebs obtained it.[1]

31. The first sanction of the validity of the *plebiscita* by the *lex Valeria Horatia* is in 449 B. C. (the year of the XII Tables). We will return to it later.[2]

32. **Comitia Tributa:** Ought the comitia tributa to be attached to this period? The 'tribus' here in

[1] Cuq, *Institutions*, vol. i, p. 458.   [2] See §§ 42, 43.

question have nothing in common with the ethnic tribes of which we have spoken above. These are the quarters of Rome;[1] there are four urban tribus (Suburan, Collatine, Palatine, Esquiline) and twenty-six suburban (or rural).[2]

The grouping by tribus was applied by the tribunes at the concilium plebis from 371 B. C.

33. The comitia tributa were held at the forum: they were convoked by a magistrate of the people (*populi* and not *plebis*); they must not be confounded with the concilium plebis; practically they yielded the same results as the plebeian assemblies because the patricians who voted in the comitia tributa were overwhelmed in the number of the plebeians.

The date of the introduction of the comitia tributa, which seems indeed to be only a generalization for the benefit of the whole people of the system in use for the concilium plebis, becomes so much the more uncertain in that one is liable to confound these assemblies with the assemblies of the plebs.

The decemviral law speaks of a *comitiatus maximus*, which would presume the existence of a *comitiatus minor*. Ought we to see in this comitiatus minor the comitia tributa already created at this time?[3]

---

[1] That is, the *district*, *ward*, or *region* (in the sense of the Italian *rione*). Says a modern writer, in treating of the fourteen "rioni" of Rome at the present time: they are wards "into which the city was divided, with occasional modifications, from the time of Augustus to the coming of Victor Emmanuel, and which with some further changes survive to this day." Crawford, *Ave Roma Immortalis*, vol. i, pp. 100, 101. See, also, Morey, *Outlines of Roman Law*, p. 11. — S.

[2] This number was raised to twenty-seven, then to thirty-one.

[3] Cuq, *Institutions*, vol. i, p. 121.

TITLE II

SECOND PERIOD — HISTORIC REPUBLICAN PERIOD

CHAPTER I

THE RISE OF THE PLEBS

34. Compilation of the Law of the XII Tables: In spite of all these reforms and admitting that certain laws of a political order were previously enacted (for example, *lex Valeria*[1] *deprovoc. ad populum*), the law of the Roman people had not ceased to be unwritten.

35. The plebs demand a written law. A proposal made by the tribune Terentillus Arsa results, at the end of eight years, if not in the compilation at least in the preparation of the law: according to the historians, at this time commissioners charged with studying Hellenic laws should have been sent into Greece (more likely into Magna Graecia, that is into the Greek colonies of southern Italy).[2]

36. On the return of the commissioners, in 451 B. C., ten magistrates were appointed, nearly all patricians, of whom the most celebrated was Appius Claudius. These magistrates were the *Decemvirs* (*Decemviri legibus scribendis*).

---

[1] The lex Valeria circumscribed the power of the magistrates to fine, as did the lex Aternia fifty-five years later. See Colquhoun, *A Summary of the Roman Civil Law*, vol. iii, § 2383. — S.

[2] The opinion of Cuq, *Institutions*, vol. i, p. 131, relative to their going to Greece to study the laws is quite skeptical. — S.

37. The first year of their magistracy ten tables were published in the forum; but the work was not complete. Decemvirs were again appointed who published two more tables. The power of the decemvirs ended tragically in the popular uprising which the trial and death of Virginia excited.

38. **Character of the Law of the XII Tables:** The law of the XII Tables is as little Hellenic as can be. The patriarchal family based on the absolute power of the head of the family, — transactions governed principally, perhaps even exclusively, by the system of formalism, — the procedure of legal actions wholly original in its archaism, all that is essentially Roman.

39. **Struggle of the Patricians and Plebeians:** That which characterizes the first three centuries of the Republic is the furious and victorious struggle of the plebeians against the patricians. This struggle is a war of classes, a social war, in the sense which we actually give to this word, quite different from the wars of factions, in the midst of which Roman liberty was to sink, two centuries later.

40. The events of this struggle group themselves about three principal ideas: (1) the destruction of the obstacles which stood in the way of the fusion of the castes; (2) the recognition of the validity of the plebiscita; (3) the conquest of the magistracies.

41. **The Fusion of the Castes:** The law of the XII Tables prohibited marriage between patricians and plebeians. This prohibition was raised in 445 B. C. by the *plebiscitum Canuleium*. From this time there

were formed families who had in their veins both the blood of the gentes and of the plebs.

42. Recognition of the Validity of the Plebiscita: The plebiscitum is the law made by the plebs on the proposal of a tribune: regularly it ought not to be binding on the patricians who did not take part at all in its enactment. The obligatory force of the plebiscita was proclaimed three times: by the *lex Valeria Horatia* 449 B. C., by the *lex Publilia* 339 B. C., and the *lex Hortensia* 288 B. C., which would give rise to the belief either that the first two 'leges' contained some restrictions, or that they had, one after another, ceased to be enforced.

43. To believe the paraphrases of the Institutes of Theophilus, the lex Hortensia should have been a "double stroke" by validating at the same time the plebiscita and the *senatusconsulta*. This affirmation cannot be accepted unreservedly, for it seems out of harmony with the constitutional principles of Roman law.

The Senate, under the Republic, was the true sovereign; but a sovereign perhaps very completely armed without possessing the legislative power; — in order to understand, we have only to consider, in France, the constitution of the second Empire.

The Roman Senate had the right of public administration, of the preparation of bills, of the approval by means of its *auctoritas* of the resolutions of the comitia, but not the right to make laws. So the Senate, before the time of Tiberius, should legislate but rarely, and probably through encroachments rendered more easy by the confusion of powers which existed at this period.[1]

[1] Cuq, *Institutions*, vol. i, pp. 459–462 ; *ibid*. vol. ii, pp. 22–24.

44. Conquest of the Magistracies: The plebeians pursue the division of the supreme authority represented by the consulship. The tactics of the patricians are both simple and curious. When they cannot defend their ground they limit it.

The plebeians are on the point of reaching the consulship as early as 444 B. C.; to save the principle the patricians bring it about that the power shall be exercised by military tribunes, who shall be taken indifferently from the patricians and the plebeians: the *title* alone of consul is temporarily saved.

45. In 367 B. C., the *lex Licinia* definitely opens the consulship to the plebeians: the patricians dismember the consulship by creating at its expense two patrician magistracies, the praetorship and curule edileship.

Labor lost! the plebeians invaded successively all the newly created magistracies: the praetorship, the curule edileship, the censorship; their last conquest was that of the sovereign pontificate in 296 B. C.

46. The Praetorship: One of the institutions created by the patricians in the course of the struggle had a consequence which they did not expect, and played an immense part in the history of the Roman law. We mean the *praetorship*. The praetor, first magistrate of Rome after the consuls, whom he replaced in their absence, had at the same time, like all magistrates of the epoch, administrative, judicial, military powers; but it is above all as a magistrate of the judicial order that the praetors have left in history a profound trace.

47. The praetor appears to us as if invested with both legislative and judicial power. As an instrument

of this legislative power he has the *jus edicendi*, right to make edicts which have for their object the administration, or the completion, or even the *correction* of the civil law (*jus civile*).

48. When the praetor entered into office, he published his edict, that is the collection of rules which he intended to apply while in office, and as to which he was in a short time forbidden to make any change during his magistracy; this edict was posted near the tribunal of the praetor, on a white board called the *album*. It was called the *edictum perpetuum* (permanent edict) in contrast to the *edicta repentina* (unexpected edicts), decisions which the praetor was obliged to make suddenly when there arose a difficulty for which his permanent edict had not provided.

49. The perpetuity of the edictum perpetuum was quite relative, since in law the edict did not survive the power of the magistrate who had made it.

The legislative activity of the praetor caused enormous progress to be made in Roman law.

50. **Jus Honorarium:** By the side of the civil law (jus civile), narrow, brutal, formalistic, the praetors created a law more humane, more philosophical, more spiritualized, more freed from formality. This is the *praetorian law:* it is spoken of, in a larger sense as the "*jus honorarium*" because the jus edicendi belongs not only to the praetors, but also to the *ediles*, magistrates charged with the policing of markets, and to the governors of provinces (*praesides*): all these magistrates have the *jus honorum:* hence the name given to the law which emanates from their initiative.

51. Abolition of Nexum: To complete the picture of plebeian emancipation we will notice, in 326 B. C., the abolition or, more exactly, the attenuation of the consequences of nexum by the *lex Poetelia Papiria:* this measure was considered as marking the entrance of a new era; *aliud initium libertatis.*[1]

CHAPTER II

THE DECADENCE OF THE REPUBLIC

52. In 266 B. C. the conquest of Italy is accomplished. This date marks both the beginning of the immense external expansion of Rome and the commencement of her internal decadence. In the great juridical events of this period, there is recognizable no longer the effort of a people to found institutions, but the convulsions of a people struggling against the general corruption, the ambition of factionists, the rivalries of the parts of the institutions already crumbling.

53. We shall notice in the course of this period only the creation of the *quaestiones perpetuae*, the agrarian laws, and the *leges judiciariae.*

54. **Quaestiones Perpetuae:** The leges Valeriae had assigned criminal justice to the Roman people as a whole assembled in the comitia centuriata: but the people in practice used to intrust the trial of criminal causes to commissions (quaestiones) appointed for the occasion.

[1] Livy, 8, 28.†

55. These commissions took on a general character. Instead of the appointment of commissioners for a given case, the comitia or Senate yearly appoint a permanent commission designated to try such and such kinds of crimes. The commissions were appointed for the entire year: hence the name of quaestiones perpetuae. Each crime had "its tribunal, its procedure and its punishment." The principle of quaestiones perpetuae was laid down in 149 B. C. by the *lex Calpurnia repetundarum* (law against embezzlements).

56. **Agrarian Laws:** These laws do not aim at the division of actual individual estates, but clearly at the division of conquered lands which belonged to the State, and which were granted to individuals in consideration of a rent. The patricians, more wealthy, naturally secured more extensive grants: in course of time they had ceased to pay rent and treated the territorial domain as their own property. — The agrarian laws, with which are associated the names and fame of the Gracchi, had for their object a new distribution of the conquered territory among all the citizens. — We know that the agrarian laws came to no result; the last agrarian law known, the *lex Thoria*, 107 B. C., is a law of reaction.

57. **Leges Judiciariae:** These are the monuments of the struggle between the senators and the knights (equites) on the occasion of the recruiting of the tribunes.[1]

[1] See *infra*, § 477.

CHAPTER III

SOURCES OF LAW DURING THIS PERIOD

58. These sources are: (1) the 'lex;' (2) the 'plebiscitum;' (3) the edicts of magistrates; (4) the 'responsa prudentum.'[1]

59. (1) and (2) **Leges and Plebiscita:** Some of these sources are already well known to us: the 'plebiscitum,' enacted by the plebs alone on the proposal of a tribune in the concilium plebis; the statute (lex), enacted by the entire people on the proposal of a magistrate of senatorial rank, as the consul, either in the comitia centuriata, or in the comitia tributa.[2]

60. The name of 'leges,' however, is not given solely to legislation enacted by the comitia: it is attached also to institutions elaborated by a person charged with the organization of a province and who receives the mandate of the Roman people to endow this province with laws. These laws receive the name of *leges datae*, in contrast with the *leges rogatae*, enacted by the comitia. (The proposal of the magistrate who convokes the comitia is called *rogatio*.[3])

---

[1] Roby, *Roman Private Law*, vol. i, 6, translates these terms as follows: *lex*, "statute," *plebiscitum*, "commons' resolution;" *responsa prudentum*, "answers of skilled lawyers." His attitude as to the retention or translation into English of Roman legal terms is set forth in the Preface of the above work, p. xiii. — S.

[2] For an excellent account of the making of leges and plebiscita, see Colquhoun, *A Summary of the Rom. Civ. Law*, vol. i, 299–304. — S.

[3] We possess some of these *leges datae*: *lex coloniae Genetivae Juliae* (tablet of Orsuna), Girard, *Textes*, p. 87; *lex Salpensana*, *ibid.* p. 107; *lex Malacitana, ibid.* p. 110.

SOURCES OF LAW DURING THIS PERIOD 21

61. The name of 'lex' is furthermore equally given to plebiscita which have, as we know, the same authority as 'leges:' many of the famous 'leges,' the lex Falcidia, the lex Aquilia, the lex Cincia are plebiscita.

62. A 'plebiscitum' is quite easily distinguished from a 'lex' in that the plebiscitum bears the single name of the tribune who proposed it, while the 'lex' bears the names of the two consuls: "Lex Fufia Caninia, lex Poetelia Papiria, lex Valeria Horatia."

63. The 'senatusconsulta' do not count, in the course of this period, as a source of private law.[1]

64. (3) **Edicts of the Magistrates:** (See what has been said on the powers of the praetors and the ediles.) The 'jus edicendi' belongs also to provincial governors.

65. (4) **Responsa Prudentum:** Jurisprudence or the science of the law had been for a long time the secret of the *pontifices*. Cnaeus Flavius, secretary of the pontifex maximus Appius Claudius Caecus, divulged the secret of the *dies fasti* and *nefasti*. To believe Cicero, the pontifices confined themselves to the composition of *formulae*, hoping that this other secret would be better guarded;[2] but their hope was disappointed: Tiberius Coruncanius, the first plebeian pontifex maximus (toward the beginning of the sixth century of Rome), commenced to "*publice respondere*," *i. e.* to give public consultations. This example was followed and gratuitous juridical opinions formed one

[1] See *supra*, § 43.
[2] Cicero, *Pro Murena*, 11.† See, nevertheless, Cuq, *Institutions*, vol. i, pp. 445-448.

of the great means of obtaining the honors which ambitious persons were seeking.

66. Jurisprudence being thus founded and the texts of the laws divulged, Sextus Aelius Catus (consul in 198 B. C.) published a work which was called the *tripertita*.

The tripertita comprised: —

(1) The law of the XII Tables;
(2) Its interpretation;
(3) The actions of the law (*legis actiones*).

The whole of this collection constitutes the *jus Aelianum*.[1]

67. The work of the jurisconsults (*prudentes*) then becomes more easy and frequent. Their functions were: (1) *respondere*, to give opinions; (2) *agere*, to act in court for their clients; (3) *cavere*, to draw up contracts.

[1] *Dig.* 1, 2, 2 (Pomponius), 7.

TITLE III

THIRD PERIOD — THE IMPERIAL DUARCHY

68. The Duarchy: In 27 B. C. Augustus abdicated the dictatorial powers which had been confided to him and made the State to revert — so he says — to the authority of the people and of the Senate. This absolute master of the Roman world posed until his death as an individual, — and the world seemed to believe him!

69. The régime founded by Augustus and perpetuated until Diocletian, régime of unacknowledged despotism, has been called by the Romanists the *duarchy*. The power, in effect, is divided — more theoretically than practically — between the emperor and the Senate. There are the provinces of the Senate and the provinces of Caesar: the *stipendium*, tax from the senatorial provinces, is turned into the *aerarium* (public treasury); the tax from the imperial provinces into the *fiscus* (treasury of the *princeps*).

The Senate can pronounce the deposal of the emperor: it did this with respect to Nero, whom it condemned to death: it can, posthumous justice, cause his statues to be broken. On principle, it appoints the emperor. Finally, it will preserve for some time the appearance or illusion of legislative power.[1] Appearances are saved (quite badly, at least, when the emperor is a Tiberius, a Caligula, or an Elagabalus). The

---
[1] Cuq in his course on Roman public law.†

mask of despotism will not be torn off until by Diocletian.

70. **Sources of Law during this Period:** The 'lex' and the 'plebiscitum' tend to disappear from the commencement of the Empire. There will still be some leges. There are even some celebrated ones among them, as the leges Julia and Pappia Poppea: but under Tiberius the comitia will cease to meet.

71. **The Senatusconsulta:** The second year of the reign of Tiberius (16 A. D.) the legislative power was transferred from the comitia to the Senate, and the people, says Tacitus, protested only by vain murmurs.[1] From this time the 'senatusconsulta' become the normal source of private law. Several senatusconsulta of this epoch are juridical monuments of the first importance: the senatusconsultum Neronianum on legacies;[2] the senatusconsulta Trebellianum and Pegasianum on *fideicommissa*,[3] the senatusconsultum Velleianum on the *intercessio* for women, the senatusconsultum Macedonianum on loans to *filiifamilias*.

72. After a while the senatusconsulta derive their name from one of the consuls for the year: senatusconsultum Trebellianum rendered under Nero, during the consulship of Trebellius and Seneca; — soon they bear the name of the emperor himself: senatusconsultum Neronianum. At other times they derive their

---

[1] Tacitus, *Annales*, 1, 15, gives rise to an ambiguity : *"Tum primum e campo comitia ad patres translata sunt."* It has been held, in arguing from this passage, that it is a question here of the electoral comitia and not of the legislative comitia. Which would leave open the question of knowing at what time the Senate began to exercise legislative power.†

[2] See § 874.   [3] See §§ 816, 817.

name from the person on account of whom they were rendered: senatusconsultum Macedonianum (Macedo was a filiusfamilias who assassinated his father in order to pay the money-lenders by whom he had been exploited).

73. The senatusconsultum is called forth by a request from the emperor termed "*oratio principis.*" It is often designated by the name of Oratio followed by the name of the emperor: "*Oratio Antonini,*" senatusconsultum on gifts between husband and wife passed on the proposal of Antoninus Caracalla. The Senate, through terror or servility, passed into the condition of a chamber of registry, and the senatusconsulta become a form more or less hypocritical of the imperial constitutions which will soon replace them.

74. **Imperial Constitutions:** The emperor united in his person every power and noticeably the 'jus edicendi:'[1] the absolute authority of the emperor in legislative matters is expressed by the maxim: *Quidquid principi placuit legis habet vigorem.*

75. This absolute authority is conferred upon him by the very law which invested him with his powers (*lex regia*).[2]

76. The constitutions of the emperors assume three forms: —

(1) The *edictum*, general ordinance.

(2) The *decretum*, judgment rendered by the emperor in a suit which is submitted to him. This judg-

---

[1] See *supra*, § 47 *et seq.*

[2] We possess in part the *lex regia de imperio Vespasiani* (tablet of bronze discovered at Rome in the fourteenth century). Girard, *Textes*, p. 105.

ment *makes law*, that is, the judges are obliged hereafter to apply the imperial solution to analogous cases.

(3) The *rescript*, of which the *epistola* and the *mandatum* are but varieties: this is an opinion given by the 'princeps' on a point of law submitted to him: the name of 'mandatum' is given to it when it is addressed to an official who has solicited the advice of the emperor; 'epistola' or 'rescriptum' when it is addressed to an individual.

77. Responsa Prudentum: It is fitting to notice the importance which, in the course of this period, the opinions of jurisconsults acquire (responsa prudentum). Before the time of Augustus, the *jus publice respondendi* belonged to all those who felt conscious of the necessary aptitude, but did not confer any official authority upon the opinions emitted.

Augustus, according to a passage of Pomponius (*de origine juris*), the import of which is disputed, conferred on certain jurisconsults a *permissio jura condendi*, that is, of imposing upon the judge the authority of their decisions. This authority would have been, thereafter, demanded as a favor; so that among the prudentes it is necessary to distinguish, from Augustus, two classes: the official jurisconsults having received the 'permissio jura condendi,' and the unofficial jurisconsults having only the 'jus publice respondendi,' whose opinions the judges could disregard.[1]

78. The first period of the principate is the beautiful era of legal literature, — especially the period which

[1] *Dig.* 1, 2, 2 (Pomponius), and § 49. Did this *permissio jura condendi* assign authority to general and abstract decisions or to concrete opinions given on the occasion of a lawsuit ? See *infra*, § 90.

elapses from the dynasty of the Antonines (96 A. D.) to the last years of the dynasty of the Syrian emperors (222 A. D.). This last period is what is called, properly speaking, "the classical era."

79. *Schools of the Jurisconsults:* The Roman jurisconsults themselves are divided, in their writings, into two schools, the Sabinians and the Proculians. These two schools recognized as their leaders the republican Labeo and the imperialist Capito, both of whom lived in the time of Augustus. Labeo is the leader of the Proculians, Capito of the Sabinians: the two schools took, therefore, the names, not of their founders, but of one of their successors (Proculus of the school of Labeo, Sabinus of the school of Capito).

The *essential* difference in doctrine between the two schools escapes us completely, so much so that it has been asked if it was not a matter of the organizations for teaching less differentiated by their doctrine than by their location and their personnel.

80. (1) The most celebrated jurisconsults prior to the accession of the Antonines are: —

(*a*) On the side of the Proculians: Labeo, Proculus, Nerva, Pegasus.

(*b*) On the side of the Sabinians: Capito, Massurius, Sabinus, Coelius Sabinus, Cassius.

81. (2) The great jurisconsults contemporaneous with the Antonines are: Neratius, Javolenus, Julian (author of the codification of the edict), Africanus, Pomponius, Gaius. This last, whose history is unknown to us, and who is believed to have been a jurisconsult of the East, plays in the contemporary teaching of Roman law a part out of proportion to the fame which he appears to

have enjoyed in his own time. This is because his Institutes, discovered in 1816 by Niebuhr under the works of St. Jerome, in palimpsest manuscript of the library of the chapter-house of Verona, are the most complete original juridical document that we possess.

82. (3) The period of the Syrian emperors witnessed the flourishing of Papinian (called the *prince of jurisconsults*), Paulus, Ulpian, all three successively praetorian prefects, and finally Modestinus, the last of the classical jurisconsults, who was 'praefectus vigilum' under Alexander Severus.[1]

83. **The Perpetual Edict:** We have seen that the edict given by each praetor upon his entrance into office did not survive the magistracy of its author. But the rules which had been found good were renewed by the next praetor; so that little by little the permanent edict of the praetor (edict perpetuum) was found to comprise two parts: (1) the 'edictum tralatitium,' composed of rules which were transmitted from praetor to praetor; (2) the 'edictum novum,' composed of new rules which the praetor entering into office proposed to apply. This branch of the law acquired a growing importance, and also, by means of selection, greater and greater stability of ground.

Under Hadrian it was thought that the evolution of the praetorian law could be considered as accomplished, and a senatusconsultum gave directly or indirectly the force of permanent law to the praetorian law codified at this time by the jurisconsult Julian (Salvius

---

[1] *Lis fullonum de pensione solvenda*, 244 A. D. Girard, *Textes*, p. 846.

Julianus).¹ The expression "perpetual edict" changed its meaning: there is no longer a permanence measured by the time of a praetorship, but a real perpetuity *of law* substituted for the perpetuity in fact. The edictum tralatitium became immutable. Nevertheless the magistrates did not lose the right to create new rules for cases not foreseen; that is indisputable, since Gaius, who lived at a later era (he seems to have finished his career under Marcus Aurelius), still writes "*jus edicendi habent magistratus populi Romani;*"² but all the inheritance of the past was put beyond attack by the legislative measure which gave the force of law to the work of Salvius Julianus.³

[1] Eutropius, *Breviarium historiae Romanae*, 8–17; Aurelius Victor, *De Caesaribus*, 19.†
[2] Gaius 1, § 6.   [3] *Code*, 1, 17, 2–18 (Justinian).

TITLE IV

FOURTH PERIOD — THE TRUE MONARCHY

84. Characteristics of this Period: The second period of the principate (period of *monarchy properly so called*) is characterized by the definite disappearance of the senatorial influence and the acknowledged absolutism of the ' princeps.'

85. A new order of succession to the Empire is established by Diocletian: the emperor, the *Augustus*, shares his power with a colleague who bears also the title of *Augustus*. The two Augusti (Diocletian and Maximian) join to themselves two *Caesars* (Galerius and Constantius Chlorus) appointed to govern with the Augusti, but with an inferior authority, and later to succeed them in the first rank and to choose for themselves new Caesars. The senate henceforth will be no longer consulted.

86. New Divisions of the Roman World: Beginning with Diocletian (284 A. D.) the aspect of the empire is completely transformed; the Roman world is divided into four prefectures, the East, Illyria, Italy, and Gaul, governed by four *praetorian prefects*. The prefectures are divided into dioceses administered by *vicarii*, the dioceses into provinces placed under the authority of a *praeses* or *rector*.

87. New Transformation under Constantine: The transformation will become more profound from the accession of Constantine (325 A. D.). A new religion, a new capital; new titles are seen to arise, such as *patricius* (honorary retirement rather than office), *comes consistorianus, quaestor of the imperial palace*. A new nobility (for life and also not hereditary) is established, comprising the *nobilissimi*, the *illustres*, the *spectabiles*, the *egregii*.[1] Rome is ended: the Byzantine empire begins.

88. **Juridical Documents of the Era:** No more great jurisconsults; the juridical documents of this last period consist of the Gregorian and Hermogenian Codes, — which are but individual compilations of imperial constitutions composed by the jurisconsults Gregorius and Hermogenianus, — and the Theodosian Code, the official collection of the constitutions of the emperors, published in 438 A. D. under Theodosius II, and of which a part only has come down to us. There are no longer, furthermore, any sources of law other than the manifold forms of imperial decisions.[2]

89. **The Law of the Citations:** To this last period is attached the constitution which has been called the *law of the citations*. Subsequent to the division of the empire of which we shall speak in the following paragraph, this law of 426 A. D. emanated really from Theodosius II, emperor of the East, but it was published at first in the West in the name of Valentinian III, still a child: this constitution said in substance, "We confirm all the writings of Papinian, Paulus, Gaius, Ulpian, and Modestinus: if they disagree, the majority prevails; if no majority exists on the

---

[1] Joannes Lydus, *Notitia dignitatum Orientis et Occidentis.*†
[2] The last senatusconsultum that we know of is of the reign of Alexander Severus (222–235 A. D.).†

question, the judge should follow the opinion of Papinian."

90. How ought this constitution to be interpreted? According to Accarias it would suppress the 'jus jura condendi.' After the jurisconsults designated in the constitution, all legislative authority is denied to subsequent jurisconsults.

91. Girard thinks, on the contrary, (1) that the 'permissio jura condendi' always referred simply to the 'responsa prudentum' called forth in the suit *for which they had been given ;* (2) that the writings of the jurisconsults had no legislative force; (3) that the law of the citations had had for its object the granting of the posthumous favor of this authority to the five jurisconsults whom it designates.[1]

92. **Formation of the Empires of the East and the West:** On the death of Theodosius I (395 A. D.), the Roman world was divided into two empires, the empire of the East and the empire of the West. The empire of the West, which exists only in name ever since the great invasion overflowed the Roman world, falls in 476 under the blows of the Herulan Odoacer.

But the Roman empire survived on the banks of the Bosphorus. And there we shall meet with a Roman jurisconsult emperor to whom we owe the preservation of the most important part of the Roman law: this emperor is the celebrated Justinian.

[1] Girard, *Manuel*, pp. 68, 72.

TITLE V

FIFTH PERIOD — THE LATER EMPIRE — JUSTINIAN

(527 A. D.)

93. **The Corpus Juris:** The immense work of Justinian is entirely contained in the *Corpus juris:* the Corpus juris comprises, in an inverse order to that which is here adopted and which is the chronological order, the Code, the Digest, the Institutes.

94. **The Code:** Is the compilation of the imperial constitutions down to Justinian.

95. **The Digest:** The Digest is a collection, in the order of the subject-matter, of the fragments of the works of the ancient jurisconsults. It is through the Digest (which is also called the *Pandects (pandectae Justinianeae)* that the most important portion which we possess of the writings of the ancient ' prudentes ' was preserved for us.

96. The text unfortunately is not reliable. Justinian, to adapt the decisions of the jurisconsults to the coloring of the law of his own time, did not fail to have the original texts altered by his commissioners, whose president was *Tribonian*, quaestor of the imperial palace. These alterations constitute what are called the *interpolations* or *tribonianisms*.

97. The discovery of some pure sources has permitted the recovery of many of them, and modern

science applies real skillfulness in the restoration of texts.[1]

98. The Institutes: The Institutes of Justinian are a *text book* designed for the law students of that time. They are the work of Tribonian, of Theophilus, professor of law at Constantinople, and of Dorotheus, professor of law at Berytus. There is attributed to Theophilus a Greek paraphrase of the Institutes, to which not long ago resort was still had quite commonly in order to clear up disputed points.

99. The Fifty Decisions (decisiones): Thus are termed the fifty constitutions by which Justinian decided points left uncertain by the preceding imperial constitutions before proceeding with the publication of the Code.

100. The Novels: Justinian modified several points of law by subsequent constitutions to which was given the name of *novels* (*novellae constitutiones*). These novels complete and conclude the Corpus juris.

101. The Basilica: Roman law has been made subsequently, in the East, the subject of various works of which the most important consists of the Basilica, which, undertaken under Basil the Macedonian, whose name they bear, were finished under Leo the Philosopher (888–911 A. D.). The Basilica represent to us the last state of the Roman or Byzantine law at the time of the fall of Constantinople, and were in our time the chief law in Greece after the obtainment of freedom: they have ceased to be the common law of the Greeks only upon the compilation of actual Greek Codes.

[1] We should notice especially the admirable "*Palingenesia juris civilis*" of Lenel.

BOOK II

PERSONS

TITLE I

PRELIMINARY CONCEPTIONS

102. **Personality:** Persons are the *subjects* of rights. *Person* and individual must not be confounded. The word *person* (*persona*, theatrical mask), is applied rather to the part played in society by the individual than to the individual himself; the latter can fill successively different parts. The same person can be considered as playing in turn the part of father, tutor, creditor, owner: as many parts, so many masks, if desired.[1]

103. On the other hand, collective bodies play an individual part, so to speak, upon the legal stage. They are called *moral persons*: for example, the state, cities, corporations (*collegia*).[2] We would say, in French law, that these collectivities have civil personality. This personality, which is revealed by the existence of a property distinct from that of the collectivity, can exist, at Rome, only by virtue of a grant made by a law.[3]

104. Personality, in the original Roman conception, does not belong to all men.

---

[1] Aulus Gellius, 5, 7.†   [2] *Dig.* 3, 4, 1 (Gaius).
[3] *Dig.* 47, 22, 3, § 1 (Marcianus).

It is necessary, in order to have a complete personality (*caput*), to be born free and not a slave, to be a citizen and not a 'peregrinus' or even a Latin, to be a head of a family and not in power.

105. The three elements of personality are therefore the *status libertatis*, the *status civitatis*, the *status familiae*.[1] Whoever loses one of them loses his 'caput.'[2]

106. Whoever does not unite these three elements of caput is afflicted by an *incapacity of law* more or less complete. With *incapacities of law*, the consideration of which forms the object of the following chapters, are contrasted *incapacities of fact*, which will be studied later.[3]

[1] *Dig.* 4, 5, 11 (Paulus).   [2] See *infra*, §§ 341 *et seq.*
[3] See *infra*, §§ 355 *et seq.*

TITLE II

STATUS LIBERTATIS

CHAPTER I

FREEMEN AND SLAVES

SECTION I. — **Condition of Slaves**

107. Freedom and Slavery: Freedom is the natural right of each one to do what he pleases.[1] As to slavery (*servitus*), the Institutes of Justinian defined it as "an institution of the *jus gentium*, by virtue of which an individual, contrary to natural law, is subjected to the ownership of another."[2] It was attempted to justify by the law of war this institution contrary to natural law which is attached to the jus gentium. "From the moment, it was said, that one had the right to kill his enemy, *à fortiori* he has the right to spare (*servare*) him." Hence the rather doubtful etymology of the word *servus*, which Justinian wishes to connect with the word *servatus*.[3]

108. (Slaves are also called *mancipia*, from *manu capti*.[4])

109. Freemen and Slaves — freeborn and freed: From the point of view of status libertatis persons are divided into freemen and slaves, and free persons are subdivided into *ingenui* (freeborn) and *liberti* (freed).

[1] *Inst.* 1, 3, pr. and § 1.   [2] *Ibid.* § 2.
[3] *Ibid.* § 3.   [4] *Ibid.* § 3.

110. Personality of the Slave: "Persons," we have said: but is the slave indeed a *person?* In general the slave is held to be a thing, a simple object of property. Yet the Roman law, in spite of its harshness, considers him, in many respects, as a person. It allows him to figure in contracts, very often as creditor, in certain cases as debtor. It must be added that in such case the slave acquires or engages only for his master; he is for the latter an instrument of acquisition or obligation. But that does not prevent the law from holding his activity or his will to be of some account.

When the slave dies, he recovers his dignity of a man, and the earth where he lies is not less sacred than where is buried the body of a freeman.

111. Rights of the Master over the Person of the Slave: During his life he is submitted to the good pleasure of the master, who has over him the power of life and death. This rigor was relaxed under the influence of Stoic philosophy and of Christianity.

112. The first influence is manifested in a perceptible manner in the era of the Antonines.

Hadrian seems to have laid down the principle of prosecuting masters who should kill their slaves.[1] A constitution of Antoninus Pius decides that the master who kills his slave should be punished like one who kills the slave of another.[2] The same emperor ordered that, when slaves maltreated by their masters should take refuge in a temple or at the foot of the emperor's statue, the master should be constrained to sell them *bonis conditionibus*[3] (*i. e.* without those unfavorable

---

[1] Spartianus, *Hadriani vita*, 18.†
[2] *Inst.* 1, 8, § 2.   [3] *Ibid.*

clauses which the rancor of masters too often would insert in contracts of sale: obligation upon the buyer to employ the slave at hard labor, — to deliver over a woman to prostitution, etc.).

Constantine later confirmed these provisions in only permitting masters to moderately whip their slaves.[1]

113. **Condition of Slaves:** In fact the situation of slaves was very unequal. The slave to whom the master relinquished the management of an important 'peculium,' whom he made captain of a ship (*magister navis*), the Greek teacher to whom was intrusted the education of his children, were not materially assimilated to the slave workman or laborer or to the *servus vicarius* who is the slave of another slave. In law all are equal: *in conditione servorum nulla est differentia.*[2]

114. *Public Slaves:*[3] It is necessary, nevertheless, to make an exception as to the *slaves of the Roman people*, "*servi publici*," partly slaves, partly inferior officers who might dispose by will of one half of their peculium.[4]

115. *Peculium:* The peculium is anything valuable intrusted by the master to the free management of the slave: it remains (save what has just been said of public slaves) the absolute property of the master, who can retake it at will, although in fact he seldom uses this right during the life of the slave.[5]

Section II. — **Sources of Slavery**

116. **Sources of Slavery:** "*Servi nascuntur aut*

[1] *Cod. Theod.* 9, 12, 1 and 2.   [2] *Inst.* 1, 3, § 4.
[3] That is, slaves of the state. — S.
[4] Ulpian, *Reg.* 20, § 16.   [5] *Frag. Vat.* 261.

fiunt," says Justinian, "slaves are born or become such." [1]

117. (1) **Birth**: Slaves by birth are the children born of a slave woman. It is sometimes a delicate problem to determine the status of a person, whose parents have been neither always free nor always slaves; here is the *criterion* of Roman law: *the child born of a lawful marriage follows the condition of his father from the moment of conception; the child born out of marriage, the condition of the mother at birth.*[2]

Consequently, if a woman should conceive while free and be delivered while a slave, the child would be born a slave; a child born *ex justis nuptiis* having a free father at the time of conception, is therefore born free, even though the father should subsequently have lost his freedom.[3]

118. Such were the primitive principles: but they did not entirely conserve their strictness: in the classical era it was held that if only the mother had been free *for a single moment during gestation*, the child would be born free.[4]

119. (2) **Event subsequent to Birth**: The events subsequent to birth whence slavery results belong either to the jus gentium or to the jus civile.

120. (*a*) *Event derived from the Jus Gentium:* The source of slavery with which the jus gentium is concerned is captivity.[5]

The consequences of captivity are mitigated by two theories: the theory of the postliminium; the theory of the lex Cornelia.

---

[1] *Inst.* 1, 3, § 4.   [2] Ulpian, *Reg.* 5, § 10.
[3] *Ibid.*   [4] *Inst.* 1, 4.   [5] *Ibid.* 1, 3, § 4.

121. *Jus Postliminii:* The jus postliminii is a rule by virtue of which, when a Roman citizen who is a prisoner of war escapes, is exchanged, or succeeds somehow in returning to his own country, his captivity is effaced *retroactively*, in such a manner that he is considered as never having been a slave.[1]

122. However, the jus postliminii produces a retroactive effect only as to *res juris* and not as to *res facti*. So, in the case where the wife of the captive has married again, her second marriage is not annulled by the return of the first husband.[2]

123. *Theory of the Lex Cornelia:* This theory has been inferred by the jurisconsults from a law of the dictatorship of Sulla, the *lex Cornelia de falsis*, a provision of which punished with the penalties for forgery the alteration of a will made during the status libertatis by a man who subsequently dies a captive of the enemy. From this provision the jurisconsults inferred the validity of the will made by a person dying in captivity, and more generally the validity of all acts prior to this captivity. This theory has been called quite improperly the *fiction* of the lex Cornelia.[3]

124. In short, the fiction of the postliminium consists in assuming that the returning captive never was a captive, and the alleged fiction of the lex Cornelia in assuming that the individual dying in captivity lost his life the moment he became a captive.

[1] *Dig.* 49, 15, 9 pr.
[2] It is necessary to distinguish, however: the texts speak only of marriage without *manus*. *Dig.* 49, 15, 12, 4 (Tryphoninus). It was doubtless admitted that manus subsisted like the patria potestas. See Girard, *Manuel*, pp. 103, 104.
[3] *Dig.* 28, 3, 15 (Javolenus).

125. (b) *Events derived from the Jus Civile:* Slaves become such *jure civili:* *¹ (1) The free individual of the age of puberty who causes himself to be sold by an accomplice with the object of afterwards causing his freedom to be established, and of sharing with the accomplice the profit from this fraud.

126. (2) The free woman *sui juris* who maintains relations with a slave belonging to another in spite of the prohibition of the master. This rule was established by the senatusconsultum Claudianum; the master should give to the free woman three notices, and it is only when she persists, after the third notice, in the culpable relations that he can cause her to be claimed as his slave (abolished by Justinian).[2]

127. The woman, before the last notice, may agree with the master of the slave that she shall be only his freedwoman, and continue this immoral intimacy at the price of sacrificing her free birth. — A freeborn person may, by virtue of a similar agreement, become a *freed* person without passing through slavery.[3]

128. The *incensus:* namely, one who, in order to avoid military service, does not have himself enrolled on the register of the census.[4]

129. (4) The ungrateful freedman (*revocatio in servitutem*).[5]

---

*[1] The term "*Jus civili*" is here understood in a sense in contrast to the *jus gentium*. For it is a provision of the Edict which deprives of his freedom the person causing himself to be sold by an accomplice. See *Dig.* 40, 12, 23 pr.

[2] Paulus, *Sent.* 2, 21 A, §§ 1–18.   [3] *Ibid.*
[4] Cicero, *Pro Caecina,* 34.†
[5] Suetonius, *Div. Claud.* 25.†

FREEMEN AND SLAVES

130. (5) Those condemned to certain punishments (*ad bestias, in metallum, i. e.* to penal servitude in mines): these condemned persons are called *servi poenae*, for they have no other master save the punishment.[1]

Section III. — Quasi-Slavery

131. **Cases of Quasi-Slavery:** Certain individuals, without losing freedom or even the right of citizenship, are in a *state of actual slavery*. These are:

132. (1) *The liber homo bona fide serviens:* The freeman who believes himself to be a slave; in reality he is free; however, he acquires for his supposed master, as if he were a slave, whatever is the product of his work (*ex operis suis*) or of the management of the peculium which is intrusted to him (*ex re ejus cui servit*).[2]

133. (2) *The addicti, judicati, nexi,* namely those who, either by the effect of the contract of nexum,[3] or by the effect of the award (*addictio*) to their creditor, could be arrested by the latter, carried away into his private prison (*ergastulum*), and employed at slave work (private prisons were not suppressed until 388 A. D.).[4]

134. (3) The *auctorati:* gladiators of free condition

---

[1] *Inst.* 1, 12, § 3. The servitude of those condemned in metallum was done away with by *Nov.* 22, ch. 8.

[2] Gaius, 2, § 92; 3, § 164.

[3] Modified in 326 B. C. See *supra,* § 51.

[4] See Girard, *Textes,* p. 134. [Roby, *Roman Priv. Law,* vol. ii, pp. 423–431; Culquhoun, *A Summary of the Rom. Civ. Law,* §§ 2358, 2359.]

hired by the organizers of games to combat in the circus.¹

135. (4) The *redempti:* ransomed captives who cannot reimburse him who furnished their ransom.²

136. (6) **Persons in Mancipio:** These are the children of free condition sold by the paterfamilias. These individuals do not become slaves properly speaking; but they are said to be in mancipio; however, they retain their political rights.³

137. (7) **The Coloni:** Finally, the Christian, empire saw a new class of non-free persons developed: these are the coloni, the men whom the Middle Ages will call serfs of the soil.⁴

These coloni are not attached to the person, but to the land. The colonus can marry, be owner, creditor, but he cannot alienate, his estate being answerable for the rent, also permanent, which he owes to his master.⁵

138. One becomes a colonus, either by birth or in consequence of the thirty years' prescription (when a freeman has lived for thirty years in the situation of a colonus),⁶ or by an agreement (when distress compels a freeman to accept the servile condition).⁷

139. The time of the creation of the *colonatus* is not precisely known: some have wished to date it back to

---

¹ Gaius, 3, § 199.
² *Code,* 8, 50, 20 (Arcadius and Honorius); *Dig.* 28, 1, 201.
³ Gaius, 1, §§ 116, 117, 162 ; 3, § 104.
⁴ *Code,* 11, 48, 2 (Constans); *ibid.* 7 (Valentinian I, Valens, and Gratian).
⁵ *Code,* 11, 50, 1 (Constantine); *ibid.* 2 (Arcadius and Honorius).
⁶ *Code,* 11, 48, 23, § 1 (Justianian).
⁷ Salvius, *De Gubernatione Dei.*†

the time of Severus, a few even to the Antonines, — perhaps to Augustus; but the only exact sources of information which we have at our command at the present time do not permit us to place its origin much before the reign of Diocletian.[1]

CHAPTER II

FREEBORN AND FREED

SECTION I.— Manumission

140. Freeborn and Freed: The freeborn is the man who never has been a slave, the freed person one who has been: "*ex justa servitute manumissus.*"[2]

Ex justa servitute: Suppose in reality that a free individual passes for a slave and that he comes to be enfranchised: will he be *libertus*? no; he will remain freeborn.[3]

141. Modes of Manumission: In this matter there were distinguished the formal and the informal modes of manumission.

142. Formal Modes of Manumission: These modes are the vindicta, the census, by will.[4]

143. (1) *Manumission vindicta:* namely by the rod. The rod which is often seen to intervene in Roman transactions is nothing else than the representation of

[1] Girard, *Manuel*, pp. 129 and 130. See, however, Esmein (*Melanges*) on the inscription of Soukh-el-Khmis (pp. 306–321). Cf. Girard, *Textes*, p. 160.
[2] *Inst.* 1, 4 pr. ; 1, 5 pr.
[3] *Inst.* 1, 5 pr.
[4] Ulpian, *Reg.* 1, §§ 6–9.

the spear, symbol of quiritary ownership.¹ The master and the slave presented themselves with a third person before the magistrate, and there they simulated the ceremonies of the procedure which was called *causa liberalis*, procedure which aimed at declaring free an individual whose status was contested. The third person playing the part of *assertor libertatis* alleged that the slave was free *according to the law of the Quirites*. The master, instead of touching the slave with his rod while uttering a contrary allegation, declared that he would not oppose it. Consequently, the magistrate adjudicated in favor of freedom.²

144. (2) *Manumission censu:* Manumission by the census consisted in the master presenting the slave before the censor and asking for his enrollment on the register of citizens.³ The slave thus registered took the name *gentilicie* of his master, followed by his name and by the indication of his rank of freedom; for example, the freedman of Lucius, member of the *gens Cornelia*, will be: Lucius *Cornelius* Lucipor,⁴ L. L. (*Lucii libertus*, the freedman of Lucius).

145. (3) *Manumission by Will :* This manumission took place in two ways: 1. The master could charge by will his heir to free the slave by the vindicta or by the census, in which case the slave became the freedman of the heir.⁵ 2. The master could directly bequeath

---

[1] Boèce, *in Ciceronis topica*, 1, 2, 10†; Gaius, 4, § 16 in fine.

[2] *Dig.* 40, 2 ; [Colquhoun, *A Summary of the Rom. Civ. Law*, § 713 ; Roby, *Rom. Priv. Law*, vol. i, p. 25, 26 n.].

[3] Ulpian, *Reg.* 1, § 8.

[4] Lucipor: *Lucii puer*, slave of Lucius ; the freedman keeps as surname the name which he bore in servitude.

[5] Will of Dasumius, line 79. Girard, *Textes*, p. 770.

freedom to the slave, who consequently found himself a freedman without a patronus and took the title of *Libertus Orcinus*, freedman of Orcus, Pluto: "*Eros, Phoebus liberi sunto.*"[1] Σαράπιας δούλη μου ... ἐλευθέρα ἔστω.[2]

145. *Cont.* .... (4) *Manumission in sacrosanctis ecclesiis:* At the time of Justinian formal manumission is made in sacrosanctis ecclesiis, in churches, in the presence of the faithful (*Christianis adstantibus*).[3]

146. **Informal Modes of Manumission:** Besides these formal modes there were informal modes of manumission: *per epistolam*, by a letter in which the master said to the slave that he gave him his freedom, *inter amicos*, when the master made known before several friends his will to free the slave — *pileo*, to the advantage of the slaves, who, by virtue of a testamentary provision of the master, have followed his funeral procession wearing the cap of freedom (the Phrygian cap).

147. According to the opinion of the most trustworthy contemporaneous interpreters, these modes of manumission were destitute of validity: the slaves who benefited therefrom were simply *statuliberi*. The praetor prevented a change of mind by the master and maintained them in freedom, but their status appears to have been discussed until the Lex Junia Norbana.[4]

148. **Lex Junia Norbana:** Its date is uncer-

[1] Will of Dasumius, line 51. Girard, *Textes*, p. 769.
[2] Will of Longinus Castor, line 17. Girard, *Textes*, p. 773.
[3] *Inst.* 1, 5, § 1.
[4] Gaius, 3, § 56.

tain; the Romanists settle it, some 18 A. D., others 83 B. C.; we abide by this latter date.*[1]

According to this law, slaves freed by an informal mode become indeed free, but instead of becoming at the same time citizens, they are simply Latins.[2] And, from the name of the law, this class of Latins was called "Latini Juniani."

149. The Lex Junia Norbana should not belong, then, in our opinion, to the series of laws restricting manumissions; it would be, on the contrary, a law of favor, the object of which would have been to substitute, for the benefit of those to whom it referred, an established status for the precarious status of the 'statuliberi.'

150. **Lex Fufia Caninia:** We shall elsewhere meet this series of restrictive laws, dictated by an anxiety which is perhaps already apparent in the Lex Junia Norbana, in spite of its liberal character.

151. Manumissions presented a peril which aroused the legislator. They crowded the city with a mob of electors infected with every vice of slavery, and whose increase resulted in forming a peril to the State. The manumissions most feared (because they did not impoverish those who made them) were manumissions by will. They are aimed at by the Lex Fufia Caninia the

---

*[1] According to the lex Aelia Sentia, freedmen who are minors of twenty years become Latins (Gaius 1, §§ 28, 29). Now, it follows from the so-called fragment of Dositheus (§ 12, Girard, *Textes*, p. 478), that the lex Junia "*Latinorum genus introduxit.*" The lex Aelia Sentia is in 4 A. D. It can refer to the Latini Juniani created by the lex Junia Norbana only unless the latter is prior.

[2] See *infra*, § 160.

exact¹ date of which we do not know, and of which Justinian does not speak except to annul it.

152. This law restricted the number of manumissions by will to a figure proportional to the total number of slaves of the testator, unless the number of freedmen should exceed one hundred. If that figure was exceeded, the manumissions were valid in the order of the will; those which exceeded the legal number were not counted. All were void if the deceased had amused himself in writing in a circle the names of the freedmen in such a manner that there was neither first nor last.²

153. **Lex Aelia Sentia:** Quite different is the significance of the Lex Aelia Sentia (4 A. D.).

154. (1) It forbids masters under twenty years of age to free their slaves otherwise than by the rod (vindicta), and without showing a weighty reason (*justa causa*) which should be approved by a special council composed at Rome of five senators and five knights, and, in the provinces, of twenty recuperators (persons enrolled on the list of judices).³ It is a lawful cause for manumission when the slave is the father, the son, the brother of the master, when the slave has saved the life of the master, when the master wishes to free a slave to marry her, etc.⁴

155. (2) It prohibits manumission in fraud of creditors.⁵ Slaves constitute in reality an important part

[1] It is of the reign of Augustus. See Suetonius, *Octavius*, 40.†
[2] Gaius, 1, § 42 *et seq.; Inst.* 1, 7.
[3] See *infra*, §§ 479, 480; [Gaius, 1, 20].
[4] Gaius, 1, § 39 ; *Inst.* 1, 6, §§ 4, 5, 7.
[5] Except this be to institute a slave as *heres necessarius* (see *infra*, § 800). [See, also, *Dig.* 40, 9, 10 (Gaius) ; *ibid.* 27 pr. (Hermogenianus).]

of property, and a master who is in debt can render himself insolvent by dissipating through manumissions the human cattle which form the security of his creditors. In both cases which we have just treated, the manumission is void: *lex impedit libertatem.*

156. (3) Every slave freed before thirty years of age becomes, by the terms of the law, Latinus Junianus, and not citizen.[1]

157. (4) Slaves who during their servitude were subjected to severe punishments (*vincti tortive*) become, if they are freed, *peregrini dediticii.* They are assimilated to peoples upon whom victorious Rome imposed the harshest conditions: the freedman 'dediticius' cannot reside within a radius of one hundred miles from Rome without running the risk of being sold as a slave with his entire family.[2]

SECTION II. — **Condition of Freedmen**

158. **Different Classes of Freedmen:** There are then, at the beginning of the empire, three classes of freedmen, namely (we commence at the lowest point, *pessima libertas*):

159. (1) *The dediticii:*[3] they can neither give nor receive by will and cannot obtain Roman citizenship.[4]

---

[1] Compare will of Longinus Castor, lines 4 and 5: Μαρκέλλαν . . . Κλεοπάτραν δούλην μου μίζονα ἐτῶν τριάκοντα. Girard, *Textes*, p. 773.

[2] Ulpian, *Reg.* 1, § 11; Gaius, 1, §§ 26, 27.

[3] " Dediticii are foreigners who had fought against the Romans and surrendered (cf. Liv. vii, 31, 9). They occupied the lowest place in the rank of freemen (Gaius 1, § 14)." Roby, *Rom. Priv. Law*, vol. i, p. 19. — S.

[4] Gaius, 1, § 26.

FREEBORN AND FREED

160. (2) *The Latini Juniani:* They are free during their life, but die slaves; *i. e.* their possessions at their death return to their master: *libertatem simul et animam in ultimo spiritu amittebant.*[1] We shall see that they can acquire Roman citizenship.[2]

161. (3) *Freedmen who are Roman Citizens:* The freedman who is a citizen does not have indeed all the prerogatives of the freeborn.

He is an elector, but to render his vote less important, he is put into one of the four urban *tribus.*[3]

He is not eligible to the magistracies (he has not the *jus honorum*).

He has not the *jus aureorum annulorum*,[4] the right to wear a gold ring, mark of the freeborn citizen.

162. But he can obtain, and also does obtain frequently under the empire, the grant of the prerogatives which he lacks. This grant is called the *restitutio natalium.*[5]

163. **Elevation of the Latini Juniani to the Rank of Citizens:** A Latinus Junianus can subsequently acquire the quality of citizen.[6]

164. (1) *Iteratione:* when the quality of Latinus Junianus results from the manumission of the slave by an informal mode, the *iteratio*, repetition by a formal

[1] *Inst.* 3, 7, § 4; Gaius, 3, § 56 *et seq.*
[2] See *infra*, § 163 *et seq*
[3] That is, *district.* See *supra*, § 32, note 1. — S.
[4] *Dig.* 40, 10, 3, 5, and 6.
[5] Concession much more complete than the *jus aur. annul.*; since it caused the disappearance of the rights of the patronus to *operae* and to succession, it cannot be granted without the consent of the latter. *Dig.* 40, 11, 2.
[6] Ulpian, *Reg.* 3, § 1, for the entire enumeration.

mode of the *manumissio*, imparts to him the quality of citizen.

165. (2) *Causae probatione :* The causae probatio is a favor made to fruitfulness. The Latin who has married a Roman or a Latin woman before seven witnesses and who has had from this union a child a year old (*puer anniculus*) can obtain citizenship for himself, his wife, and his children.

166. (3) *Liberis:* Favor to the freedwoman Latina Juniana who has had three children (*ter enixa*).

167. (4) *Erroris causae probatione:* Differing from the causae probatio: When a Roman or Latin husband or wife has wrongfully believed his or her spouse in the case of causae probatio.

168. (5) *Militia:* By service for six years in the brigade of night watchmen (*vigiles*) of Rome.[1]

(6) *Pistrino:* By establishing a bakery at Rome.

(7) *Nave:* By commerce by sea in corn intended for the provisioning of Italy.

(8) *Aedificio :* By being a builder of edifices.

169. Reforms of Justinian: Justinian did away with the classes of freedmen dediticii and Latini Juniani. All freedmen, in the last state of the law, are citizens.

170. Duties of Freedmen toward their Patroni: Freedmen, even citizens, are held to certain obligations toward their patroni. These obligations are reduced to three: (1) Obsequium; (2) operae; (3) bona.

171. (1) *Obsequium :* The obsequium is a duty of

---

[1] Provision of a *Lex Visellia*. Ulpian, *Reg.* 3, § 5.

respect: thus the freedman runs the risk of prosecution if he sues his patronus without the authorization of the praetor.[1]

172. (2) *Operae.* The operae consist in the duty of rendering to the patronus certain dutiful services (*operae officiales*); they are sanctioned only by a moral obligation. The patronus wishing to secure from the future freedman more extended services (*operae fabriles*), takes care, before emancipation, to bind the slave by an oath before the pontifices; this is the *jurata promissio liberti.*[2]

173. (3) *Bona:* This is the word which serves to designate the right of succession of the patronus and his family. The family of the freedman being none other than that of his former master, it is to this family that the succession *ab intestato* to the freedman dying without issue should return.[3]

174. It follows, therefore, that the tutela of the freedman who is impubes or of the woman manumitted belongs to the patronus or to his descendants by virtue of the Roman principle, "*ubi emolumentum successionis ibi et onus tutelae.*"

175. **Emancipation of the Coloni:** The coloni emerge from their condition by promotion to the episcopate; they do not escape from it either by emancipation or by the thirty years' prescription.

[1] *Dig.* 37, 15; Gaius, 4, § 46.
[2] Gaius, 3, §§ 95, 96.
[3] Add that the freedman is bound toward the patronus in need by an obligation to support him. Paul. *Sent.* 2, 32.

TITLE III

STATUS CIVITATIS

176. Division of Persons from the Point of View of Citizenship: Persons are divided, from the point of view of status civitatis, into Roman citizens and peregrini,[1] — but among the peregrini two great classes must be distinguished: the Latins, and the peregrini properly so-called. The quality of Latin carries with it subordinate distinctions which will be shown later.[2]

[1] Translated "aliens," Poste, *Gaius*, pp. 72-75, also Sohm, *Institutes of Roman Law* (trans. by Ledlie, *q. v.*); "foreigners," Roby, *Rom. Priv. Law*, vol. i, p. 19.

"Foreigners (peregrini) may be shortly defined as freemen who were not either Roman citizens or Latins (though the Latins were foreigners, Gaius 1, § 79)." Roby, *ibid*.

"*Cives non optimo jure*," *i. e.* citizens of the Roman State not possessing the full rights, but enjoying those privileges in a modified degree. Colquhoun, *A Summary of the Roman Civil Law*, § 374.

"All who were not citizens were, strictly speaking, *Peregrini*, whether they were Latins or Italians, or had the rights of such. After the extension of the citizenship by Caracalla to all *Ingenui*, this *Peregrinitas* applied only to freedmen being Latins and *Dediticii*, such not being *ingenui*. When, however, Justinian further extended the franchise to *Libertini*, the very word *Peregrin* became obsolete, and the word *Barbarus* was substituted for it in contradistinction to *Romanus*." Colquhoun, *ibid*. 394. — S.

[2] See *infra*, §§ 195 *et seq*.

CHAPTER I

CITIZENS

**177. Sources of the Quality of Citizen
(1) Birth:** We shall again find here a certain number of rules analogous to those formulated as to the subject of status libertatis. Thus, citizens are born or become such.

An individual is born a citizen whose parents have had Roman citizenship from his conception to his birth inclusively.

When parents are of different conditions, the child follows the condition of his father at the moment of conception if he is born *ex justis nuptiis*.

178. But here the analogy stops; if the child is born out of marriage, which will be the most usual case (the jus connubii not existing between Romans and peregrini), he will be a foreigner (peregrinus) by virtue of a lex Minicia of unknown date, *lex Minicia deterioris parentis conditionem sequi jubet*.[1] An idea identical with that which our old *coutumiers*[2] expressed

---

[1] Gaius, 1, § 78.

[2] Written documents of the thirteenth, fourteenth, and fifteenth centuries preserving the expression of the pure customary law of France which prevailed in the north and centre of France. Esmein, *Cours élémentaire d'histoire de droit français*, pp. 711–713, 722. "By *coutumier* is meant a private treatise in which an individual has collected the provisions of one or more customs (*coutumes*). Generally, the compiler is an officer of justice who lived and exercised his functions in the country . . ." (of the custom or customs). Esmein, *opus cit*. p. 722. See, also, § 790, note 2, *infra*. — S.

in the matter of serfdom, "the bad prevails over the good."[1]

There was never granted to the peregrina who had been a Roman citizen during gestation the favor granted to the slave who had had, in the course of pregnancy, a moment of freedom.[2]

179. *Cont.* (2) **Acquisition of the Right of Citizenship after Birth:** The acquisition of citizenship is a consequence of the favor of the law (for example, to the benefit of the peregrinus who has informed against a peculating magistrate),[3] or of naturalization granted, under the Republic, by the comitia, and, under the empire, by the emperor.[4]

180. Rome had been in her infancy very prodigal of the right of citizenship, she then had need of recruiting her corps of citizens; under the Republic she became very miserly: quite often, in this era, she consented to bestow on peregrini only the *civitas sine suffragio*, civil rights without political rights.

181. The emperors did not often cheapen for their peregrini-subjects the grant either general or individual of the right of citizenship. Claudius, born at Lyons, showed himself generous to the Gauls; the Spaniards were favored by Trajan and Hadrian, both natives of Spain.

182. **Constitution of Caracalla:** In 212 A. D. Caracalla granted the right of citizenship to all the inhabitants of the empire. This grant, dictated by an

---

[1] "*Le mauvais emporte le bien.*"
[2] See *supra*, § 118.
[3] Lex Acilia, repetundarum, line 76. Girard, *Textes*, p. 32.
[4] Tacitus, *Annales*, 11, 23.†

anxiety entirely fiscal, had for its purpose to place all the subjects of the empire under the tax of one twentieth on successions (*vicesima hereditatum*) which was paid only by citizens.

183. It is still a very much debated question whether, after the constitution of Caracalla, there were non-citizens in the empire, and particularly if, by virtue of this constitution, the right of citizenship was bestowed in advance on all those who subsequently became subjects of the empire.

According to the theory generally accepted, the constitution of Caracalla would be inapplicable to the natives of regions then alien to the Roman world.

Ortolan has combated this theory and held that, starting from the constitution of Caracalla, the quality of subject of the empire and that of citizen are mingled in such a manner that the one cannot be acquired without the other also. How, then, can *peregrini* be found in the empire? As in France, to-day, are found foreigners, persons traveling.

There is a weak point in this theory: Ortolan seems to confuse the alien outside of the Roman power (*hostis, barbarus*) with the *peregrinus* (*foreigner*) who is a subject of Rome.

Girard supposes that the constitution of Caracalla did not have the generality which is attributed to it, without passing upon the restrictions which might have limited the general grant of the right of citizenship. In reality only conjectures can be hazarded: precise proofs are wanting.[1]

184. **Condition of Citizens**: The Roman citi-

---

[1] Girard, *Manuel*, p. 114, text and note 3.

zen is the *Quiris*. It is believed that this is a term of Sabine origin; [1] (the Sabines inhabited the small fortified town of Quirium). The special law for Roman citizens bore the name of *Quiritary* law (*jus quiritium*). It can be separated into three component parts of a private nature and two of a political nature. These component parts are:

185. *In private law :* (1) the *jus connubii*, right to contract 'justae nuptiae,' generative of the 'patria potestas.'

(2) The *jus commercii*, right to figure in a contract of Roman form; that is, in a contract 'per aes et libram.'

(3) The *factio testamenti*, right to dispose of or receive by will. The factio testamenti appears as an aspect of the commercium when the will is made per aes et libram, and as an appendage of political rights, when the will was made 'calatis comitiis.' It is in fact necessary to be an elector in order to enter the comitia.

186. *Of a political nature*, the Roman citizen has:
(1) The *jus suffragii* (the right to vote).
(2) The *jus honorum* (eligibility for the magistracies).

187. **Loss of Citizenship:** The right of citizenship is lost necessarily along with freedom, save for the application of the jus postliminii and the fiction of the lex Cornelia, but it is by itself lost:

188. (1) By the effect of condemnation to exile "*interdictio aqua et igni*," the interdiction of water and fire (this was the phrase employed to express the obli-

---

[1] See, however, *supra*, § 5; and Cuq, *Institutions*, vol. i, pp. 101, 102.

gation of expatriation).¹ This penalty was replaced under the empire by *deportation to an island*, which, like the former, involves loss of citizenship.²

189. Deportation to an island must not be confounded with banishment, which left the right of citizenship subsisting. Ovid banished to the Chersonesus of Thrace can write: "*Nec mihi jus civis, nec mihi nomen abest.*" ³

190. (2) By enrollment in the number of members of a Latin colony: Romans desirous of going to seek their fortunes away from home did not always find at a given place a colony of citizens: they sometimes joined emigrants going away to found a Latin colony, and assume in this case the condition of Latin colonists (*Latini colonarii*), which will be defined a little later.⁴

CHAPTER II

NON-CITIZENS

Section I.—**Peregrini properly so-called**

191. **Hostis and Peregrinus:** In the first centuries of Rome the term *hostis* had a general meaning: it served to designate foreigners and implied so little the idea of a state of war that it has been thought that an etymology common to the word *hostis* and the word *hospes* (guest) ⁵ might be given.

[1] *Inst.* 1, 16, § 2. [2] *Ibid.*
[3] Ovid, *Tristes.*† [4] Gaius, 1, § 131.
[5] It is in this archaic sense that the Law of the XII Tables says "*status dies cum hoste*" for a lawsuit with a foreigner, — or "*adversus hostem aeterna auctoritas.*"

Later 'hostis' is distinguished from 'peregrinus.'[1] The peregrinus is the subject of Rome, the individual belonging to a conquered people to whom, conformably to her invariable policy, Rome has left its national law.

192. Persons are peregrini by birth: persons become such by the effect of interdiction 'aqua et igni,' but in this case they are *peregrini sine civitate*.

193. **Condition of Peregrini:** Peregrini have neither political rights (jus suffragii, jus honorum), nor civil rights (connubium, commercium, factio testamenti): they live under the empire of their national laws, and are governed by the jus gentium as much in their relations among themselves as in their relations with the Romans.

194. **Populi Fundi:** The Romans do not impose upon subject peoples their law: but these peoples may adopt it of their own accord; they are then called 'populi fundi.' This title did not of itself create any special privilege.[2]

SECTION II. — **Latins** [3]

195. **Jus Latii:** So termed, in properly speaking of the condition fixed by Rome first for the inhabitants of Latium, and later for all the *civitates foederatae*, which composed the "Latin league," and finally for all the Italian peoples.

196. The *majus Latium* and the *minus Latium* are

---

[1] Cicero, *De Officiis*, 1, 12.†
[2] Cicero, *Pro Balbo*, 8.†
[3] "Latins meant originally inhabitants of Latium, and was afterwards applied to members of Latin colonies, who were often Roman citizens originally." Roby, *Rom. Priv. Law*, vol. i, p. 19. — S.

distinguished. In cities enjoying the 'majus Latium,' it is sufficient to have been a decurion in order to acquire Roman citizenship. In cities having only the 'minus Latium,' it is necessary to have filled a magistracy to obtain the same privilege.[1]

197. **Division of the Latins:** Latins are divided into Latini veteres, Latini colonarii, Latins without appellation[2] or Latins of Italy. To these classes must be added the Latini Juniani, of whom we have spoken above.[3]

198. (1) *Latini veteres* (the ancient peoples of the Latin league). The Latini veteres have the 'jus suffragii.' When they are at Rome they vote in the comitia and draw by lot the 'tribus' in which they should give their votes.[4] Their suits are brought before the praetor urbanus.

199. (2) *Latini colonarii:* Colonies founded by the Latin league, or even recruited in Rome, among citizens who renounced the 'jus civitatis' in order to obtain grants of land.

The Latini colonarii have the same civil rights as the Latini veteres, but they cannot have the 'jus suffragii,' which is denied even to members of Roman colonies (these last can exercise their electoral right only in the colony and not at Rome).

200. (3) *Latini* (without appellation): The Latini have only the 'commercium,' and the right to appear in court before Roman magistrates. They have the

---

[1] Gaius, 1, §§ 95, 96.
[2] "*Sans epithète.*"   [3] See *supra*, § 160.
[4] *Sitella allata est ubi Latini sortirentur ubi suffragium ferrent.* Livy, 25, 3.†

'connubium' only when it has been expressly granted to them.

201. (4) *Latini Juniani*.[1]

202. **Acquisition of Citizenship by Latins:** Latins acquire citizenship by 'causae probatio,' 'erroris causae probatio,' and in general by all the modes already noticed above which cause the 'jus civitatis' to be acquired for Latini Juniani.

203. They acquired it also by individual or collective naturalization. After the Social War, in 90 B. C., a lex Julia, the author of which was the father of Julius Caesar, granted the right of citizenship to the Italians.[2]

204. **Gradation of Citizenships:** We will complete this survey with some thoughts on the gradation of citizenships.

(1) Rome, common country of all citizens.

(2) The Roman colonies composed of citizens sent out to Romanize a region. These cities are administered by 'duumvirs' corresponding to the consuls, and a 'curia,' a sort of local senate; the members of the colonies, when they are at Rome, enjoy the private law, but not the electoral rights: they have therefore civitas sine suffragio.

(3) The cities of the Latin league (Latini veteres) endowed with the 'jus suffragii' and the 'connubium.'

(4) The Latin cities which have only the 'commercium' but not the 'connubium.'

(5) The Latin colonies are assimilated sometimes with the preceding, or, being more favored, have the

---

[1] See *supra*, § 160.
[2] Cicero, *Pro Balbo*, 8, 21.

same condition as the cities of the Latini veteres, without the 'jus suffragii.'

(6) The municipia which retain the liberty of internal administration and govern themselves.

(7) The prefectures where the liberty of internal administration is exercised only under the control of a delegate from Rome (*praefectus*).

205. **Jus Italicum :** The jus Italicum is a quality of the soil, and not a privilege of its inhabitants; we will speak of it again in treating of quiritary ownership.[1]

[1] See *infra*, § 597.

TITLE IV

STATUS FAMILIAE

CHAPTER I

THE ROMAN FAMILY

206. Character of the Roman Family: The Roman family is presented in an aspect quite peculiar. It has for its basis the *patria potestas*, the conception of which, in Roman law, is almost without analogy in other systems of law: "*Fere enim nulli alii sunt homines qui in filios suos habent potestatem qualem nos habemus.*"[1]

Understood in a large sense, the family is composed of a head, the *paterfamilias*, who is *sui juris*, that is, who is dependent upon no one, and of individuals placed under the power of this head (persons *alieni juris*).[2]

The individuals placed under the power of the head of the family comprise: —

(1) Slaves subjected to *dominica potestas*.
(2) The wife subjected to *manus*.
(3) Children and descendants under *patria potestas*.
(4) Persons *in mancipio*.

207. The head of the family, priest and judge, is the absolute sovereign of this microcosm over which he has, in principle, the power of life and death.

[1] Gaius, 1, § 55.   [2] *Dig.* 50, 16, 195, §§ 1, 2.

208. Understood in a narrow sense, the family is composed of the paterfamilias, his wife, if she is *in manu*, and his children or descendants, lawful, adopted, or legitimated; children emancipated from the patria potestas, the daughter entering another family through marriage accompanied by a *conventio in manum*, are not included.

209. **Agnation:** The tie which unites among themselves all those who are under the patria potestas of the same head of a family is called agnation or civil relationship.

This tie survives at the death of the paterfamilias: furthermore it is extended to all those who are not found under the power of a head of a common family, but who would have been had this head of the family lived long enough for that. Therefore, the children of two consanguineous brothers, although born after the death of their grandfather and in consequence not having ever been under the power of this common ancestor, do not thereby cease to be agnates.

210. **Cognation:** Cognation is the natural relationship, which we would call the blood-tie. It connects the individual not only with his paternal, but with his maternal family.

211. **Relations and Differences between Agnation and Cognation:** It would seem, after what we have just said, that a person can be an *agnate* without being a *cognate* (for example, when a person is connected with a family only by adoption), and a cognate without being an agnate.[1] But, by a veritable abuse of language, the Roman jurisconsults

[1] *Dig.* 38, 10, 10 ; *ibid.* 38, 8, 1, § 4 (Ulpian).

admit that *agnation* implies *cognation*. Whoever enters a family by adoption, becomes at the same time a cognate as well as an agnate.[1]

On the contrary, agnation is very clearly lost without cognation; the son emancipated or given in adoption ceases to be an agnate of the members of his paternal family without ceasing to be their cognate.

212. The Gens: When a person can connect himself through a paternal genealogy with a common ancestor, he is an agnate. But in the course of time the tie of agnation becomes difficult to verify. Yet, between individuals whose agnation it is impossible to prove, a tie subsists: the relationship arising from the gens (*gentilitas*). When a person is no longer agnate, he may still be *gentilis*.

213. What then was a *gentilis?* Already toward the end of the Republic it was somewhat difficult to account for them. Under the Antonines, the gentiles have so passed into a state of memory that Gaius limits himself to saying: "*Totum gentilicium jus in desuetudinem abiit.*" And yet we should know what the gentiles were since Cicero affirms that he knows of nothing more complete than this definition of Mucius Scaevola: "*Gentiles sunt qui inter se eodem nomine sunt; nec est satis; qui ab ingenuis oriundi sunt; nec est satis; quorum majorum nemo servitutem servivit; abest etiam nunc; qui capite non sunt deminuti. Hoc fortasse satis est.*"[1]

214. So then, the first characteristic which reveals a common origin is the common name.

[1] Cicero, *Topica*, 6, 29.†

The Romans have three names: the *praenomen*, the *nomen*, the *cognomen*.

Ex. Publius *Cornelius* Scipio; Caius *Julius* Caesar. The nomen or *nomen gentilicium* is that which serves for the recognition of a common origin when the tie of agnation cannot be proved.

215. But why does the definition insist upon these two points: "*qui ab ingenuis oriundi sunt; quorum majorum nemo servitutem servivit*"? Because the name of the gens is borne not only by the members, but also by the freedmen of the family. There are, then, individuals who, although bearing the name of the gens, do not belong to the gens; these are the freedmen of the gens and their descendants.[1]

216. Cicero adds a last condition: that, in order to be part of the gens to which a family belongs, the tie of agnation with this family must, furthermore, not have been broken by a *capitis deminutio*.[2]

All that is perfectly clear and agrees with the idea of a remote agnatic relationship which is no longer recognizable save by the common name and the sacrifices (*sacrificia*).

217. Also is abandoned the political theory of Niebuhr, who attempted to see in the gens a political subdivision of the curia (ten families should form a gens, ten gentes a curia, ten curiae a tribe).

218. Abandoned also is the theory according to which the gentiles should be the members of the family of the manumittor considered in relation to the members of the family of the *manumissus*.

That is one of the aspects of 'gentilitas,' but it is only

[1] See *supra*, § 144.   [2] See *infra*, § 341.

one of its aspects, for the tie of 'gentilitas' exists previously among the members of the family of the *manumissor*.

CHAPTER II

THE PATERNAL POWER

219. The Paterfamilias: The paternal power is not exercised at Rome as with us by the father over his children, but by the head of the family over his descendants of the second as well as the first degree, who are, both of them, for the same reason, *alieni juris*.

While the grandfather, head of the family, is living, he alone is master both of his sons and of his grandsons, whatever may be the age of each.

As to the mother, she never exercises, at any time or under any circumstances, the paternal power; moreover, if she is under the 'manus' of her husband, at his death she herself falls under the 'tutela' of her children who are her agnates.

220. The Patria Potestas: The patria potestas of the head of a family is exercised alike over the person of the filiusfamilias and over his property.

221. (1) Rights over the Person of the Filiusfamilias: The head of a family has over his children the power of life and death; he may kill them, sell them, expose them, and make a noxal surrender (*noxae datio*) of them, that is, mancipate them, as reparation, to the victim of the delict.

The absolute power of the paterfamilias is affirmed in the earliest times of Rome and down to the end of the Republic by some tragic examples: without speaking of Brutus and Manlius, who used severity perhaps, the first as consul and the second as general, the conspiracy of Catiline gives us an example of a family execution: the father of Fulvius, one of the accomplices of Catiline, had him arrested while he was going to rejoin the troops of Mallius and put to death by virtue of his domestic jurisdiction.[1]

222. The rigor of the law was relaxed in the course of time. Trajan forced a father who maltreated his child to emancipate him.[2] Hadrian punished with deportation a paterfamilias who had killed his son.[3] However, to find a precise and general decree we must come down to Constantine, who punished with the penalties for parricide the paterfamilias guilty of the murder of his son " *sive clam sive palam fuerit enisus.*"[4] The word palam (openly) evidently referred to the domestic execution. *Parricidium* (*paris caedes*, and not *patris caedes* as we understand it in French) is the murder by a man of *his equal*.[5]

223. The right to sell the children lasted longer, since Constantine was contented with limiting it by prohibiting parents to sell their children, except the newly-born (*sanguinolentos*), and then solely in case of extreme poverty (*propter nimiam paupertatem egestatemque victus*).[6]

224. The noxal surrender which was made by means of *mancipatio,* and resulted in placing the filius-

[1] Sallust, Catilina, 49.†   [2] Dig. 37, 12, 5 (Papinian).
[3] Dig. 48, 9, 5 (Marcianus).   [4] Code, 9, 17, 1 (Constantine).
[5] Cuq (*Institutions*) gives a different etymology : *parricidium* should come from *patris caedes,* murder of a patrician (*pater*). See *Inst.* vol. i, p. 159, note 1.
[6] Code, 4, 43, 2 (Constantine).

familias *in mancipio*,[1] was not abolished until Justinian.[2]

225. Rights over the Property of the Filiusfamilias: On principle, the filiusfamilias has nothing of his own; whatever he acquires, he acquires for the head of the family.

His obligations are nevertheless considered as valid,[3] but cannot be, during the life of the paterfamilias, reduced to execution otherwise than by imprisonment, since he possesses nothing.

226. The father is not bound by the contracts of his son — at least until the introduction of actions *adjectitiae qualitatis*;[4] he is bound by his delicts, but he has the means of freeing himself, in such case, by the noxal surrender of the delinquent.[5]

227. **Peculia:** This law was modified by the successive creation of different peculia.

228. (1) *Peculium castrense* (created at the time of Caesar): This peculium was composed of property which the filiusfamilias might acquire in the discharge of the military profession.[6]

229. (2) *Peculium quasi castrense* (creation of Constantine): Is composed of wealth acquired by the filiusfamilias in the discharge of offices of the palace.[7]

230. (3) *Peculium adventicium*, or better, *Bona adventicia*: (the expression 'peculium adventicium,' used for a long time by commentators, is not Roman). 'Bona adventicia' are what come to the son from suc-

---
[1] See § 136.   [2] *Inst.* 4, 8, § 7.   [3] *Dig.* 44, 7, 39 (Gaius).
[4] See Bernard, *La deuxième année de droit romain.*
[5] Gaius, 4, § 75.   [6] Paul. *Sent.* 3, 4, § 3.
[7] *Code*, 12, 30, 1 (Constantine).

THE PATERNAL POWER 71

cessions falling to him. Originally they fell into the estate of the father: Constantine made for the benefit of the son a distinct property of the 'bona materna' (succession from the mother);[1] to the 'bona materna' were successively added all property which does not come to the son from paternal generosity, or from the peculia castrense and quasi castrense.

231. Peculium Profecticium: This is the peculium properly speaking: *peculium a patre projectum*, composed of property the free management of which has been granted by the head of the family to the filiusfamilias: symmetrical to the peculium of the slave, it dates back, doubtless, like the latter, to the most remote era and consequently is distinct from what we have called the creation of peculia.

232. *Ownership of peculia :* The peculia castrense and quasi castrense belong in full ownership to the filiusfamilias.

The bona adventicia belong, as to the naked ownership, to the filiusfamilias, and as to the usufruct, to the paterfamilias.

As to the peculium profecticium, it does not cease to be property of the father, who retakes it on the decease of the filiusfamilias, in spite of any contrary disposition, not by right of succession, but *jure peculii*.

233. Status of the Filiusfamilias in the Political Order: The subordinated condition of children in the civil organization does not react on the political organization. The father, absolute master of his son as paterfamilias, is held to obey the son if he is a magistrate of the Republic.

[1] *Code*, 6, 60, 1, § 1 (Constantine).

Fabius the son, the consul, surrounded by his lictors, meets on the Appian way his father Fabius of consular rank who was coming on horseback in the opposite direction. Etiquette obliged horsemen to dismount when they passed a consul. Fabius, the father, pretended not to remember it, and the lictors thought it advisable to remark upon this lack of deference. "*Descendere jube*," "Make him dismount," orders the consul to the lictors. . . . And the old Fabius, dismounting, threw himself into the arms of his son, whom he congratulates that the majesty of the Roman people is thus made to be respected.[1]

CHAPTER III

SOURCES OF THE PATRIA POTESTAS

234. The sources of patria potestas are, on the one hand, justae nuptiae; on the other, adoption and legitimation.

SECTION I. — **Justae nuptiae**

§ 1. Marriage and Manus

235. **Marriage:** Marriage is the union of man and woman for the purpose of having children: but thus understood, marriage would not differ from concubinage, a non-prohibited, extra-legal union, nor from *stuprum*, transitory, and culpable union of individuals of different sex.

Marriage, properly speaking, which serves as a basis

[1] See, however, quite an ambiguous passage of Cicero, *De Inventione*, 2, 17.†

SOURCES OF THE PATRIA POTESTAS 73

for the patria potestas, is what is called, in Roman law, *matrimonium* or *justae nuptiae*. It is defined in the Institutes of Justinian as "*viri atque mulieris conjunctio individuam vitae consuetudinem continens.*" [1] "*Individuam vitae consuetudinem,*" an *inseparable* existence, but not an indissoluble coëxistence, since divorce was permitted at Rome.

236. Marriage with or without Manus: At Rome two kinds of marriage are distinguished, both lawful, but which do not create the same condition for the wife: in marriage with manus the wife enters the family of her husband; in marriage without manus the wife remains in the family of her origin.

237. Forms of Marriage: To the question, "what are the forms of the Roman marriage?" there is only one juridical answer: there are none. Marriage, in Roman law, is a purely consensual contract; to such a degree that the jurisconsults declare that the lawful wife and the concubine differ solely by the intent alone of the parties "*solo dilectu.*" [2] Doubtless, there are ceremonies consecrated by usage, but these ceremonies are accessory and not essential.

238. Thus marriage is ordinarily preceded by a betrothal (*sponsalia*): This betrothal was anciently made by means of verbal contracts,[3] or, later, by pacts,[4] of which a written statement (*instrumentum*) was drawn up; although the name of 'instrumentum' should be reserved rather for documents intended for the statement of the pecuniary agreements of the

---

[1] *Inst.* 1, 9, § 1. [2] Paul. *Sent.* 2, 20.
[3] Aulus Gellius, 4.†
[4] *Dig.* 23, 1, 4 (Ulpian) ; *ibid.* 11 (Julian).

spouses: it is in this latter sense that we say "*instrumentum dotale*" (contract of marriage).

The betrothal, moreover, does not constitute marriage; at most, it may lead, in the last state of the law, to damages in case of a breaking off without cause.[1]

239. *The festivitas nuptiarum*, the formal ceremony, the garlands, the songs, the cries of "Talasse" uttered by the young people, the *flammeum*, — veil over orange-flowers worn by the bride, all that is consecrated by usage, but is not indispensable to the validity of the marriage.[2]

240. *Delivering over the wife :* It may be assumed, however, that the validity of the marriage is subordinated to the delivering over the wife to the husband (*deductio in domum mariti*), and in this sense the principle can be invoked: "*Vir absens uxorem ducere potest, femina absens nubere non potest.*"[3]

241. **Marriage with Manus:** Marriage by itself does not produce manus.

To begin with, what is manus? We shall not say that it is the marital power, for the marital power exists even in marriage without manus, and is established by the interdict given to the husband in order to obtain the surrender and control of his wife, by the rights which the *lex Julia de adulteriis* gives to the husband; . . . but it is a *more complete* power of the husband over the wife, a power very analogous to the patria potestas, since the wife in manu is deemed with regard

---

[1] *Code*, 5, 1, 5 (Leo and Anthemius).
[2] Festus, *De Verb. Signif.* † See, also, Colquhoun, *Rom. Civ. Law*, § 549. — S.
[3] Paul. *Sent.* 2, 19, § 8.

to her husband as in "*loco filiae*," with regard to her children born of the marriage as in "*loco sororis*" (whence results to the benefit of the wife a right of succession identical with that of her children considered as her brothers).

242. It will be, however, a mistake to believe that manus necessarily belongs to the husband: it belongs to the head of the family if the husband himself is under paternal power, and will not pass to the husband until at the death of the paterfamilias.

243. **Modes of acquiring Manus:** Manus would be acquired in the ancient law by three proceedings: (1) confarreatio; (2) coëmptio; (3) usus.[1]

244. (1) *Confarreatio:* It has for its essential ceremony the sacrifice of a cake of meal (*farreum*) to Jupiter. To be a priest of Jupiter, Mars, or Quirinus, it was necessary for a long time to be born of *nuptiae confarreatae.*[2] This essentially patrician ceremony became in course of time so unusual that on one occasion persons presenting the requisite qualifications could not be found for *flamines diales* (priests of Jupiter), and it was necessary, under Tiberius, to modify the law.[3]

245. (2) *Coëmptio:* Marriage of the plebeians not being possible by confarreatio, it followed from this that manus could never have been acquired in a plebeian family: to remedy this disadvantage coëmptio was created.

Coëmptio, the details of which are not known, was resolved into a sort of 'mancipatio,' that is, sale of the

---
[1] Gaius, 1, § 110.   [2] *Ibid.* § 113.
[3] Tacitus, *Annales*, 4, 16.†

wife to the husband in the presence of five witnesses and a person carrying the balance (libripens).[1]

246. (3) *Usus:* When the marriage had taken place neither by confarreatio, nor by coëmptio, manus, not produced at the time of the marriage, began by law at the end of a year of cohabitation, according to the law of the XII Tables.

247. But the wife who wished to remain in her paternal family could escape this acquisition by usus by absenting herself for three nights in the year: this was called "*usurpatum ire trinoctio;*" the word *usurpare* is technical, in Roman law, to express the interruption of a prescription in the course of being accomplished. In the present instance manus is acquired by an actual *usucapion* (what French law calls a *prescription*) and the prescription is interrupted by the *usurpatio.*[2]

248. **Decadence of Manus:** Free marriage (sine manu) did not cease becoming general, and ended by remaining master of the field. It has been seen that *farreum* was fallen into desuetude under Tiberius; Cicero already notices the decadence of *usus; coëmptio* still exists at the end of the Republic.[3] Gaius mentions its survival in the era of the Antonines, but it then seems more in use outside of marriage than employed between husband and wife.

249. **Fiduciary Coëmptiones:** Coëmptio is employed as an expedient in three cases.

[1] Gaius, 1, § 113. Huschke, and Muirhead, following him, have supposed that the husband and wife bought one another. This conjecture is treated quite severely by Girard, *Manuel,* p. 149 n., 2 n. 1.

[2] Aulus Gellius, *Noctae Atticae,* 3, 2.†

[3] *Laudatio funebris Turiae,* line 14. Girard, *Textes,* p. 778.

SOURCES OF THE PATRIA POTESTAS 77

250. (1) *Coëmptio tutelae evitandae causa :* The tutor of a woman *sui juris* conscientiously believes he should refuse his authorization to an act contemplated by the latter, and yet he does not wish to make it impossible for her to do it: in order to become released from his responsibility, he authorizes the woman to mancipate herself (*convenire in manum*) to a person who is charged with mancipating her again to a third person. This third person, *chosen by the woman*, binds himself by a *fiduciary pact* to manumit: he actually manumits her, and, in the character of patronus, keeps the tutela. The woman has thus procured for herself a tutor of her own choice whom she has under her control.[1]

251. (2) *Coëmptio testamenti faciendi gratia :* The woman *sui juris* cannot make her will without the authorization of her tutors who are her agnates. She changes her tutor by the process previously indicated, and places herself under the authority of a new tutor (the one who has manumitted her) who will let her make a will as she wishes.[2]

252. (3) *Coëmptio sacrorum interimendorum causa:* The *sacra privata* were doubtless quite a heavy burden, since the Romans, in order to express "unmixed good fortune," facetiously say "*hereditas sine sacris.*" A

[1] Gaius, 1, § 115.

[2] *Ibid.* Gaius seems even to say that the woman who is mancipated and freed will be able to make a will without authorization. It is more probable that the new tutor (guardian) who, not being an agnate, has no right of succession, will let her dispose by will as she pleases. Cuq, *Institutions*, vol. i, p. 564. Hadrian gave to women the right to make a will, and the coëmptio testam. fac. gr. disappeared. Gaius, *loc. cit.*

woman called to a succession finds herself, by reason of her character as heir, obliged to maintain the domestic cult. In order to free herself from this obligation, she makes 'coëmptio' with an old man as near to his end as possible, and who binds himself by a fiduciary pact to emancipate her. After the 'conventio in manum,' it is the old man who has the obligation of the sacra 'privata:' he dies, and the obligation is extinguished with him.[1]

253. Marriage sine Manus: If marriage is not accompanied or followed by the 'conventio in manum,' the wife remains in her paternal family; she is called not by the name of *materfamilias* reserved for the wife married with manus, but by the name of *uxor*.[2]

254. Marriage without manus does not require any public or religious authority: it may be asked by what shall the existence of this marriage be known; the question will not be put often, for the spouses will generally resort to the *festivitas nuptiarum* and to an *instrumentum dotale* which will establish the situation; but all that is not necessary. From what, then, shall the marriage be inferred? From the cohabitation of the pair? But it is from the principle "*nuptias non concubitus sed consensus facit*" [3] — that the concubine and the wife differ "*solo dilectu.*"

255. The status, then, of the spouses can be established only by the aid of presumptions. Marriage or concubinage was wont to be presumed according as the persons united were or were not of the same rank. It

---

[1] Cicero, *Pro Murena*, 12.†
[2] Aulus Gellius, *Noctae Atticae*, 18, 6.†
[3] *Dig.* 50, 17, 30 (Ulpian).

was so down to the emperor Justin, uncle and predecessor of Justinian. From the constitution of Justin marriage was always presumed.[1]

§ 2. The Essential Conditions of Marriage

256. **Essential Conditions of Marriage:** The essential conditions indispensable to the validity of marriage are three in number: puberty, consent, connubium.

257. (1) **Puberty:** Is the possibility, for a man, of uniting with a woman, and, for a woman, of receiving the embrace of a man with the object of conceiving: the woman, in this event, is said to be *viri potens*.

Puberty was formerly verified by the state of the body.[2] As to boys, the heads of families met on the occasion of the feast of the Liberalia, and, before causing the youth to leave off the *toga praetexta* in order to put on the *toga virilis*, they ascertained if his physical state revealed the genital power. When manners became less gross, puberty of youths was fixed at fourteen years. An analogous practice had been early renounced as to girls, and the age of *viri potentia* was fixed at twelve years.

258. (2) **Consent:** The consents indispensable to marriage are: —

1. That of the contracting parties.[3]
2. That of their respective heads of families.
3. If the future husband is a grandson under the patria potestas of a grandfather, nevertheless the con-

[1] See *infra*, § 263.
[2] Ulpian, *Reg.* 11, § 28; Gaius, 1, § 196.
[3] *Dig.* 23, 2, 28 (Marcianus); *ibid.* 16, § 2 (Paulus); *Code*, 5, 4, 12 (Diocletian and Maximian).

sent of the father of the young man is necessary. This is in consequence of the rule, "*Nemini invito suus heres adgnascatur.*"[1] "No one should, without his consent, be exposed to exercising the paternal power" (the *heres suus* is the descendant subjected to the patria potestas). Indeed, on the death of the grandfather, head of the family, the paternal power over the wife in manu of the *nepos* (grandson) and in all cases, whether the marriage was contracted with or without manus, over the children born of the marriage, will be exercised by the father of the nepos if he has not died first.

The woman needs only the consent of the head of her family, and not that of her father. The latter, indeed, does not run the risk of having his son-in-law or his grandchildren under his power (for *sui heredes*), since the wife enters the family of her husband, and not the husband the family of the wife.

259. These principles lost much of their vigor: the *lex Julia de maritandis ordinibus* (under the principate of Augustus) permitted children to summon into court parents who refused their consent to their marriage, so that the old marriage contract, concluded by the parents with the consent of their children, became in reality a contract concluded by the children with the authorization of their parents.[2]

260. (3) **Connubium**: Connubium is the capacity to contract *justae nuptiae.*

We should distinguish between absolute connubium, general ability to contract marriage, and relative connubium, ability for a given person to contract justae nuptiae with another given person.

[1] *Dig.* 23, 2, 16, § 1 (Paulus); *Inst.* 1, 11, § 7.
[2] Girard, *Manuel*, p. 153.

SOURCES OF THE PATRIA POTESTAS

261. Thus, there absolutely does not exist any connubium for slaves, whose union is given over to nature (*contubernium*),[1] — for peregrini, — for Latins who have not received the jus connubii,[2] — down to the fourth century for soldiers in service,[3] — for the individual held in the bonds of a marriage non dissolved.

But most generally, in the want of connubium only a relative incapacity is to be seen.

262. The prohibitions, which have greatly varied in course of time, are referable either to considerations of a political nature, or to agnatio, cognatio, affinity.

263. (*a*) *Prohibition of a political nature:* Down to 445 B. C. (plebiscitum Canuleium), there was no connubium between patricians and plebeians;[4] — there was none, furthermore, between the freeborn and the freed down to the first lex Julia de maritandis ordinibus.[5] Finally, down to Justin, marriage was prohibited between senators or their descendants and women of shameful profession (*levae, proxenatae,* — female comedians and dancers *quae artem ludicram faciunt,* — courtesans *quae corpore quaestum faciunt,* etc.).[6]

Justin raised these prohibitions: this bounty for the conversion of female sinners was granted on account of the solicitations of the emperor's nephew Justinian; the latter wished indeed to wed the famous Theodora, daughter of a driver of the circus, who had been the ornament of the Embolum, the most celebrated house of prostitution in Constantinople.[7]

---

[1] Ulpian, *Reg.* 5, § 5.   [2] *Ibid.* 5, § 4.
[3] Epistula of Hadrian, line 10. Girard, *Textes,* p. 177.
[4] Livy, 1, 4. †   [5] *Dig.* 23, 2, 23 (Celsus).
[6] *Dig.* 23, 2, 44 pr.   [7] *Code,* 5, 4, 23, § 1 (Justin).

264. *(b) Prohibitions based on relationship or affinity.* Cognatio is an eternal obstacle to marriage in the direct line (between ascendants and descendants); but in the collateral line the prohibition did not extend beyond the third degree (uncle and niece, aunt and nephew). Claudius, who wished to wed his niece Agrippina (already indeed his mistress), obtained from the Senate the repeal of this prohibition of connubium between the *patricus* and his niece.[1]

> ... a law less severe,
> Put Claudius in my bed and Rome at my knees.
> RACINE, *Britannicus.*

This law, made for the occasion, was abrogated by Constantius and Constans.[2]

265. As for *agnatio*, it prevents marriage between the adopter and the descendants of the adopted, between the adopted and natural children of the same father.

266. *Affinitas* (affinity) is the tie which unites a husband or wife to the members of the family of the other. Affinitas, which was not perhaps an obstacle to connubium under the Republic (the mother of Cluentius married her son-in-law),[3] became, under the pagan emperors, a cause of eternal prohibition in the direct line, and under the Christian emperors, in the collateral line, but solely between the brother-in-law and sister-in-law.

267. *(c) Prohibitions laid down by positive laws:* Of this class are the prohibition of marriage: (1) between the adulterous spouse and the paramour;[4] (2) between the guardian (tutor) or the son of the

---

[1] Tacitus, *Annales*, 12.†
[2] *Cod. Theod.* 3, 12, 2 (Constantius and Constans).
[3] Cicero, *Pro Cluentio.*†   [4] *Dig.* 48, 5, 41 (Paulus).

guardian and the ward;[1] between the governor of a province and the women of the province (among whom it was, however, explicitly allowed him to take a concubine);[2] (4) under the Christian emperors, between Jews and Christians.[3]

268. The absence of connubium vitiates the marriage, but incest alone (violation of a provision of law relative to relationship or affinity) has a penal sanction which varies, according to the gravity of the facts (exile, flagellation, *cinguli privatio*, that is, military degradation, capital punishment in certain cases).[4]

§ 3. Effects of Marriage

269. **Effects of Marriage**: These effects vary according as marriage is or is not accompanied with the *conventio in manum*.

270. (1) *Between the spouses:* By the 'conventio in manum' the wife becomes the daughter of her husband; every tie between her and her former family is broken never to be renewed, even in case of the dissolution of the marriage.

The tie which is established between her and the family of her husband is a tie of agnation: whence this consequence that the husband has over her the same rights as over his children: he can condemn his wife to death, but not without taking the opinion of a council composed of the nearest cognates of the wife,

---

[1] *Dig.* 23, 2, 36, 37, and 59 (Paulus).
[2] *Ibid.* 38, 65, § 1 (Paulus); Lamprid. *Alexandri Severi vita*, 42.†
[3] *Code*, 1, 9, 6 (Gratian).
[4] *Cod. Theod.* 3, 12, 1.

namely, the members of her former family.[1] He can also emancipate his wife.

As for the wife, she is heir of her husband and of the paterfamilias of the latter since she is in regard to him *loco filiae*, in regard to the former *loco neptis*.

271. When marriage is not accompanied by the 'conventio in manum' the wife remains under the power of the head of her family, or if she is *sui juris*, under the tutela of her agnates, and cannot claim in the family of her husband any right of succession.[2]

272. Nevertheless she is subject to the domestic jurisdiction, and in order to restore the conjugal domicile if she happens to desert him, her husband has the interdicts *de uxore ducenda, exhibenda*. She is also subject to the suits and penalties of the lex Julia de adulteriis.[3]

273. In marriage with manus, the property of the wife is absorbed in her husband's, since at least on principle the filiifamilias have no property distinct from that of the paterfamilias.[4]

In free marriage (*sine manu*) the wife (uxor) retains the ownership and administration of her property. Under all systems the spouses are incapable of making gifts to each other.[5]

274. (2) *Between the mother and her children:* If the wife is in manu, she is the sister of her children (*loco sororis*) as the daughter of her husband (*loco filiae*),

[1] Denys of Halic. 2, 25 ; Tacitus, *Annales*, 13, 32.†
[2] *Dig.* 43, 30, 1, § 5.
[3] Esmein, *Mélanges*, pp. 92 *et seq.* ; Paul. *Sent.* 2, 26, § 14.
[4] Cicero, *Topica*, 4.†
[5] See § 839.

SOURCES OF THE PATRIA POTESTAS

and the relations of succession between the mother and children are the same as between brothers and sister.

275. If the wife is not in manu, the mother and children *are not of the same family:* no rights, nor duties consequently on either side. These provisions were modified in the second century by the senatusconsulta Tertullianum and Orphitianum, which established succession of mothers to their children and of children to their mothers.

276. (3) *Between the father and his children:* Here, it matters little whether there was or was not a 'conventio in manum:' justae nuptiae always produce *patria potestas*.

277. . . . Upon condition, however, that the child be born from the acts of the husband: It is supposed that at a very early epoch the child was, immediately after birth, laid at the feet of the husband, who raised it or left it on the ground according as he acknowledged or repudiated the paternity. In the expression "*tollere suscipere liberos*"[1] the basis of this conjecture may be found (?).

We have only certain ideas as to the epoch when the question was already solved by the presumption still admitted to-day in French law: presumptions based on the birth of the child more than one hundred and eighty days after the celebration of the marriage or less than three hundred days after its dissolution, and which go back to Hippocrates. But the Roman law

[1] Epistula of Hadrian (Girard, *Textes*, p. 177), "*eis quos patres eorum militiae susceperunt* (ἀνείλαν) *temporibus* . . ."

appears to have admitted contrary evidence much more largely than the French law.[1]

§ 4. Dissolution of Marriage

278. Dissolution of Marriage: Dissolution of marriage may be voluntary or forced.

279. A. Forced Dissolution: It results: —

(1) From the death of either husband or wife.

(2) From the captivity of either; and in this case the 'jus postliminii' does not manifest itself at all. If the captive spouse returns a new marriage with the former conjoint should be contracted, if the latter is free. Under Justinian the wife whose husband has fallen into captivity is obliged to wait five years before contracting a new marriage.

What we have just said concerning captivity among the enemy applies to all cases of slavery (*maxima capitis deminutio*).[2]

(3) From the loss of citizenship (*media capitis deminutio*[3]) since connubium does not exist among the peregrini, and the husband or wife losing citizenship becomes a peregrinus.[4]

280. (4) In marriage with manus, from the loss of family rights (*minima capitis deminutio*): The loss of family rights is without influence on marriage sine manu, unless the new situation of the husband and

---

[1] *Dig.* 2, 4, 5 (Paulus) : *Pater vero is est quem nuptiae demonstrant.*

[2] See §§ 341 *et seq.*

[3] See § 345.

[4] This is the rigor of the early law ; it no longer exists under the Severi (third century A. D.) : see *Dig.* 48, 20, 5, § 1 (Ulpian), and *Code*, 5, 17, 1 (Alexander Severus).

SOURCES OF THE PATRIA POTESTAS 87

wife creates a tie of a nature prohibiting connubium.

281. Thus, a father-in-law adopts his son-in-law; the latter becomes the adopted brother of his wife, and the marriage is dissolved. This may be avoided, however: the father-in-law, before adopting his son-in-law, has only to emancipate his daughter. The son-in-law indeed enters the family, but the daughter is no longer therein.[1]

282. **Voluntary Dissolution: Divorce and Repudiation:** It is manifested either by the *repudium*, act of one party, or by *divorce*, which is, on the contrary, an agreement of the parties. Divorce by mutual consent did not exist, perhaps, on principle, for the 'nuptiae confarreatae;' it was introduced at all events beginning at a certain epoch, since mention is made in the texts of a *diffarreatio*, — save for the marriage of the *flamen dialis*, which is indissoluble.[2]

283. Excepting 'nuptiae confarreatae,' *divortium* was always allowed, although rare, during the first five centuries of Rome, and the contract *ne diverteretur* was held to be invalid.[3]

284. Abolished by Justin, it was reëstablished almost immediately by Justinian: the indissolubility of marriage prevailed in the Christian law only in the West and toward the beginning of the ninth century.

285. *Repudium* emanates either from the sole will of one of the married pair, or even from the will of the head of the family: a paterfamilias could dissolve the

[1] *Inst.* 1, 10, § 2.
[2] Aulus Gellius, *Noct. Att.* 10, 15. Cf. Esmein, *Mélanges*, p. 17. †
[3] *Code*, 8, 38, 2 (Alexander Severus).

marriage of his daughter without her consent (provided the marriage had been made without the 'conventio in manum,' for in this event the paternal power is extinguished).[1]

286. In the time of the Antonines (under Antoninus Pius, according to Paulus, under Marcus Aurelius, if a constitution of Diocletian and Maximian is to be believed) a father was prohibited from dissolving the marriage of his daughter without her consent, "*nisi adjecta filiae persona.*" [2]

287. The *repudium* persisted under Christian law, which was content with punishing *unjustified* repudiations, but without ever contesting the principle of the institution.[3]

288. **Forms of Divorce and Repudiation:** *Divorce* takes place by the simple agreement of the parties without any particular form.

According to the lex Julia de adulteriis, *repudium* requires notice to be given in the presence of seven witnesses of a *libellus repudii.*[4]

§ 5. Second Marriages

289. **Second Marriages:** Among us, the widow or divorcee cannot remarry until at the end of ten months (to avoid the *turbatio sanguinis*, confusion of offspring). The rules of the Roman law were less fixed: the lex Julia did not render the wife *caelebs*

---

[1] Cicero, *Rhetorica*, 2, 24.†

[2] Paul. *Sent.* 5, 6, § 15; *Code*, 5, 17, 5 [where Diocletian attributes the rule to Marcus Aurelius. See, also, *Dig.* 43, 30, 1, 5, and *ibid.* 2].

[3] *Nov.* 22 and 117.

[4] Juvenal, *Sat.* 6, verse 147.†

SOURCES OF THE PATRIA POTESTAS

until a year after the death of her husband, but she attained it six months after divorce; therefore the period of widowhood did not exceed six months in this second case.[1] The Christian law prohibited the wife from remarrying before the expiration of a year.[2]

The wife of the *hostis*, of the person condemned for high treason (*perduellio damnatus*), of certain suicides, could, in the classical era, remarry immediately.[3]

290. The senatusconsultum Plancianum, rendered under Hadrian or a little before, obliged the wife enceinte at the time of the divorce to declare her pregnancy within thirty days, and fragment 1 of the Digest, book 25, title 3, *De Agnoscendis Liberis*, makes us acquainted in detail with the minute precautions which are or might be taken by the husband to prevent supposititious offspring.

291. The pagan law is favorable to second marriages: it forces by every possible means the wife who is divorced or repudiated to contract a new union. Thus, men and women not remarrying within a certain period of time are afflicted by the *leges caducariae* (leges Julia and Pappia Poppea, which deprive the caelibes and the orbi of the benefit of gifts by will)."[4]

Section II. — Adoption

§ 1. Adoption in General

292. Of Adoption in General: Adoption *lato sensu* is a proceeding of the civil law (jus civile) de-

---

[1] Ulpian, *Reg.* 14, § 1.
[2] *Code*, 5, 9, 2 (Gratian, Valentinian III, and Theodosius II).
[3] Neratius cited by Ulpian, *Dig.* 3, 2, 11.
[4] See *infra*, § 755.

signed to create artificially the patria potestas for the benefit of a head of a family over a person who is not subject thereto by birth.

This person may be absolutely unrelated to the adopter, — he may also be connected with him by natural filiation as a *liber naturalis;* or by the tie of cognation, as, for example, when a maternal grandfather adopts the child born *ex justis nuptiis* of his daughter.

293. The Romans attached a great importance to adoption which was a means of preventing the *sacra privata* from being extinguished when there were not descendants to perpetuate them.

294. Adoption had sometimes for its end the satisfaction of a political interest. Thus, Clodius, patrician, had himself adopted by the plebeian Fonteius in his canvass for a plebeian magistracy, the tribuneship.[1]

295. **Essential Conditions of Adoption:** (1) In the last state of the law, the adopter should be a full *pubes*, that is, eighteen years older than the adopted. — Had this requirement always existed? It is allowable to doubt it: Fonteius was younger than Clodius, adopted by him, and Cicero, who violently criticises this adoption, does not go so far as to declare it clearly illegal. The question was still controverted in the time of Gaius.[2]

296. (2) Adoption is prohibited for eunuchs because adoption *imitates nature;* but it is not prohibited for impotent persons (*spadones*).[3]

---

[1] Cicero, *Pro Domo*, 13.†
[2] Cicero, *ibid.* 13; Gaius, 1, § 106; *Inst.* 1, 11, § 4.
[3] Girard, *Manuel*, p. 173; [*Inst.* 1, 11, 9].

297. (3) Adoption, in the general sense of the word,[1] is also prohibited for women, since women cannot exercise the paternal power. We have, however, a rescript of Diocletian and Maximian of 291 A. D. which permits adoption by a mother who has lost her children; it can be a matter here only of adoption restricted to the consequences alone possible for the benefit of a woman.[2]

298. We shall, in studying the adoption of persons *sui juris* (arrogatio), notice some more restrictions.[3]

299. **Adoption and Arrogatio:** Adoption is the general term: but in this matter are distinguished *arrogatio*, which is the adoption of a person *sui juris* (head of a family) by another head of a family; and *adoption properly so-called*, which is applicable to a person already placed under the authority of a paterfamilias (a person *alieni juris*).[4]

§ 2. Arrogatio

300. **Importance of Arrogatio:** Arrogatio presented a special importance because it caused a family to disappear in the person of the *arrogatus*, and, consequently, extinguished a domestic cult.[5]

301. **Forms of Arrogatio:** By reason of its importance, arrogatio could not be performed save at a meeting of the pontifices and with the consent of the people assembled in the comitia curiata (*calatis comitiis*), consequently by virtue of a *lex curiata* passed probably with the pontifex maximus presiding.[6]

Furthermore, if the people, on principle, really assembled to sanction arrogationes, they were later satisfied

---

[1] See *infra*, § 299.   [2] *Code*, 8, 47, 5; *Inst.* 1, 11, § 10.
[3] See *infra*, § 302.   [4] *Dig.* 1, 7, 1, § 1 (Modestinus).
[5] Aulus Gellius, *Noctae Atticae*, 5, 19.†   [6] *Ibid.*†

with a meeting of thirty lictors who were deemed to represent the thirty curiae, and it was before these thirty lictors that arrogatio occurred.

302. In order that arrogatio might be had, the arrogans and the arrogatus must present themselves before the comitia; consequently both of them must have access to the comitia curiata (we would say to-day "that they must be *electors*").

This explains why neither women, nor peregrini, nor slaves, nor impuberes, could be arrogated: for indeed women, peregrini, slaves, impuberes had not access to the comitia.[1] This is what is expressed, as regards women, by the phrase of Gaius: "*per populum feminae non adoptantur.*"[2]

303. **Arrogatio by Rescript of the Emperor:** Later, for arrogatio by virtue of a lex curiata is substituted arrogatio by rescript of the emperor. It must not be wondered that in this era the *arrogatio of women* becomes possible: it was indeed introduced or authorized by Antoninus Pius.[3]

304. In the same era we find established the arrogatio of minors (impuberes); but special precautions were taken that the arrogatio might not lead to the ruin of the arrogatus.[4]

305. **Arrogatio by Will:** Along with arrogatio by lex curiata there was arrogatio by will (often improperly called adoption by will), the most celebrated example of which is the adoption by will made by

---

[1] Aulus Gellius, *Noctae Atticae*, 5, 19. †
[2] Cf. Ulpian, *Reg.* 8, § 5.
[3] *Dig.* 1, 7, 21 (Gaius).
[4] Gaius, 1, § 102; see *infra*, § 311.

Julius Caesar in favor of his sister's son, Octavius.[1] Precise information as to this arrogatio is lacking, but it is generally thought that it ought to be confirmed by a lex curiata.

306. **Effects of Arrogatio:** We have to examine the effects of arrogatio: (1) On the person; (2) On the property of the arrogatus.

307. *Effects on the person of the arrogatus:* The patria potestas with all its extreme consequences (*jus vitae necisque*) is acquired by the arrogans over the new filiusfamilias.

308. In return, the arrogatus acquires in the family of the arrogans all the rights of a legitimate child; he becomes the 'heres suus' of the arrogans and the agnate of his agnates.

It results, therefore, that he sees rising before him all the obstacles to 'connubium' caused by the tie of agnation.[2]

309. The effects of arrogatio were not manifested solely in the person of the arrogatus, but also in the persons of his children who become the grandchildren of the arrogans. A celebrated example to cite on this point is: Augustus adopted Tiberius, but he did so only after the latter had adopted Germanicus. What Augustus wished, indeed, was, quite agreeably to his wife Livia, to secure Germanicus as heir by making him his grandson. Unfortunately the predecease of Germanicus rendered Tiberius master of the Roman world.[3]

310. *Effects on the property of the arrogatus:* The

[1] Suetonius, *Div. Julius*, 83.†
[2] See *supra*, § 265.   [3] *Inst.* 1, 11, § 11.

entire property of the arrogatus is absorbed in the property of the arrogans.

Hence this consequence that, if the arrogatus happened to leave by emancipation the family into which he had entered by arrogatio, he would lose his property.

The law does not seem to be moved by this danger concerning those more than twenty-five years of age; but it would seem that, from the time of Claudius, the minor under twenty-five years of age could not give himself in arrogatio without the consent of a curator.[1]

311. This is certain that, by the terms of a rescript of Antoninus Pius, the paterfamilias arrogating an impubes, was held, if he emancipated him *ante pubertatem*, to restore him his property; and, if the emancipation took place *sine justa causa*, not only had the arrogatus a right to all his property, but he had furthermore, after the decease of the arrogans, the right to demand the fourth part of what would have come to him by succession, had he not been emancipated. This is called the *quarta Antonina*.[2]

312. These restitutions and indemnities were assured by means of a verbal promise of the arrogans secured by bondsmen (*fidejussores*). This promise of the arrogans and the bondsmen was received by a *servus publicus*, later by a *tabularius*, subordinate officer of free condition, sort of notary or clerk of court.[3]

313. *Effect on the debts of the arrogatus*: Arrogation (like all *capitis minutiones*) does away with the pro-

---

[1] *Dig.* 1, 7, 8 (Modestinus).
[2] *Dig.* 38, 5, 13 (Paulus).   [3] *Inst.* 1, 11, § 3.

perty of the individual, *not only as to assets, but also as to debts.* The arrogatus has no longer either property or debts; but while his assets are gathered by somebody, his debts pass to nobody; such was the rigor of the ancient law.[1]

314. The praetor earnestly believed himself authorized to remedy the shocking injustice of this early doctrine: he gave to the creditors of the arrogatus an action *de peculio*, the resultant of which was to compel the arrogans to pay the debts of the arrogatus to the extent of the property of the latter, property which the praetor considers as a *peculium.* — Or again, the praetor worked by way of *restitutio in integrum;* namely, that, putting back things in the same status as before arrogatio, he gave to the creditors, in spite of the civil law (jus civile), a right of action against the property of their debtor as if the arrogatio had not occurred. — Then one of two things happened: the arrogans must pay, or the creditors seized the assets of the arrogatus which had not ceased to be their pledge, since these were deemed not to have ceased to be the property of their debtor.[2]

§ 3. Adoption properly so-called

315. **Purpose of Adoption:** It does not affect a head of a family, but a filiusfamilias: a person *alieni juris* passes out from the patria potestas of his natural family's head to fall under the patria potestas of a new paterfamilias.

In order that adoption may be accomplished, it is therefore necessary: (1) To extinguish the power of the old paterfamilias; (2) to create the patria potestas of the new paterfamilias.

[1] Gaius, 3, § 84. [2] *Ibid.*

96 THE FIRST YEAR OF ROMAN LAW

316. **Forms of Adoption:** Hence the very Roman procedure of this operation.

317. A. *Extinction of the* PATRIA POTESTAS *of the first paterfamilias:* It is known that the law of the XII Tables permitted a Roman paterfamilias to sell, or rather to mancipate, his children. But the mancipated son did not remain indefinitely *in mancipio*. The censor could give him his freedom. He fell back then under the power of his paterfamilias, who could mancipate him again. Now the law of the XII Tables had decided that this speculation could be done but three times. After the third mancipation, the child given his freedom fell back no more under the power of the paterfamilias. "*Si pater filium ter venumduit filius a patre liber esto.*" [1]

To attain the destruction of the paternal power, the Roman jurisconsults came to utilize this principle: the paterfamilias mancipated his son three times successively to a friend who set him free each time; after the third setting at liberty the son fell back no more under the paternal power.[2]

318. B. *Creation of the* PATRIA POTESTAS *of the new paterfamilias:* The task is only half done. The child is freed from the patria potestas of his paterfamilias. He must be subjected to the power of his adopted father; for that, recourse is had to another proceeding: the *cessio in jure* which is the imitation of a suit in revindication. The adopter and the paterfamilias present themselves before the magistrate (it is not necessary, however, that the scene occur in court),

[1] Ulpian, *Reg.* 10, § 1.
[2] Aulus Gellius, *Noctae Atticae*, 5, 19 †; Gaius, 1, § 134.

SOURCES OF THE PATRIA POTESTAS 97

and the adopter claims the child as his son. The paterfamilias does not deny this claim, and the magistrate, by an act of gracious jurisdiction, awards the child to his new paterfamilias.[1]

318. *Cont.* A single mancipation suffices to extinguish the paternal power in respect to girls and grandchildren.[2]

319. **Effects of Adoption:** (1) *On the person of the adopted:* The adopted passes under the patria potestas of the adoptive father, *but he alone passes:* his children, if any, remain under the paternal power of their old paterfamilias.[3]

320. The adopted may enter into his new family either as son or grandson. In the latter event two hypotheses may be offered: either the adopter does not designate, among his sons, a father for the adopted, and this latter is assimilated to a child of a predeceased son; — or the adopter assigns his adopted grandson to be the child of one of his sons particularly designated. The consent of the designated son is in such case necessary, because he is called upon, in the event of the death of the adopter, to exercise the paternal power over the adopted, to have the latter as a suus heres, and we have already cited the rule by the terms of which no one can have an heir against his will "*nemini invito suus heres adgnascatur.*"[4]

321. (2) *On the name of the adopted:* The adopted loses his name *gentilicie* and retains it only as a surname, transforming the last name into an adjective. Thus Scipio, the second Africanus, did not belong at

[1] Gaius, 1, § 134.   [2] *Ibid.*
[3] *Dig.* 1, 7, 40 pr. (Modestinus).   [4] *Inst.* 1, 11, §§ 5–7.

all to the gens Cornelia, but to the gens Aemilia (he was son of the celebrated Paulus Emilius): after his adoption he becomes *P. Cornelius Scipio Aemilianus*, otherwise called "Scipio Aemilianus." C. Octavius became likewise *C. Julius Caesar Octavianus*.[1]

322. (3) *On the rights of succession of the adopted:* The adopted acquires in his new family all the rights of succession of a son or grandson of the paterfamilias, he becomes 'suus heres.' In return, he loses all the rights of succession in his original family.

323. **Reforms of Justinian:** Justinian completely overturned this system. According to Code, 8, 47, *de adoptionibus*, 10, the adopted child loses in no case his rights of succession in his natural family, and he acquires new ones in the family which he enters by adoption.

So far as the paternal power is concerned, Justinian distinguishes between the case where the child is adopted by a stranger and that where he is adopted by one of his maternal ascendants. In the first case, the adoption is said to be *minus plena*, and the adopted remains under the paternal power of his original paterfamilias. Adoption has no effect other than to confer on him rights of succession in the adoptive family. In the second case, the adoption is said to be *plena*, and the child passes under the patria potestas of the maternal ascendant who adopted him.[2]

Section III. — Legitimation

324. **Liberi Naturales — Spurii:** Children born out of marriage were divided at Rome into two

---

[1] Girard, *Manuel*, p. 176. [2] *Code*, 8, 47, 10 (Justinian).

classes: (1) those born from concubinage; (2) those born from accidental relations. The first are called 'liberi naturales,' the second 'spurii' or *vulgo concepti*. For each there exists no tie with the father who begat them, which caused it to be said with considerable pertinence that at Rome there are only *lawful fathers* and *natural mothers* (we know, indeed, that the lawful mother exercises no authority over the children born of her marriage).

325. The *liberi naturales* are not at all tainted; but no more for them than for the 'spurii' is there any civil relationship with their father, and it is by virtue of a privilege that Hadrian confers on soldiers the right to have for heirs *ab intestato* and ranking only as cognates the natural children which they have had during their service.[1]

326. The Christian law profoundly modified this situation: quite contrary to the 'spurii,' it rendered natural children, properly so-called, susceptible of legitimation.

327. **Legitimation:** Legitimation is a new proceeding put at the disposal of natural fathers to acquire the patria potestas over children whom they have had outside of 'justae nuptiae.' Legitimation differs essentially from adoption in that it is applicable only to the 'liber naturalis,' while adoption was applicable indifferently to the 'liber naturalis,' the 'spurius' or the 'extraneus.'

328. **Modes of Legitimation:** There are three of them: (1) legitimation by *subsequent marriage* ; (2) legitimation by *imperial rescript* ; (3) legitimation by *oblatio to the curia*.

[1] Girard, *Textes*, p. 176.

100 THE FIRST YEAR OF ROMAN LAW

The first two proceedings offer no difficulty of comprehension. The first consists in a regular marriage evidenced by a contract (*instrumentum*) between the parties in concubinage.¹ The second is an act of imperial omnipotence.

329. The third merits some explanation. It is necessary to call to mind that the 'curia' was the body (*collegium*) of *decurions*, magistrates charged with the collection of taxes and responsible for their receipt. The honor of belonging to the curia was onerous and to be dreaded; so the emperors resorted to every proceeding either of enticement or compulsion in order to recruit the corps of decurions (or *curiales*): legitimation by 'oblatio' to the 'curia' was one of these means: the 'curialis' who had a natural child could legitimate him by merely making him a member of the collegium to which he himself belonged.²

CHAPTER IV

DISSOLUTION OF THE PATERNAL POWER

330. **Causes of the Dissolution of the Paternal Power:** The paternal power is dissolved: (1) and (2) by the death of the paterfamilias or the filiusfamilias; (3) by the three 'capitis deminutiones' of either; (4) by emancipation; (5) by elevation of the child to certain dignities; (6) by certain penal forfeitures pronounced against the paterfamilias.

330. *Cont. Death:* The paternal power is extin-

[1] *Code*, 5, 27, 5 (Zeno); *Inst.* 1, 10, § 13.
[2] *Code*, 5, 27, 3 (Theodosius II and Valentinian III).

DISSOLUTION OF THE PATERNAL POWER 101

guished : (1) by the death of the person subject to it.

(2) By the death of the person exercising it. But in this case the person subject to the patria potestas, according to the cases, will become *sui juris* or fall under the power of another paterfamilias (for example, on the death of a grandfather the grandchildren find themselves under the power of their father).[1]

330. *Cont. Capitis deminutiones :* (3) by the three 'capitis deminutiones' of the paterfamilias or of the filiusfamilias.[2]

331. **Emancipation :** (4) by emancipation. Emancipation is, as was seen above,[3] the first part of adoption. It is recalled to mind that three successive sales to a friend followed by three liberations by the latter resulted in the destruction of the paternal power, which was reconstituted for the benefit of the new paterfamilias by means of an *in jure cessio*.

If the second part of adoption is omitted, that is the 'in jure cessio,' emancipation will be had, since after the third liberation by the friend the filiusfamilias will be freed from the paternal power.[4]

332. We should mention on this point the existence of a twofold proceeding: (1) There is a halt at the last liberation by the figurant, and the figurant becomes the patronus of the emancipated. (2) Most generally, after the third emancipation, instead of liberating the filiusfamilias, the figurant sells him back to the paterfamilias, who himself emancipates him and consequently reserves the rights of patronus.

[1] *Inst.* 1, 12 pr.
[2] See *infra*, §§ 341 *et seq.*
[3] See § 317.
[4] Gaius, 1, § 132.

102 THE FIRST YEAR OF ROMAN LAW

All these measures were concerted between the paterfamilias and the friend who lends himself for their operation, in a contract which is called *contract of fiducia*.

333. Anastasian Emancipation: In 502 A. D., under the emperor Anastasius, these ceremonies were replaced by a rescript of the emperor, which is called the *Anastasian emancipation*.[1]

334. Justinianian Emancipation: The Anastasian emancipation was only optional, and was concurrent electively with the old proceeding. But some thirty years later, in 531 A. D., Justinian definitely abolished the old ceremony, and in making allusion to the rod (*vindicta*) which was used in the emancipation, he declares that he wishes no more of these blows of the stick (*rhapismata*) which he finds to be injurious; emancipation shall be hereafter either by imperial rescript (*Anastasian emancipation*) or by a simple declaration of the paterfamilias before the magistrate (*Justinianian emancipation*).[2]

335. Extinction of the Paternal Power by Certain Dignities: (5) The paternal power is also extinguished: in the Pagan era by elevation of the filiusfamilias to the dignity of a priest of Jupiter (flamen dialis), by entrance of the filiafamilias into the college of the Vestal Virgins.[3] Under Justinian, by elevation of the filiusfamilias to the dignities of patricius, consul, praetorian praefect, praefectus urbi, magister militum, and bishop.[4]

[1] *Code*, 8, 48, 5 (Anastasius).
[2] *Code*, 8, 48, 6 (Justinian) ; *Inst.* 1, 12, § 6.
[3] Gaius, 1, § 130.
[4] *Inst.* 1, 12, § 4 ; *Code*, 10, 32, 67 (66) (Justinian) ; *Nov.* 131, c. 3.

336. **Forfeiture:** (6) Finally, in Byzantine law, certain offenses of the pater freed the children from the paternal power, but without losing their rights in the family; for example, the exposing of a child, the fact of delivering over a daughter to prostitution.[1]

337. **Effects of Emancipation:** Emancipation results in causing the child of a family to disappear completely from it. In the rigor of the ancient law, the filiusfamilias who is emancipated had no rights of succession, and found himself without property. Also certain Romanists suppose that in theory emancipation was a penalty.

338. But it changed its character:[2] first, after the creation of the *peculium castrense*, the emancipated child retained this peculium (it was also the same later of the *peculium quasi castrense*).

The *peculium profecticium*, being the property of the father, should have remained his; but it came to be considered as granted to the child by gift which was presumed in case of silence: in order that the father might retain the peculium profecticium it must be reserved in the emancipation.[3]

As to the *bona adventicia* (of which the father had but the usufruct), the Christian emperors granted them to the child, excepting an indemnity to the father for the loss of his enjoyment, — indemnity which was fixed by Constantine at one third of the entire property, and by a scarcely happy innovation of Justinian, at one half of the usufruct.[4]

[1] *Code*, 8, 51, 2 ; *Code*, 11, 41, 6 ; *Nov.* 12, c. 2.
[2] Paul. *Sent.* 2, 25, § 5. "*Filiusfamilias invitus emancipari non cogitur.*"
[3] *Frag. Vat.* 260.   [4] *Inst.* 2, 9, § 2. See, also, 3, 28.

339. Quite early, the praetorian law (jus honorarium) did away with the loss of the rights of succession by giving to the child possession of the property 'unde liberi' (*bonorum possessio unde liberi*) which permitted him to share with the 'sui heredes' as if he had not gone out of the family.

340. On the other hand, the father succeeded to his predeceased son in spite of emancipation, but for that there was no need of new law; the father became ordinarily indeed the *patronus* of the emancipated, and we shall see later that it was the patronus who, in default of children, inherited from the emancipated.[2]

APPENDIX

To Titles I to III, and to Sections I to IV of Title IV of Book II

Capitis Deminutiones

341. **Caput**: 'Caput' is the juristic personality of the individual. It is composed of three elements: (1) freedom; (2) citizenship; (3) family. Sometimes a fourth is added, which is the *civic honor* called by the Romans 'existimatio.'

342. *Capitis deminutio*: When there is a disappearance of one of these three elements, it is said that there is a capitis deminutio.

Does this expression cause to arise the idea of lessening?[3] This is one of the explanations given of it;

---

[1] See *infra*, § 794.   [2] See *infra*, § 793 and note.
[3] That is, "*impairment.*" Cf. Roby, *Roman Priv. Law*, vol. i, p. 41, "*head-abatement.*" — S.

however, it may be objected that the filiusfamilias who is given in adoption suffers no lessening, and that nevertheless his change of status is, by the acknowledgment of all the jurisconsults, a capitis deminutio.[1]

There is another explanation which is derived from the manner in which the rolls of the census were kept: every time a person is affected by a capitis deminutio, the entry concerning him is struck out on the roll of the census, leaving it open for him to be reëntered in another section if occasion demand, and the section where it was first made is thus lessened by an entry (caput).

This suppression of an entry on the roll would be what would have given rise to the expression "capitis deminutio."

343. **Various Capitis Deminutiones:** There are three capitis deminutiones: (1) maxima capitis deminutio, loss of freedom; (2) media capitis deminutio, loss of the right of citizenship; (3) minima capitis deminutio, loss of family rights.

344. *Maxima capitis deminutio (loss of freedom):* Results from captivity; but it is more theoretical than practical, for captivity becomes effaced, in case of a return home, by the jus postliminii,[2] and, in case of death while a captive, by the fiction of the lex Cornelia.[3]

On the other hand, there is a very practical loss of freedom by reason of certain condemnations.[4] Most generally in reality, for the most part, however, a freeman loses his freedom by causing himself to be sold by an accomplice.[5]

---

[1] The theory mentioned is Savigny's: *contra*, Gaius, 1, § 162.
[2] See *supra*, § 121. [3] See *supra*, § 123.
[4] See *supra*, § 130. [5] See *supra*, § 125.

345. *Media capitis deminutio (loss of citizenship)*: It results also from certain condemnations.[1]

346. *Minima capitis deminutio*: As to minima capitis deminutio, it is produced whenever an individual, being free and a citizen, loses his family rights. For instance, a woman who falls under 'manus,' a head of a family who is arrogated, a filiusfamilias given in adoption, a legitimated child (the legitimated child leaves the family of his mother to fall under the paternal power).

347. **Effects of Capitis Deminutio:** The fundamental principle in this matter is that the civil capacity of the 'capite minutus' is destroyed by a sort of *civil death*.

348. From the point of view of the individual, all ties of civil relationship based on the paternal power are broken; — the ties of natural relationship subsist, whence it results that capitis deminutio, which produced enormous effects in the epoch when civil relationship was everything, became of little importance in the epoch when natural ties prevailed over civil relationship.

349. From the point of view of property, capitis deminutio took away the property of the 'capite minutus,' both liabilities and assets. We have already studied this doctrine in its most interesting consequences while treating of arrogatio: we therefore refer to the explanations given above.[2]

In case of capitis deminutio media or maxima there is no ground for the 'restitutio in integrum;' but the praetor gives to the creditors of the 'capite minutus' an

[1] See *supra*, § 188.   [2] See *supra*, §§ 310 *et seq.*

action against him who has benefited by his property, and, if the latter refuses to pay, they proceed to seize the property of the 'capite minutus.'

Such was the praetorian doctrine; but as generally the person who benefited by the property of the condemned is none other than the State, seizure became impossible. What then? The question was perhaps unanswerable had not the State, when it confiscated the property of a 'capite minutus,' adopted the practice of paying the debts to the extent of the assets.

350. **Reforms of the Byzantine Law:** The effects of 'capitis deminutio minima' were greatly changed in Byzantine law: the persons who suffered it no longer lose their property; this property is simply transformed into 'peculium castrense,' 'quasi-castrense,'[1] or 'adventicium.' The result is that it does not cease to be the security of the creditors of the capite minutus, excepting the deduction of an indemnity to be awarded to the new head of the family for the loss of the enjoyment to which he has a right of the 'bona adventicia.'[1]

351. **Breaches of Existimatio:** Existimatio, accessory element of status, the signification of which we have given above, is impaired by infamia, by being intestabilis, and by turpitudo.

352. *Infamia:* This is a general term in which are included all the various forfeitures pronounced by different magistrates (censorian, consular, praetorian infamia); these forfeitures might extend from prohibition to come into court (praetorian infamia) to deprivation of electoral rights (censorian infamia).

[1] Girard, *Manuel* (cap. dim.), p. 194.

353. *Being intestabilis:* This is the incapacity of being a witness or to have others for witnesses:[1] it affects the author of a libellous writing (*carmen famosum*).

354. *Turpitudo:* Actual dishonor afflicting by operation of law, or by means of a decree of a magistrate, certain persons or professions; turpitudo resulted in creating certain obstacles to 'connubium,' exclusions from the 'tutela,' or incapacities in testamentary matters. Thus by the terms of a constitution of Domitian, *mulieres probrosae*, namely, women given over to immoral practices (*quae lenocinium faciebant*) were declared incapable of receiving legacies.[2]

CHAPTER V

INCAPACITIES OF FACT

Section I. — **Preliminary Notions**

355. We have passed in review incapacities in law, which are veritable *civil deaths*. But it is possible that owing to certain circumstances of fact (age, sex, mental condition), some individuals in possession of a complete personality (of their 'caput') find themselves "unable to play in the juristic life the rôle incumbent upon them."

These individuals are not *incapable in law*, but *incapable in fact*. The enjoyment of their rights is intact and not assailed, but the exercise of these rights by

---

[1] Or to make a will, *Dig.* 28, 1, 18, § 1 (Ulpian). The statement of the text is supported by Gaius in *Dig. ibid.* 26. — S.

[2] Cf. Machelard (survivorship), pp. 76 *et seq.*†

them, or at least by *themselves alone*, becomes a peril of which they would be the first victims.

To provide against the inconvenience of these conditions of fact, the law invented the tutelae and curatelae.

Section II. — **Tutela**

§ 1. Tutela in General

356. **Origin:** The institution of guardianship (tutela) is based on the actual incapacity resulting from being a minor (impubes), — or from sex, — a very real incapacity in the first case, and, in the second, an artificial incapacity which is but the creation of customs or statute.

§ 2. Guardianship of Minors

357. **Guardianship of Minors:** It is not sufficient to be *sui juris* in order to be able to manage one's affairs; it is necessary, furthermore, to have the intelligence needed for this purpose. The infant child has indeed legal capacity as soon as he becomes head of the family; but he lacks actual capacity. Hence, the guardianship of minors, that is the placing of a minor (impubes) *sui juris* (*caput liberum* as the definition of Servius says) under the authority and protection of a person (*tutor*, from *tueri*, protect) who will look after his affairs for him.[1]

358. **Various Kinds of Guardianship:** The guardian (tutor) may be appointed either by the will of the minor's head of the family, or by law, or by the magistrates, or by means of a contract called 'fiducia.' Therefore there are four kinds of tutela:

---

[1] *Inst.* 1, 13, §§ 1, 2.

(1) testamentary guardianship; (2) statutory guardianship (tutela legitima); (3) guardianship established by the magistrate; (4) fiduciary guardianship (tutela fiduciaria).

359. *Testamentary guardianship:*[1] This guardianship necessitates no development: it is established by the will of the paterfamilias and its existence depends upon the validity of the will. It is, however, important to bear in mind that the appointment of a guardian by the paterfamilias, even when this guardian has himself excused, is appointed only *ad tempus,* or dies before the testator, is always sufficient to avoid the statutory guardianship. In the provision of the testator is to be seen both an expression of confidence in the guardian whom he appoints and a want of confidence as to guardians by law whom he repudiates; if the appointment of guardian fails, the want of confidence remains and suffices for the appointment by the magistrate of a guardian, on the failure of the testamentary guardian.[2]

360. *Statutory guardianship:* This is derived from the law and particularly the law of the XII Tables. The principle which controls this matter is stated in the adage: "*Ubi successionis emolumentum est, ibi et onus tutelae esse debet.*"[3]

Actually there are but two guardianships by law, tutelae legitimae, of agnates and of patroni.

The agnate to exercise guardianship is he who would inherit; if there are several agnates of the same de-

[1] This tutela dates from the XII Tables: "*Uti legassit super pecunia* TUTELAVE *suae rei, ita jus esto.*" Ulpian, *Reg.* 11, § 14.
[2] *Dig.* 26, 2, 11, §§ 3, 4 (Ulpian); *Dig.* 26, 4, 6 (Paulus).
[3] *Inst.* 1, 17.

gree, they share the tutela as they would share the inheritance from the minor, if the latter happened to die.[1]

The guardianship of patroni rests on the same principle. The patronus who would inherit is therefore he who should exercise guardianship.*[2]

361. *Fiduciary guardianship:* To these two tutelae legitimae is ordinarily added a third, *that of the father* of *the manumitted child;* but this guardianship is called statutory only in respect to the mancipating father; it belongs, in reality, to another class of guardianship called by the Romans 'tutelae fiduciariae.'

Let us take the proceeding of manumission such as we have described: a paterfamilias mancipates his son three times to a figurant, who liberates him three times; who should be the patronus of the emancipated? Evidently the third party, who is manumissor.

But by a contract of fiducia the father reserves for himself this last liberation. It is only by virtue of this contract of fiducia that the son reënters the family during an instant of full capacity, when the patria potestas is exhausted by three successive sales. The father no longer derives his rights from the law, but from the contract of fiducia; if he becomes guardian it is by virtue of this contract. He receives, therefore, the name of 'tutor legitimus' only by courtesy: the

[1] *Inst.* 1, 16, § 7.
*[2] *Inst.* 1, 17, *de leg. patr. tut.* A peculiarity is to be noticed here. When two persons have over a slave, one quiritary ownership, the other bonitary ownership (see *infra*, §§ 597 *et seq.*), according to the lex Julia Norbana, the tutela belongs after manumission to the quiritary owner, although the right to inherit belongs to him having the slave *in bonis.* Ulpian, *Reg.* 11, § 19.

proof is that the guardianship takes the name of fiduciary when it passes his children.[1]

362. Why is not this guardianship a statutory guardianship like that of the sons of the patronus of the freedman? *Because there is no right of succession;* they who become guardians do not inherit from the ward (pupillus); therefore, since statutory guardianship is but a consequence of being presumptive heir, their guardianship is not statutory.[2]

363. *Guardianship established by magistrates:* There is ground for this guardianship when there are not any statutory guardians, or an appointment, fulfilled or non-effective, of a testamentary guardian has disclosed the distrust of the head of the family of the statutory guardians.[3]

364. Guardians by magisterial appointment are called *Atilian* guardians and *Juliatitian* guardians, from the name of the lex Atilia which established them for the city of Rome, and the leges Julia and Titia which established them in the provinces.

365. The magistrates who appointed guardians were, at Rome, the praetor conjointly with the majority of the tribunes of the plebs. The lex Atilia is prior to 187 B. C.; during this year the freedwoman Hispala Fescennia, who had revealed the mysteries of the Bacchanalia, is known to have asked for a guardian from the praetor urbanus and the tribunes of the plebs. Therefore the lex Atilia was passed.

Claudius transferred the appointment of guardians

---

[1] *Inst.* 1, 19.   [2] *Ibid.*
[3] *Inst.* 1, 20 pr., and § 1. See *supra*, § 359.

to the consuls,¹ and Marcus Aurelius intrusted it to a special *praetor tutelaris*.²

As for the leges Julia and Titia (some writers believe that it is a matter of but one law, the lex Julia Titia), they date from the reign of *Augustus*.

366. The guardians of children of illustrious families were appointed by the *praefectus urbi*.

367. **Administration of the Guardian:** The intervention of the guardian is manifested under two forms:³ —

(1) The guardian *negotia gerit:* that is, he acts alone in behalf of the ward.

(2) The guardian *auctoritatem interponit:* That is, he lends his assistance to the act done by the ward himself. "*Auctorne fis?*" the guardian is asked by the person contracting with the ward. "*Auctor fio,*" replies the guardian.⁴

368. The act of *negotiorum gestio* creates some complications owing to the Roman doctrine of *non-representation*. In contracts where the guardian figures alone, he acts on his own account; he becomes creditor, debtor, acquirer, save that he returns later to the ward the benefit of the contracts he has made in his interest. But in spite of the inconveniences which it presents, the act of 'negotiorum gestio' is required so long as the ward himself is not essentially capable of figuring in any transaction.

369. Furthermore, the Romans distinguished in the status of wardship three periods: (1) The period of

---

[1] Suetonius, *Div. Claud.* 23.†
[2] Julius Capitolinus, *M. Antonini philos. vita*, 10.†
[3] Ulpian, *Reg.* 11, § 25. [4] *Dig.* 26, 8, 3 (Paulus).

infantia (*in* privative, *fari* to speak); (2) the period *infantiae proxima;* (3) the period *pubertati proxima.* During the first two the guardian is certainly obliged to resort to the act of 'negotiorum gestio' since the ward is incapable of speaking or at the very least of understanding what he does. During the third the guardian causes the ward to intervene personally in transactions and contents himself by interposing his 'auctoritas.'

370. There are cases where, even during the first two periods, recourse to the 'negotiorum gestio' is impossible, when it is one of those transactions which Roman law called *actus legitimi*, and which do not permit of agency; of this number are 'legis actio,' 'mancipatio,' acceptance of a succession, 'acceptilatio' (release or discharge in civil form of an obligation existing for the benefit of the ward).

371. As to the 'legis actio,' the law was relaxed from its original rigor, and a guardian was permitted to sue at law in the name of the ward (*lege egere pro tutela*).[1]

372. Was it the acceptance of a succession fallen to the ward? In the ancient law the hereditas was accepted by a slave of the ward: later the praetorian law [2] permitted the guardian to make 'aditio hereditatis' for the ward: but in this event the ward was a simple praetorian heir, a *bonorum possessor*. In Byzantine law the 'aditio hereditatis' made by the guardian ends by rendering the ward the civil heir.[3]

---

[1] *Inst.* 4, 10 pr.

[2] *The jus honorarium*, more exactly. — S.

[3] *Code*, 6, 30, 18, § 2 (Theodosius II and Valentinian III). The ward, however, could not accept a succession without the authorization of his guardian. See Labbé, append. to the second vol. Ortolan, *Inst.* p. 705. †

373. The intervention of a slave of the ward seems to have been also the proceeding indicated for permitting the ward who is 'infans' to acquire property by means of 'mancipatio.'

374. *Acceptilatio* required manœuvres still more complicated, for it could not be done by a slave. Recourse was had to a *novation*, that is, the guardian became creditor or debtor in place of the ward, and the extinguishment of the new debt or obligation thus established took place between the guardian and the individual, who, originally the debtor or creditor of the ward, had become, through the novation, the debtor or creditor of the guardian.[1]

375. **Acts prohibited to the Guardian:** The guardian cannot, under any form and by any proceeding whatever: —

(1) Dispose gratuitously of[2] (*i. e.* give away) the property of the minor.[3]

(2) Manumit his slaves.

(3) Alienate, after a senatusconsultum of Septimus Severus (oratio Severi), 'praedia rusticana' or 'suburbana' of the minor (farms and pleasure domains situated in the suburbs of Rome).[4] This prohibition was extended by Constantine to 'praedia urbana' and to precious movables.[5]

The act done by the guardian in violation of the senatusconsultum was void, and to invoke its nullity the ward was not obliged to plead any injury.

[1] *Dig.* 46, 4, 13, § 10 (Ulpian).

[2] "*Disposer à titre gratuit.*"

[3] *Dig.* 26, 7, 12, § 3; *ibid.* 7, 22; [Colquhoun, *A Summary of the Roman Civil Law*, § 754].

[4] *Dig.* 27, 9, 1 pr.   [5] *Code*, 5, 37, 22.

376. **Restitutio in Integrum:** Even in the case where the act was done by the guardian within the limit of his powers, the ward who is thereby injured can ask the praetor to nullify it. This is what is called 'restitutio in integrum.' It is not granted to the ward unless he shows an injury, and that the insolvency of the guardian does not permit the latter to repair the damage by means of an indemnity. *Minor restituitur non tanquam minor sed tanquam laesus.*[1]

377. **Acts done by the Ward Himself:** We should finally examine the validity of acts done by the ward himself without the auctoritas of his guardian.

Are these acts invalid or valid? It is necessary to draw this distinction: *the ward is capable of making his condition better, but he is incapable of making his condition worse.*[2]

That is to say that, in transactions where an advantage is obtained only with a detriment, the transaction is considered in both aspects. Valid in so far as it procures an advantage to the minor, it is invalid in so far as casts upon him an obligation. Thus, should the minor make a sale, he certainly becomes creditor for the price, but he does not become debtor for the thing sold; should he receive a payment of money, the money received in payment is certainly acquired by him, but his claim is not extinguished, and the guardian can recover *de novo* the amount.[3]

378. The rigor of these principles is tempered by the application of the maxim: "*nemo cum alterius detrimento locupletari potest.*" I will explain: a ward

---

[1] Girard, *Manuel*, pp. 227, 228, note 4.
[2] *Inst.* 1, 21 pr.   [3] *Dig.* 19, 1, 13, § 29 (Ulpian).

has sold something and has bettered his condition. He cannot lay claim to the retention of this price from which he has profited, and the return of the thing sold.[1]

Again, a ward receives a payment of money, and has turned it to a profitable use: he cannot combine the advantage of the payment received with the preservation of his claim.[2]

But suppose that he has spent the money received, nothing will hinder him, in case of a sale, from recovering the thing sold, and, in case of payment of a claim, from demanding a new payment.[3]

The party contracting with him is therefore at the mercy of the utility more or less advantageous which he derives from the contract; indeed, he will refuse to proceed with a ward in a transaction the benefit of which he would have only on condition that ward does not waste the sums received by him.[4]

379. **Powers of the Guardian over the Person of the Ward:** In French law, the care of the guardian is generally extended over the person and property of the ward. It is not so in Roman law. The tutor is charged only with the pecuniary interests of the minor. The care of the minor is intrusted by the magistrate either to his mother, if she is alive, or to a maternal relative who is not the presumptive heir.[5]

The *garde noble* of our feudal law [6] offers analogous provisions.

380. **End of Guardianship:** Guardianship is ended either ex parte minoris, or ex parte tutoris.

[1] *Dig.* 26, 8, 5, § 1 (Ulpian); *Dig.* 44, 7, 58 (Licinius Rufinus).
[2] *Dig.* 44, 7, 58 (Lic. Rufinus); Gaius, 2, § 84.
[3] Gaius, *loc. cit.* [4] *Dig.* 44, 1, 4 (Paulus).
[5] *Dig.* 27, 2, 1 and 2, 3, 6. [6] That is, *French law.* — S.

381. A. *Ex parte minoris:* (1) By the puberty of the ward.

(2) By his death.

(3) By the three 'capitis deminutiones' of the ward (indeed, the 'maxima' and the 'minima capitis deminutio' of the ward make him a person *alieni juris*. As for the 'minor capitis deminutio,' this takes away from him the quality of Roman citizen, and the Roman 'tutela' is exercised only over citizens).[1]

382. B. *Ex parte tutoris:* (1) By the death of the tutor.

(2) By the 'maxima' or 'minor capitis deminutio;' but it is only the statutory guardianship of the agnates which ends by the 'minima capitis deminutio' of the guardian. Indeed, upon entering a new family, the guardian ceases to be the agnate of his ward and his powers lose their reason of existence.

(3) By the conviction of the guardian for unfaithfulness.

(4) By his discharge when he is excused *a suscepta tutela*.[2]

(5) By expiration of the time if he was appointed guardian but for a limited period (this mode of extinction is applicable only to testamentary guardianship).[3]

383. **Guardianship Account:** The guardian has to render an account of his management to the ward who is of age (pubes), or to the new guardian if his duties end before the puberty of the ward, or to the heirs of the ward, if the guardianship comes to an end by the death of the latter.

[1] *Inst.* 1, 22.   [2] *Ibid.* See *infra*, § 391.   [3] *Inst.* 1, 22.

384. **Responsibility of the Guardian:**
(1) *Actio de rationibus distrahendis:* In the ancient law there was against the unfaithful guardian a penal action, perhaps contemporaneous with the XII Tables, and called 'actio de rationibus distrahendis. It had for its object and consequence the condemnation of the guardian for the ward to a fine double the value of the property converted.[1]

It aimed only at acts of unfaithfulness and not at the damage caused by a guardian at once honest and incapable, and, like all penal actions, it did not survive against the heirs of the guardian.[2]

385. (2) *Crimen suspecti:* The ward was also protected by the 'crimen suspecti,' action involving forfeiture against the suspected guardian. This second action is an *actio publica*, that is to say, at Rome, where there was not any *minister of justice*, the action might be brought by any one: it was open even to women who have a tie of relationship or affection with the ward.[3] The 'crimen suspecti' dates from the XII Tables.[4]

386. (3) *Actio directa tutelae:* Sanction of the responsibility of the guardian took on definite form at the time of the creation of the ' actio directa tutelae ' (which we do not believe was prior to the lex Aebutia), and which has a general bearing: negligence or fraud, it embraces all injuries to the property of the ward.[5] — The guardian who has made expenditures for the management of the tutela, has himself against the

---

[1] *Dig.* 27, 3, 1, § 20; [Girard, *Manuel*, p. 215].
[2] *Dig.* 27, 3, 1, § 23.　　[3] *Inst.* 1, 26, § 3.
[4] *Inst.* 1, 26 pr.　　[5] *Dig.* 27, 3, 1, § 21 (Ulpian).

ward, in order to reimburse himself for his advances, a concurrent action called *actio contraria tutelae*.[1]

387. Securities for the Ward: The right of the ward has been successively protected: —

(1) At about the era of Claudius, by the *satisdatio rem pupilli salvam fore*: this security consisted in a promise of the guardian secured by bondsmen (*fidejussores*).

The question necessary to the stipulation (*Spondes ne?*) was asked by the ward himself. If the ward was infans, some of his slaves intervened to stipulate for him; — if he had no slave, one was bought for him; — if there was no money for this purchase, the words of the stipulation were uttered by a public slave. — The 'servus publicus' belonging indeed to the entire Roman people, thereby belonged to the ward as to the other citizens. This slave acquired the security promised for the benefit of the ward by virtue of the principle according to which the slave owned by several masters can acquire for one of them the exclusive benefit of a contract if he stipulates *nominatim* for his account.[2]

388. (2) According to the terms of a senatusconsultum rendered under Trajan,[3] by a subsidiary action (*actio subsidiaria*) which is given, in case of the insolvency of the guardian,[4] against magistrates *nominatores tutorum*. In these 'nominatores tutorum' should be found not the high magistrates invested with the duty of appointing guardians, but the subordinate officials charged with making an examination as to the sol-

---

[1] *Dig.* 27, 4, 1 pr. (Ulpian).
[2] *Dig.* 46, 6, 2 (Ulpian).
[3] *Code*, 5, 75, 5 (Diocl. and Maxim.).
[4] *Code*, 5, 75, 4 (Gordian).

vency of the tutors prior to their appointment, and of accepting the sureties offered.[1]

389. (3) In the classic era, by a *privilegium inter personales actiones* which allows him to obtain payment before the unsecured creditors, but after the mortgage creditors [2] of the guardian.[3]

390. (4) From Constantine, by an implied hypothec on the property of the guardian which dates from the time the tutela is undertaken.[4]

391. **Excuses and Discharges:**[5] The tutela is a public burden (*munus publicum*), that is to say, no more in Roman law than in French law can a person escape therefrom except in a case of exemption, a case of excuse, to use the established term.

Excuses are divided into excuses *a suscipienda tutela*, — or summary excuses, — which dispense with an acceptance of the guardianship, and discharges (*excusationes a suscepta tutela*), which permit a person to free himself from the burden of a guardianship he has undertaken.

The principal excuses are:

(1) Three living children at Rome, or four in Italy, or five in the provinces. Children who died in military service count as if still living.

(2) Three burdens of guardianship at one time. But the tutelae are reckoned by the number of the estates to manage, and not by the number of the wards.

---

[1] *Inst.* 1, 24, § 4.
[2] "*Créanciers hypothécaires.*"
[3] *Dig.* 27, 3, 22 (Paulus); *ibid.* 25 (Hermogenianus).
[4] *Code*, 5, 37, 20.
[5] See *Inst.* 1, 25, *de excusationibus*.

(3) Certain public functions, for example, those of the administrators of the treasury; those necessitating absence on public business.

(4) Poverty.

(5) Ill-health.

(6) Illiteracy.

(7) Over seventy years of age.

The intervention of public functions referred to in (3) above, poverty, illness, the age of seventy, are discharges as well as excuses.

392. **Incapacity:**[1] Excuses must not be confounded with cases of incapacity.

Those incapable of being guardians are:

(1) Peregrini; (2) minors (impuberes),—but not the filiusfamilias, who is pubes; (3) women (Justinian, however, decided that the mother and grandmother could be guardians); (4) Soldiers (at least in the time of Justinian); (5) the mute; (6) the deaf; (7) the fool; (8) under Justinian, the minor under twenty-five years.

The incapable person cannot be guardian even though he wishes to. If the excusable person does not become a guardian, this is only because he so desires; he is even obliged to establish his reasons of excuse if he desires to escape the duties which are devolved upon him by the testator, by statute, or by magisterial appointment.

§ 3. Guardianship of Women (tutela mulierum)

393. In general: The guardianship of women was perpetual:[2] it existed even in the time of Diocletian, but it was singularly attenuated from the end of the Republic.

[1] *Inst.* 1, 25.   [2] Gaius 1, § 144.

The woman under guardianship can, at the beginning of the Empire, dispose of her property, — except res mancipi. The intervention of the guardian by means of his auctoritas is not required save for certain exceptional transactions.[1]

Moreover, guardians other than statutory guardians may be compelled to give their auctoritas;[2] wherefore the result that, after the lex Claudia abolished the statutory guardianship of the agnates over women, the guardianship of women ceased to be important.[3]

394. Statutory Guardianship and Testamentary Guardianship:

It was not rare that a husband appointed the guardian of his wife. Very often he left to her the care of choosing herself the guardian, who was then called *tutor optivus*: "*Titiae uxori meae optionem do.*"[4]

395. For want of a testamentary guardian the statutory guardianship of agnates was occasioned.[5]

396. *Jus liberorum:* From the earliest times of the Empire, women escaped the tutela when they had acquired the jus liberorum,[6] granted to the freeborn woman who had three children (*ter enixa*), or to the freedwoman who had four, it mattering little whether these children are legitimate or not.

When Theodosius and Honorius granted the jus liberorum to all women in the Empire, the guardianship of women definitely disappeared.[7]

[1] Ulpian, *Reg.* 11, § 27.   [2] Gaius, 1, §§ 190–194.
[3] Ulpian, *Reg.* 11, § 8.   [4] Gaius, 1, §§ 150, 154.
[5] Which disappeared under Claudius. — [See *supra*, § 250, what was said of the *coëmptio tutelae evitandae causa.*]
[6] Gaius, 1, § 145.
[7] *Code*, 8, 58, 1.

124 THE FIRST YEAR OF ROMAN LAW

397. **Tutor Cessicius:** Guardianship of a minor cannot be the object of an assignment (*cessio*): it is not so with the tutela mulierum. The assignee of the tutela is called, in such case, cessicius tutor. The reason of this difference seems to be that the guardianship of minors would necessarily have a limit, while the guardianship of a woman might last indefinitely unless it was possible to be freed from it.[1]

Section III. — Curatelae

§ 1. Of Curatela in General

398. **Sources of the Curatorship (Curatela):** There are not only minors and women who are incapable of managing their affairs: an indefinite number of accidental incapacities may occur of which the most important are the various derangements of the mental faculties, the profuseness of expenditure which may happen as a consequence of a weakness of mind.

The adult (*pubes*) himself, when he has reached the age of sixteen years, has a very disputable capacity.

Accidental incapacities the Roman law relieves against, so far as it could, by the institution of curators.

399. The principal curatorships are those of the 'furiosus,' of the 'mente captus,' of the spendthrift, of the adult (pubes) under twenty-five years.[2] It is impossible to formulate general rules as to the powers and

---

[1] Gaius, 1, §§ 168, 169. The *cessio* of the tutela was made by means of an *in jure cessio*.

[2] Let us mention, also, the curator given to the impubes when his interests are in conflict with those of the *praetorius tutor* of ancient law; the curator *ad ventrem* appointed for a child not yet born who may be called to a succession; the curator of the property of a person in captivity, or of an *hereditas jacens*, etc.

INCAPACITIES OF FACT

administration of curators. The powers and modes of intervention vary with the different curatelae.

§ 2. Curatorship of the Furiosus

400. *Furiosi and mente capti:* The 'furiosus' is the madman who has lucid intervals: the 'mente captus,' the madman who has not. The law of the XII Tables had established the curatorship for the 'furiosus' alone.

401. The *mente captus* was considered as not having need of a curator, because his condition, which rendered him incapable of mind, affected all his acts with absolute nullity and, by that very thing, sufficiently protected him.

Later the institution of the curatela was extended by the praetor to all deranged persons.

402. The curatorship of a madman might be testamentary, statutory, or by magisterial appointment.[1]

403. **Administration of the Curator of the Furiosus:** It is necessary to again distinguish between the curator of the 'mente captus' and of the 'furiosus.'

If the 'furiosus' has a lucid interval, he can and should act alone;[2] if he has an attack of madness, the curator acts in his stead by way of 'negotiorum gestio.'

The 'mente captus' having no lucid intervals, the curator always manages for him. So, then, in this matter *there is never any occasion for the intervention of the curator by way of assistance:* the curator acts alone, — or not at all.

---

[1] *Code*, 4, 38, 2 (Diocletian and Maximian).
[2] Ulpian, *Reg.* 12, § 2; *Code*, 5, 70, §§ 6 and 7.

§ 3. Curatorship of the Spendthrift (prodigus)

404. Decree of Interdiction: He who wasted his family property which he had inherited *ab intestato* (*bona paterna avitaque*) was, from the time of the XII Tables, subjected to magisterial interdiction: "*quando*," said the decree, "*bona paterna avitaque tua nequitia disperdis, liberosque tuos ad egestatem perducis ob eam rem tibi ea re* (*or aere?*) *commercioque interdico.*"[1] — In the classical era the origin of property wasted by the 'prodigus' has ceased to be considered, in order to interdict him and place him under a curatorship.

405. Curatorship of the Spendthrift: The curatorship of a spendthrift belonged to his agnates; for want of agnates, the curator was appointed by the magistrates.[2]

406. Administration of the Curator: For a long time it was taught that the spendthrift acted with the assistance (consensus) of his curator, like, in French law, one of full age who has been provided with a *conseil judiciaire*.[3] — This doctrine is to-day very much assailed, and it is thought that the curator of the spendthrift acted by way of the 'negotiorum gestio.'[4]

407. Personal Acts of the Prodigus: The spendthrift is like the minor, incapable of making his condition worse. Contrary to the minor, he can make an 'aditio hereditatis.'

---

[1] Paul. *Sent.* 3, 4a, § 7.   [2] Ulpian, *Reg.* 12, §§ 2 and 3.
[3] Girard, *Manuel*, p. 225. — Contra, Accarias, *Précis*, 1, p. 442.
[4] A person appointed by order of court to assist the spendthrift in the management of his affairs, without whom the spendthrift cannot act. See *Code civil*, arts. 513-515. — S.

INCAPACITIES OF FACT

§ 4. Curatorship of Minors under the Age of Twenty-five Years[1]

408. Historical: The legal situation of minors under twenty-five years has passed through five periods:

1st Period: prior to the lex Plaetoria, or period of full capacity of the adult (*pubes*) under twenty-five years of age.

2d Period: from the lex Plaetoria to the edict of the praetor concerning the 'restitutio in integrum.'

3d Period: from the 'restitutio in integrum' furnished by the edict to the constitution of Marcus Aurelius, or period of casual curators.

4th Period: from the constitution of Marcus Aurelius to Diocletian and Maximian (293 A. D.), or period of permanent curators.

5th Period: period of incapacity subsequent to 293 A. D.

409. Lex Plaetoria: On principle the adult (pubes) became absolutely capable of all acts of civil life at the age of sixteen years. The first restriction on his capacity was made by the lex Plaetoria (about 191 B. C.) which was familiarly called *lex quinavicennaria*, statute of twenty-five years. The real name of this lex which the ancient commentators called lex Laetoria has been revealed to us by the discovery of the bronze tablet of Heraclea. It is mentioned in the Pseudolus of Plautus where Calidorus cries: "*Lex me perdit quinavicennaria, Metuunt credere omnes.*"

The lex Plaetoria established a *judicium publicum*, a public suit against him by whom a minor under

[1] *Minores xxv annis.* — S.

128 THE FIRST YEAR OF ROMAN LAW

twenty-five years had been imposed upon (*deceptus*) or taken advantage of (*circumscriptus*).[1]

If the lex Plaetoria punished him who had imposed an obligation on the minor, it did not annul this obligation.[2]

410. Restitutio in Integrum : There was a gap which was filled up, towards the end of the Republic, by the praetor: the praetor used his new powers which he held from the lex Aebutia to furnish the minor under twenty-five years injured by a contract the 'restitutio in integrum.'[3]

411. The edict of the praetor opens the period of casual curators; the praetor admitted, indeed, that the act done by a minor under twenty-five years, without escaping the 'restitutio in integrum,' was less suspicious if it occurred with the assistance of a curator. What happened? That individuals who had to deal with a minor under twenty-five years and who well knew that the contract entered into might be annulled by the praetor, refused to contract unless the minor, by having a curator appointed to assist him, consented to give to the act a relative solidity which, under other conditions, was wanting.

412. Minors under twenty-five years of age found themselves therefore, in fact, under the impossibility of contracting without the assistance of a curator; but in law their capacity remained entire: and it is only

---

[1] *Lex Julia municipalis* (tablet from Heraclium), line 111. Girard *Textes*, p. 85.

[2] See, however, Girard, *Manuel*, p. 226, and note 1, p. 227.

[3] Edict of Praetor, x, 3 (Girard, *Textes*, p. 135) ; *Dig.* 4, 4, 1, § 1 (Ulpian).

INCAPACITIES OF FACT

on their request that a curator can be appointed for them, "*inviti adolescentes curatores non accipiunt.*" [1]

413. In contrast to the guardian who is appointed permanently and not for a certain piece of business, who is given *personae non rei vel causae*, the curator of the 'adolescens' is appointed for a special piece of business (*res vel causa*);[2] and the minor requesting his appointment ought to show the motive of his request (*reddere causam*).

This liberty of the 'adolescens' is more theoretical than practical, for if he did not wish to ask for a curator, he would find no one who would agree to contract with him.

414. **Reform of Marcus Aurelius:** This law was modified under Marcus Aurelius. He, according to his historian Julius Capitolinus,[3] "*ita statuit ut omnes adulti curatores acciperent non redditis causis.*" [4]

415. This text has received several interpretations: the most plausible is that Marcus Aurelius permitted minors under twenty-five years to ask for a curator without establishing any of the situations provided for by law (*non redditis causis*); but it is a disputable question whether it was from that time on that absolute permanence of curatorships was attained.

416. At all events, in the time of Severus, the property of the minor under curatorship is administered not by him but by his curator;[5] — which certainly

---

[1] *Inst.* 1, 23, § 2. [2] *Ibid.* [and *Dig.* 26, 5].
[3] Not regarded as "*a very satisfactory authority*" by Roby, *Roman Private Law*, vol. i, 1, p. 124, and note 3. — S.
[4] Julius Capitolinus. *M. Antonini Vita*, 10.
[5] *Dig.* 4, 4, 1, § 3 (Ulpian).

proves that the permanency of his functions was then admitted at least for certain curators (for example those appointed by the will of the paterfamilias).

Furthermore, it seems that the 'adolescens,' even provided with a curator, obtains 'restitutio in integrum' only by showing an injury. Modestinus, contemporaneous with the last Syrian emperors, writes: "*Puberes sine curatoribus suis possunt ex stipulatu obligari.*" [1]

417. The Minor under Twenty-five Years in the Time of Diocletian: Under Diocletian and Maximian the nullity of acts done by the minor under twenty-five years without the assistance of a curator is definitely introduced and established by a constitution of 293 A. D. At this time 'adolescentes' have became incapable of making their condition worse without the 'consensus' of their curator. This is a real prolongation of the state of wardship.[2]

418. Consensus of the Curator: We recall here that 'consensus' is far from being a mode of intervention common to all curators. 'Consensus' is manifested only in the late law, in the curatorship of minors under twenty-five years, and nothing is shown that it was extended to the other 'curatelae.'

419. 'Consensus' differs from 'auctoritas tutorum' in this way: (1) that it is divested of all formality.

(2) That it may be given before or after the event, while the 'auctoritas' should be concurrent with the authorized act.

(3) That the want of consensus does not nullify the

---

[1] *Dig.* 45, 1, 101.
[2] *Code* 2, 21, 5 (Diocl. and Maxim.); *ibid.* 3 (Diocl. and Maxim.).

act done by the adolescens, but only exposes it to be shattered by an 'in integrum restitutio.' This difference, according to Girard, would be effaced in the last state of the law, and the 'adolescens' would become like the 'pupillus' incapable of making his condition worse (in consequence of obligating himself) without the consent of his curator.[1]

420. **Venia Aetatis:** To grant to the individual *sui juris* capacity at the age of sixteen years was too early. — To grant it to him at the age of twenty-five years was too late. — Under the reign of Septimus Severus this last inconvenience was palliated by means of the 'venia aetatis.'[2]

By obtaining the dispensation which the texts call by this name, the 'pubes minor' under twenty-five years could raise himself to full capacity.

421. The 'venia aetatis,' dangerous favor, was granted to the man over twenty years, to the woman over eighteen years, and made them capable of contracting, but not, however, of alienating or hypothecating their 'praedia rustica' or 'suburbana.' Alienation or hypothecation of a 'praedium rusticum vel suburbanum' belonging to a minor under twenty-five years could take place only by virtue of a magisterial decree.

422. **Accounts of the Curatorship:** It has been seen that accounts between guardians and wards were regulated by the *actio directa* or *contraria tutelae*.[3] Accounts between curators and persons sub-

[1] Girard, *Manuel*, pp. 226, 227, 230, 231.

[2] *Code* 2, 44, 1 (Aurelian), but the constitution declares the previous existence of the *venia aetatis* rather than creating it.

[3] See *supra*, § 386.

ject to the curatela were regulated by the *actiones — utilis negotiorum gestorum* and *utilis contraria negotiorum gestorum* given, the first to the adolescens against the curator, the second to the curator against the adolescens.[1]

423. Securities for the Curatela: These are the same as for the tutelae, namely: (1) *satisdatio rem pupilli vel adolescentis salvam fore.*[2]

(2) The subsidiary action against officials charged with receiving the 'satisdatio' of curators.

(3) The 'privilegium inter personales actiones;' (4) the 'crimen suspecti curatoris '; (5) after the constitution of Constantine of 326 A. D., an implied hypothec on the property of the curator.[3]

[1] *Dig.* 27, 4, 1, § 2 (Ulpian).
[2] See *supra*, §§ 387 *et seq.*
[3] Same texts as for the tutela. [See § 390, *supra*, note 1.]

BOOK III

THINGS

TITLE I

DIVISION OF THINGS

424. If persons are the *subjects of rights*, things are the *objects of rights*. Many divisions thereof have been made: we will retain here only the most important.

425. **Things extra Patrimonium and in Patrimonio:** In things which are "beyond ownership" must be distinguished those which are not yet but which may become such, and those which will never be such. Both are called *res nullius;* but this last expression is more often applied to things which having actually no owner may have one.

426. Things *extra patrimonium* for the present and for the future are: —

(1) *Res sacrae:* consecrated to the *dii superii:* temples.[1]

(2) *Res religiosae:* consecrated to the *dii manes:* tombs.[2]

(3) *Res sanctea:* protected by a sanction of a primitively religious order: walls and gates of cities, for example.[3] 'Res sanctae, religiosae, sacrae' form the group of *res divini juris*.[4]

[1] Gaius, 2, § 4. [2] *Ibid.* [3] *Inst.* 2, 1, § 10. [4] *Ibid.* 2, 1 pr.

427. Some things, although *res humani juris*, are, however, *extra patrimonium:*

(1) *Res publicae:* things forming part of the public domain of the state or of cities: public places, baths, theatres.[1]

(2) *Res communes*, the use of which belongs to all and the ownership to no one: the air, sea, running water, seashore.[2]

428. Things *in patrimonio* comprise those belonging to collectivities (*collegia*), which are called *res universitatis*, and those belonging to individuals.

429. **Res Mancipi and nec Mancipi:** This is the most important division from the point of view of the study of the law of things *in patrimonio*.

Mancipium is the Roman ownership, which is exercised over a Roman thing, for the benefit of a Roman citizen.[3]

Res mancipi have been classified from the earliest times of Rome: their enumeration already evidently enlarged comprises: (1) Italian land (fundi Italici);[4] (2) slaves and beasts *quae dorso collo ve domantur* (beasts of burden or of draught); (4) rural servitudes of 'fundi Italici.'[5]

All the rest constitutes the category of *res nec mancipi*.[6] What characterizes 'res mancipi' is that they can be transferred only through the means — eminently *quiritary* — of *mancipatio:*[7] mancipatio was a

---

[1] *Inst.* 2, 1, § 6.   [2] *Ibid.* 2, 1, § 1.
[3] Girard, *Manuel*, p. 260.
[4] Land originally within Roman territory. — S.
[5] Ulpian, *Reg.* 19, § 1.
[6] *Ibid.*
[7] Gaius, 2, §§ 18–22.

formal sale made in the presence of five witnesses who are Roman citizens and of a libripens.

If it is asked why all the objects composing the property of the ancient Romans do not present the same character, it is doubtless because the Romans, an agricultural people, had wished to give a certain fixity to the things which were considered to be the essential capital of the farmer, while allowing on the contrary a greater facility of handling to things of less value (cattle, provisions) which, at a time when coined money was unknown, constituted the medium of exchange.[1]

Things unknown to the early Romans are not made part of the ' res mancipi,' and this is explainable: ' mancipatio ' is the formal mode of transferring ownership in a society in its infancy when transactions are few and have no need for rapidity. In proportion as the legal conception is freed from the formalism of the early ages, ' mancipatio ' tends to become more rare and to give way to the less complicated method of delivery (tràditio).

430. **Corporeal and Incorporeal Things:** Corporeal things, according to the established definition, are those *quae tangi possunt;* — incorporeal things, those *quae in jure consistunt :* — corporeal thing: the fundus Cornelianus: incorporeal thing: a hypothec on this same fundus Cornelianus: that is to say, that incorporeal things are any rights whatever over a thing, other than the right of ownership.

[1] According to Cuq *res mancipi* would have constituted that part of the estate which the Romans called *familia*, and *res nec mancipi* that other part designated by the name of *pecunia*. Cuq, *Institutions*, vol. i, p. 91. *Contra*, Girard, *Manuel*, p. 247 and notes.

And why is the right of ownership less incorporeal than the others? Because it is identified, it is confused with the thing over which it is exercised.

This division is without foundation. The right of ownership, considered as a relation between the subject and the object of the right, is as incorporeal as the others, and the other rights have quite often a material object.

431. Real and Obligatory Rights: But if the division of things composing property into corporeal and incorporeal things is of little importance, very important is the subdivision of incorporeal things into *real rights* and *obligatory rights*.[1]

432. A. Ownership is itself a real right: it is the most extended of all real rights: but owing to the vicious terminology which we have just noticed, ownership having been set apart by reason of the confusion made between the right of ownership and its object, the name of *real right* is reserved for *jura in re aliena* (rights over the property of another).

433. The owner can do with the object of his right whatever he likes. He who has but a *jus in re (aliena)* can do with respect to the object of his right only limited, definite acts: the owner of land can do with this land whatever he wishes: the neighbor who has over this same land a right of way, a simple real right, can make of the land only the limited use which consists in passing over it.

434. B. The right *in personam*, which is also called *obligation* in a general sense, right of *claim* if looked at from the active side, *liability* if looked at from the

---

[1] Or rights *in rem* and *in personam*. — S.

passive side, is a *right of control* over a certain person for the purpose of obtaining from him an act or an abstention.[1]

435. Differences between the Real and Obligatory Right: The *real* right is characterized by two attributes which are wanting to the obligatory right: *right to pursue;*[2] *right of preference.*

436. (1) *Right to pursue:* The obligatory right does not render the property of the debtor non-disposable; not only does it not specially affect anything of his property, but, originally, *it did not affect the property itself.* Had the creditor the right to be paid out of the debtor's property? Not at all. He brought suit against the person by *manus injectio,* and the payment made by the *nexus* was less a discharge of the debt than a ransom of his person. Even after the lex Poetelea Papiria, the obligatory right subjects the property of the individual obligated only considered as a mass susceptible of increase or diminution: anything going out from the mass escaped the obligation, while anything entering therein was affected.[3]

The real right, on the contrary, subjects the property *singulatim,* and is joined thereto: it *follows* the property into whatever hands it goes.

In other words, the action arising from an obligatory right lies only against the debtor; the action arising from a real right lies against every possessor of the property over which the right is established.

[1] See *infra,* § 440.

[2] "*Droit de suite,*" *i. e.* following the property into whatsoever hands it goes. See *infra,* §§ 604 *et seq.* as to the recovery of ownership by vindicatio, etc. — S.

[3] F. Bernard, *Cours sommaire de droit civil,* i, 494.†

437. (2) *Right of preference or exclusion:* The real right is supplied with a right of preference, while the obligatory right is not. Should a person who has promised me the fundus Cornelianus venture to promise it to another person, or undertake quite a different personal liability, contract quite another obligation, if his assets are not sufficient to satisfy his various creditors, each one of the latter will obtain only a dividend proportional to his claim. No one will be preferred to the others: what is called *the sharing of so much on the franc* will take place among them.

The real right, on the contrary, confers on its holder the right to exclude, first, all those who have only an obligatory right, and in the next place all those who have only a real right later in date.[1]

Let us suppose a conflict between Primus creditor with hypothec (holder of a *real right* of hypotheca) on the fundus Cornelianus, Secundus an ordinary creditor (*unsecured*[2] creditor as he is ordinarily termed, holder of a simple *obligatory right*). The fundus Cornelianus is sold for a sum insufficient to satisfy both creditors: from the proceeds Primus, the creditor with a hypothec, will first take what is due him; Secundus will obtain the rest: he will have nothing if the entire proceeds are absorbed by Primus.

Instead of making Secundus a simple unsecured creditor, let us suppose that he himself had a hypothec on the land, but that this hypothec is subsequent to that of Primus. In this second case, as in the first,

---

[1] Girard, *Manuel*, p. 250.
[2] *Creditor chirographarius:* Roby, *Roman Private Law*, vol. ii, p. 110. — S.

Secundus will not be considered until after Primus: "*prior tempore, potior jure.*"

438. Composition of Property: To sum up, property is composed of three constituent parts: ownership, 'jura in re aliena,' obligations.[1]

[1] *Inst.* 3, 29, § 2.

TITLE II

SUMMARY NOTIONS AS TO OBLIGATIONS [1]

CHAPTER I

THE OBLIGATORY RIGHT AND ITS SOURCES

439. Obligation: Obligation is the right *in personam* looked at from the passive point of view.

So, considered as to the individual who enjoys it, the right in personam is the power to compel a person to render a performance; considered as to the individual who is liable, it is the necessity of rendering this performance.

440. Performance: [2] The word performance, the sense of which is absolutely general, embraces every kind of advantage to be gained, corporeal things, positive acts, negative acts. *Dare, facere, non facere,* all that is *praestare*, in the large sense of the word.[3]

441. Sources of Obligations: The two principal sources of obligation are contracts and delicts (torts): delicts, namely unlawful acts committed by one person against another, and which create, chargeable upon the doer, for the benefit of the victim, the

---

[1] The study of obligations belongs to the course of studies for the second year (in the French law schools. — S.); we give here only the principles, a notion of which is indispensable to a general knowledge of Roman law.

[2] "*Prestation,*" used also in § 439. — S.

[3] Orotolan, *Explic. hist. des inst., Généralisation*, § 61.†

THE OBLIGATORY RIGHT

obligation to pay an indemnity; contracts, namely consensual agreements legally concluded between the parties.[1]

Whether obligations are *ex delicto* or *ex contractu*, they always result in rendering one person the creditor of another, and consequently they form an element of property.[2]

442. But a false idea, and above all scarcely Roman, would be given of obligations if it was imagined that in Roman law every unlawful and harmful act resulted in the creation of an obligation *ex delicto*, or that every consensual agreement between parties had for its consequence, the production of an obligation *ex contractu*.

443. In a matter *ex delicto*, the injured party becomes the creditor only as a positive law (*lex*) has established an indemnity for his benefit: *nulla poena sine lege*. — In a matter *ex contractu*, *consensus* is not sufficient for establishing the legal bond: *form* is necessary, the formality peculiar to each kind of contract. It might be said that an obligation *ex delicto* arises by statute (*ex lege*), an obligation *ex contractu*, from the form (*ex forma*).

444. **Repressive Laws:** The civil law (XII Tables and later laws) sanctioned by an indemnity only a restricted number of delictual acts: theft, 'rapina' (theft with violence), 'damnum injuria datum'

---

[1] Girard, *Manuel*, p. 387.

[2] We speak here of *offenses against individuals*. Roman law distinguishes *public* and *private wrongs*: public wrongs are unlawful acts considered to affect the general welfare: the corporal or pecuniary penalties which these involve do not benefit on principle their victims. See, also, *supra*, § 438.

142   THE FIRST YEAR OF ROMAN LAW

(damage caused by an unlawful act), 'injuria' (insult). — The praetorian law singularly enlarged the circle of delicts and repressed 'dolus,' violence, fraud against creditors, etc.

CHAPTER II

FORMALISM

445. Idea of Formalism: In French law, save for a number of exceptions, *consensus* is sufficient to create an obligation, the performance of which can be pursued before the courts, and consequently to constitute the contract: which is expressed by saying that in French law "*solus consensus obligat.*" It is not so in Roman law. The Roman doctrine is "*solus consensus non obligat;*" in order that a contract be valid, it is necessary, on principle, that the agreement of the parties be established by some formalities without which the obligatory bond would not exist.

446. These forms consisted formerly in the formalities of *nexum*, later in the writings made in the *Codex* (sort of ledger which Roman citizens had), or finally in the exchange of a question and answer which constituted the *stipulatio*.

447. Nexum: We have already spoken of the nexum, which a considerable number of writers consider as having constituted a general form of contracting, but which we on our part suppose to have been applicable on principle only for the contract of loan.[1]

448. Expensilatio: Expensilatio was the entry

[1] See § 25, *supra*.

made in the codex of a citizen of an obligation against a debtor. "*Expensum Titio centum,*" paid to Titius one hundred ——. This mention — we to-day should say this *debiting Titius* — had obligatory force.

449. Stipulatio: Stipulatio, the most used and the most tenacious of the formal contracts of Roman law, — perhaps because it was the most simple, — consisted in a question, "*Spondesne nihi centum ?*" do you promise me one hundred? followed by an affirmative answer, "*Spondeo,*" I promise.

450. Formalism in the Extinguishment of Obligations: Obligations were extinguished as they were formed: *nexum*, contract *per aes et libram*, was dissolved *per aes et libram*, that is, by an analogous ceremony, accomplished like the first in the presence of five witnesses and a libripens.

451. *Expensilatio*, contract formed *litteris*, was dissolved *litteris*, by an entry in the *codex*, the opposite of expensilatio: "*acceptum a Titio centum.*" The person who had been debited was *credited*, we should now say. This was called *acceptilatio litteris*.

452. Another *acceptilatio*, made *verbis*, extinguished stipulatio, contract formed *verbis*. "*Quod tibi spopondi habesne acceptum ?*" — "*Habeo.*" "What I have promised, have you received?" "I have received it."

453. An idea quite Roman, to which our minds to-day have difficulty in bending, is that *payment*, that is to say, the execution of the obligation, was not always sufficient to extinguish it. It was only about 53 A. D., according to Mommsen (at all events not before the last century of the Republic) that the obligation born of a formal contract ceased to survive its execution so far as it had not been dissolved by a formality inverse to that which had presided at its formation.[1]

454. **Real Contracts:** Certain contracts, however, had to remain outside the sphere of formalism. These are the contracts which are formed by the delivery of a thing. "*Nemo cum alterius detrimento locupletari potest.*" This is one of the old rules of the ancient law which the 17th title [2] of Book 50 of the Digest has preserved for us. This rule of good sense and honesty had to be written in the most rudimentary laws: and we think as Dareste, that the first contracts had to be real contracts. The obligation to return the slave or the beast of burden lent by a neighbor, to return a bailment, must have preceded the oldest formal contracts. Real contracts might take the most varied aspects, so the Romans placed in this category, along with the four contracts of *mutuum* (loan for consumption), *commodatum* (loan for use), *depositum* and *pignus*, an indefinite number of contracts for which they had found no special name (*innominate contracts*), and in which the obligation arose from a performance which, if it was retained without returning the equivalent, would constitute for the benefit of him who received it an unjust enrichment at the expense of another.[3]

455. **Decadence of Formalism:** Formalism is the characteristic of primitive law. Among people grown older, it tends to become attenuated and to disappear: the spirit of contracts prevails little by little

[1] Girard, *Textes*, pp. 820–827.
[2] *De diversis regulis iuris antiqui.*
[3] Girard, *Nouvelle Revue historique*, 1895, p. 413.†

FORMALISM

over their external characteristics, substance over form.

The Roman law did not escape from this general law: and the decadence of formalism is revealed in the course of its history by two kinds of legal phenomena.

(1) The disappearance of the most complicated formal contracts. (2) The birth of new contracts purely consensual like ours.

456. A. In the first class of ideas, we already have had to notice the desuetude of *nexum* after 326 B. C. *Expensilatio* definitely disappeared at the time of Caracalla. There still remained, at the end of the classical era, only the verbal contract *stipulatio*, which became more and more what has been ingeniously termed "a contract-mould." [1]

457. *Stipulatio* lived as long as the Roman law. That comes doubtless from its being at once very comprehensive and very simple. Very comprehensive, for it can be added, to give obligatory force to them, to the most complicated agreements; very simply, since it amounts, so to speak, to two words which the parties utter or (are deemed to utter, for quite often in the last state of the law an *instrumentum* states the ordained words without the contracting parties taking the trouble of uttering them).

458. The extinguishment of obligations followed an evolution necessarily parallel; discharge *per aes et libram* disappeared in part with *nexum*, acceptilatio *litteris* with the contract *litteris*. — Finally, during the

[1] We omit the two less usual verbal contracts, the *jusjurandum liberti* of a religious and special character, and the *dictio dotis* which will soon disappear, to make room for the *pactum dotis* freed of formalities.

last years of the Republic the payment, the execution of the obligation, became the *legal* proceeding, as it was the *rational* proceeding of discharge.[1]

459. *Acceptilatio verbis* persisted, however, like stipulatio; but it is used only to make discharges of debts, or settlement of accounts, irrespective of the character and origin of the debts which it is desired to extinguish.

460. In order to apply to all obligations the discharge by *acceptilatio verbis*, the praetor Aquilius Gallus (contemporary and friend of Cicero) invented an ingenious proceeding, which has retained his name: the *stipulatio Aquiliana*.

461. This proceeding consisted of two operations: —

First the obligation was transformed into an obligation verbis (which is called a novation): "What you owe me on such a ground" — (or "on any ground whatever," — if a general settlement of accounts is made, the ordained formula takes in all types of and grounds of debt which can be conceived of),[2] "*do you promise it to me?*" "*I promise it.*" Here is the debt or the mass of debts transformed into an obligation *verbis*.

Second operation: "What I have promised you by the stipulatio Aquiliana, do you hold it as received?" "I do."

This formalism of later times lacks, as we see, neither simplicity nor flexibility.

462. B. The second legal phenomenon which marks the decadence of formalism is the introduction of con-

[1] Girard, *Manuel*, pp. 678, 680, note 1.
[2] *Inst.* 3, 29, § 1.

FORMALISM 147

sensual contracts: they never became the rule in Roman law; but, provided with actions by the civil law or by the praetor, or by imperial constitutions, these contracts (*pacta vestita*, opposite of *nuda pacta*, not enforceable, not *clothed* with an action) ended by constituting an important group, especially as they embrace the most usual contracts: (1) sale, letting, partnership, *mandatum* (established by the civil law); (2) *pactum de jure jurando, constitutum debiti, pactum hypothecarium* [1] (sanctioned by the praetorian law); (3) *donatio* and *pactum dotis* [2] (enforceable by imperial constitutions).

463. So, in the last state of the law, obligations ex contractu are said to be formed *re, litteris, verbis, consensu*.[3]

[1] See Roby, *Roman Private Law*, vol. ii, p. 114; Colquhoun, *A Summary of the Roman Civil Law*, § 1492. — S.

[2] These are termed *pacta legitima*. — S.

[3] Gaius, 3, 89; *Inst.* 3, 13, 2. The existence of obligations *litteris*, already doubtful in the time of Gaius, seems more open to dispute in the time of Justinian. It is to be remarked that Modestinus, contemporary of Alexander Severus, does not include the obligation *litteris* in the enumeration in the Digest, 44, 7, 52 pr.

BOOK IV

ACTIONS

TITLE I

GENERAL AND HISTORICAL NOTIONS — THE COURTS

464. Meaning of the Word "Action." The word *action*, in Roman law, presents several acceptations.

In the first place, the right to sue at law on a claim of debt or a right of ownership is called *action;* [1] — but the word *action* is equally used to designate the procedure to which recourse is had in order to enforce a right through a court of justice.

465. Successive Systems of Procedure: Roman procedure passed through three periods: —

(1) The system of 'legis actiones;'
(2) The formulary procedure;
(3) The procedure 'extra ordinem.'

466. Ordo Judiciorum: The first two periods are characterized by what is called the 'ordo judiciorum,' that is, the distinction between the magistrate and the judge (judex).

During these first two periods, the Roman magistrate himself does not judge the dispute brought before his court. He contents himself with drawing up the

[1] *Dig.* 44, 7, 51 (Celsus).

GENERAL AND HISTORICAL NOTIONS 149

contention and refers its cognizance to the *judices privati* [1] who decide the matter in litigation. The magistrate does not reënter the scene except to secure execution of the judgments.

During the third period, the *judices privati* disappeared, and the magistrate combines the functions of organizer of the process of a suit with those of judge.

467. The procedure before the magistrate is called procedure *in jure;* the procedure before the judge bears the name of procedure *in judicio.*

468. **Magistrates:** In the earliest times of Rome the sole magistrate, so to speak, was the *king ;* [2] after the fall of royalty the judicial authority passed into the hands of the two consuls; [3] but the consuls did not take cognizance of all causes; those concerning religion and the sacrificia were taken before the *collegium of pontifices.* [4] This jurisdiction subsisted even in the time of Cicero, since it is before the collegium of the pontifices that Cicero delivered his address "*Pro domo sua.*" — The ascribing of jurisdiction to the pontifices arose from the fact that Cicero's house was consecrated to the goddess Liberty. [5]

469. *The praetorship:* In 367 B. C. the consuls were divested of their judicial powers for the benefit of the *praetors.*

The word *praetor* characterizes a superior function (from *praeire*, "go before"). In a Roman camp the

---

[1] That is, sworn judges who are private individuals. — S.
[2] *Dig.* 1, 2, 2, § 14 (Pomponius).
[3] *Ibid.* § 16.
[4] Denys of Halicarnassus, 2, 73.†
[5] Cicero, *Letters to Atticus,* 4, 2.†

150 THE FIRST YEAR OF ROMAN LAW

tent of the commanding general was called *praetorium*, and the gate of the camp through which the army left to be drawn up for battle, the *porta praetoria*.

470. There was at first but a single praetor: the *praetor urbanus;* in 247 B. C. there was created the *praetor peregrinus* charged with administering justice between Romans and 'peregrini' or between 'peregrini' only. — The praetor 'peregrinus' took the place of the praetor 'urbanus' while absent.

471. Then special praetors for Sicily and Sardinia were created. From four the number of these magistrates was increased to six. — This number was again increased by the creation, under the Republic, of criminal courts called *quaestiones perpetuae;* each 'quaestio' was presided over by a praetor, — next, under the Empire, by the creation of administrative praetors charged with special services like the praetor 'tutelaris' (charged with tutelae), the praetor 'fideicommissarius' (charged with fideicommissa). — The total number of praetors reached the maximum of eighteen.

472. *Curule aediles:* The curule aediles, charged with the policing of markets, also had a jurisdiction.

473. *Prefect of the city:* Finally, in the earliest times of the Empire is seen the development, especially in criminal matters, of the jurisdiction of a superior officer, the prefect of the city (*praefectus urbi*).

474. *Praesides:* In the provinces, the judicial functions were exercised by the provincial governor.

475. **Judices:** When once the contention is drawn up by the magistrate (procedure *in jure*) the parties are sent before judices (procedure *in judicio*).[1]

[1] Gaius, 4, § 15.

476. How were the judices recruited ? The recruiting of judices became the object of furious struggles between the senators and *equites*. On principle the senators had the exclusive right of figuring on the *list of judices*. This list is ready made: it is the list of the senatorial order itself, the *ordo senatorius*. But when the qualification passed to another order, it was necessary to make up an annual list; this list was publicly affixed by the praetor urbanus to the *album*.

477. *Leges judiciariae:* The laws which assigned judicial functions either to the senators or to the equites are called 'leges judiciariae.' The *lex Sempronia* of Caius Gracchus (142 B. C.) transferred the right to be a judex from the senators to the *equites;* — in 106 B. C. the *lex prima Servilia* shared the qualification between the two orders; the equites triumphed exclusively with the *lex secunda Servilia;* the senators took their revenge under the dictatorship of Sulla. — Subsequently, a *lex Aurelia* shared the right to be a judex between senators, equites, tribuni aerarii,[1] etc.

478. *Appointment of the Judex:* From the lists which thus varied the parties chose, or the magistrate appointed, if the parties could not agree, sometimes one judge, *judex*, sometimes arbiters, *arbitri* (three ordinarily).

479. The judices appointed in suits between peregrini or between peregrini and citizens were called *recuperatores*.[2]

[1] Probably a class of plebeians of wealth and importance, but not generally recognized as the equals of the equites. See Roby, *Rom. Priv. Law*, vol. ii, p. 322. — S.

[2] "Recoverers" is the term employed by Roby, *Rom. Priv. Law*, vol. ii, p. 315. — S.

480. The same name was given to the *judices* of the provinces.[1]

481. The common characteristic of all *judices* consists in that they were specially appointed for each suit.

482. *Centumviri:* The sole permanent court of Rome was the court of the centumviri, charged with the trial of questions as to ownership, freedom, wills. We do not wish to say that the centumviri continued in office *in perpetuum* — their office was annual like all the public offices of Rome, but we thereby mean that the magistrate did not appoint them specially for one suit: instead of sending the litigants before a judex whom he appointed (*judex esto N.* . . .), he sent them before the centumviral court.[2]

483. The court was divided into four sections, which were called *tribunalia* or *hastae*. This last name comes from the spear, symbol of Roman ownership, which was set up before the court of the centumviri specially charged with trying questions of ownership. — Suits brought before the centumviral court were tried sometimes by one section, sometimes by two, sometimes finally by all sections reunited.[3] Each section was convoked and presided over by a praetor, and the first president of the court was called *praetor hastarius*.

[1] Festus, *De Verb. Signif.*: *Reciperatio est quum inter civitates peregrinas lex convenit ut res privatae reddantur singulis reciperanturque*. The recuperatores would have, therefore, derived their name from commissioners charged with doing justice on frontier maraudings.†

[2] See *infra*, § 502; Roby, *Rom. Priv. Law*, vol. ii, pp. 314, 315. — S.

[3] Pliny the Younger, *Epist*. 6, 33.

TITLE II

SYSTEMS OF PROCEDURE

CHAPTER I

THE LEGIS ACTIONES

484. General Characteristics of the System: Legis actiones [1] constituted a complicated ritual, a mass of acts and formulae which the litigants could not avoid under penalty of losing their suit. — The example is cited of a litigant whose vines had been cut and who was dismissed from court for having used the word *vites* instead of the word *arbores* which figured in the legis actio.[2]

485. Secret and Divulging of the Legis Actiones: The pontifices had, naturally, carefully kept the secret of this ritual, as well as the knowledge of the *dies fasti*, that is, the only days of the year in which it was permitted to bring a suit. Gnaeus Flavius, secretary of the pontifex maximus Appius Claudius Caecus, divulged the secret of the dies fasti and of the legis actiones. His revelations were published in a collection of law to which was given the name of the *jus Flavianum*, and the secret of the dies fasti and the

---

[1] "*Procedure by statute*," Roby, *Rom. Priv. Law*, vol. ii, p. 339; "*statute-process*," Poste, *Gaius*, pp. 467 *et seq.* — S.

[2] Gaius, 4, 11.

legis actiones came into public possession.¹ It is this event which certain Romanists of to-day call the *secularization of jurisprudence*.²

Nevertheless the procedure of the legis actiones was so delicate that it was not prudent to venture by one's self into a suit, and Cicero, who jests with much humor about the old ritual, shows us the litigants escorted before the court by a prompter who dictates the words and makes them give the gestures prescribed by the lex.³

486. Names of the Legis Actiones: The legis actiones were five in number: (1) The sacramentum; (2) judicis postulatio; (3) manus injectio; (4) pignoris capio; (5) condictio.⁴

487. The Sacramentum ⁵ (or better the *legis actio sacramenti*): The 'legis actio sacramenti' was a sort of wager. The 'sacramentum' consisted in a sum of money which each of the parties deposited in the hands of the collegium of pontifices. The party whose 'sacramentum' was declared *injustum*, that is, who lost his suit, forfeited also his stake, which became appropriated to the *sacra publica*. The 'sacramentum' was fifty *asses* or five hundred *asses*. In suits concerning freedom, the 'sacramentum' was reduced to the minimum, that is, fifty *asses*.⁶

488. Judicis Postulatio: The second legis actio is the judicis postulatio: the formula by which

---

¹ Cicero, *Pro Murena*, ii.†
² Cuq, *Institutions*, vol. i, pp. 445, 446.
³ Cicero, *Pro Murena*, 12.†
⁴ Gaius, 4, § 12.
⁵ "*Stake or Deposit*," Poste, *Gaius*, p. 468. — S.
⁶ Gaius, 4, §§ 13, 14.

this action was demanded from the magistrate has been preserved for us by the Notae of Valerius Probus. "I. A. V. P. V. D." i. e. *judicem arbitrumve postulo uti des.* This is all we know of it.[1]

489. It appears from the manuscript of Gaius that recourse was had to this action, but very exceptionally, and that the procedure was by the 'sacramentum' whenever the law had not decided otherwise.[2]

490. **Manus Injectio:**[3] Manus injectio consisted in arresting the body of a debtor in the presence of the magistrate by pronouncing certain prescribed [4] words, and in leading away to the creditors house this debtor whom the creditor could sell or even kill if he did not obtain satisfaction from him; the debtor might be cut up, according to the law of the XII Tables (*partis secanto*), if there were several creditors. — We know from Aulus Gellius that the rigor of the law of the XII Tables never was but a theoretical rigor. Certain contemporary Romanists go so far as to say that the *alleged cutting* up of the debtor never existed even in theory, and that the Romans, in the time of Aulus Gellius, no longer understood an archaic expression "*secanto*," which never meant "to cut up." [5]

---

[1] Girard, *Textes*, p. 198. "It was apparently the prototype of actions ex fide bona, that is, of actions which required an equitable balancing of opposite claims, and an assessment by the judex of the damages, if any, due the plaintiff." Poste, *Gaius*, p. 472. But cf. Roby, *Rom. Priv. Law*, ii, p. 345, and Muirhead, *Roman Law*, § 35. — S.

[2] Gaius, 4, § 13.

[3] "*Arrest*," Poste, *Gaius*, p. 472; "*Bodily arrest*," Roby, *Rom. Priv. Law*, vol. ii, p. 426. — S.

[4] Gaius, 4, 21; Jobbé-Duval, *Hist. de la proc. civ.* 6–9.†

[5] See Cuq, *Institutions*, vol. i, p. 425, note 2.

491. Sometimes manus injectio is employed after a judgment "*manus injectio judicati;*" sometimes it was employed as if there had been a judgment "*manus injectio pro judicato;*" which occurred especially in virtue of the *leges Furia* and *Publilia de sponsu*, when the principal debtor had not reimbursed within the period of six months the surety who had paid the debt for him.[1]

492. There also was a *manus injectio pura*, which was employed without judgment and in virtue of the contract itself. It took place somewhat analogously to what happens in our time as to *actes authentiques*[2] clothed with executory form. As a creditor of to-day secured by an *acte notarié exécutoire*[3] can seize the property of his debtor, without having to first look to the court, even so the Roman creditor whose right conferred the 'manus injectio pura' could seize the person of his debtor without first taking him into court.

493. *Manus injectio pro judicato* was employed in case of 'nexum,'[4] of a legacy 'per damnationem,'[5]

---

[1] Gaius, 4, § 22.

[2] *Acte authentique:* a transaction entered into before or recorded by a public official, such as a notary, clerk of court, etc. Boitard, *Leçons de procédure civile*, pp. 344 *et seq.* — S.

[3] The *acte notarié exécutoire* refers to a document authenticated and recorded by a notary wherein the creditor is given power to take the debtor's property upon the happening of a contingency therein stated. Boitard, *Leçons de procédure civile*, pp. 555, 556. "The seizure of immovables can be had only by virtue of an *acte exécutoire*, that is, an *acte notarié* or a judgment." Boitard, *ibid.* p. 339. — S.

[4] See *supra*, § 25.

[5] See *infra*, § 870.

manus injectio pura, for the restitution of usurious interest (*lex Marcia de foeneratoribus*), etc.[1]

494. Between *manus injectio judicati*, or *manus injectio pro judicato* on the one side, and *manus injectio pura* on the other, there was this difference, that in the first two cases it was impossible to defend one's self against execution, and it was necessary, in order to escape arrest and its consequences, to employ the intervention of a *vindex*, that is, of a third person who, contesting the legality of the ' manus injectio,' brought the question before the court. — If it was a case of 'manus injectio pura,' the arrested debtor could personally resist and dispute before the court the legality of the measure of which he was the object.[2]

495. To thus object to 'manus injectio' (which was done by the debtor or by a vindex), was called "*depellere manum.*" It was "playing for a discharge or a double forfeiture," for the debtor or the vindex whose resistance was declared not to be well founded was condemned *in duplum*, that is, for twice the amount of the debt.[3]

496. The interest of the distinction just shown was effaced when a lex Vallia (between 194 and 87 B. C.) permitted *in every suit* "*Sibimet depellere manum,*" that is, to resist in all cases 'manus injectio' without the assistance of a vindex.[4]

[1] Gaius, 4, § 23. See, also, Colquhoun, *opus cit.* § 2410. — S.
[2] Gaius, 4, § 23.
[3] *Lex coloniae Genetivae Juliae*, 61; Girard, *Textes*, p. 88.
[4] Except in the cases of *judicatum* and *actio depensi*. — In the time of Gaius the *judicatus* and he who is sued in the *actio depensi* are bound only to give security: the *manus injectio* no longer exists, but the addictio by the magistrate is still possible. Gaius, 4, §§ 25, 26.

497. **Pignoris Capio:**[1] Pignoris capio, or the taking of a pledge, consisted, for the unpaid creditor, in seizing something belonging to the debtor. It took place out of court, which has caused its quality as a legis actio to be disputed. This measure is so conformable to the early law that Girard, who calls it "a procedure without a lawsuit,"[2] does not hesitate to state that it may be considered as the most ancient of the legis actiones. It survived, however, in the law only as an exceptional right, for example, in favor of soldiers who had not been reimbursed the price of their horses (*aes equestre*), or who had not received grain (barley) for their maintenance (*aes hordearium*); — in favor also of those who had furnished cattle for sacrifice and had not received the price for them.[3]

498.[4] **Condictio:** The four legis actiones previously explained are probably contemporaneous with the law of the XII Tables: at a time very much later as to which the Romanists do not agree and which is quite arbitrarily fixed at the beginning of the sixth century of Rome (254 B. C.) was introduced a fifth legis actio called *condictio*.

499. *Condicere*, according to Festus, is "*dicendo*

---

[1] "*Distress*," Poste, *Gaius*, p. 482; "*Levying a distress*," Roby, *Rom. Priv. Law*, vol. ii, p. 115. — S.

[2] Girard, *Manuel*, pp. 26, 960, 963, 971, 972, note 1. See, also, Cuq, *Institutions*, vol. i, p. 429. — S.

[3] Gaius, 4, § 26. What if the debt on account of which the *pignoris capio* was employed is contested? See Jobbé-Duval, *Études sur l'hist. de la proc. civ.* pp. 10 and 11.†

[4] "*Notice*," Poste, *Gaius*, p. 471. It was first introduced by the lex Silia about 244 B. C., and afterwards extended by the lex Calpurnia about 254 B. C. Cf. Poste, *Gaius*, p. 472. — S.

denuntiare." [1] Condictio seems analyzable into a simple summons before the magistrate (*vocatio in jure*) after which on a second appearance of the parties, thirty days later than the first, a judex was appointed without any other formalities, to hear the dispute.

500. Gaius wonders why 'condictio' was created when 'sacramentum' and 'judicis postulatio' were sufficient for all needs. It is, according to the greatest number of writers, for the purpose of simplification. Cuq supposes that the introduction of 'condictio' had for its purpose the giving of a civil sanction to new contracts which previously had created only debts of honor (obligations resting on confidence).[2] This very alluring theory is contrary to the text of Gaius, who positively states that 'condictio' was applicable to obligations previously enforced by 'sacramentum.'[3]

501. **Decadence and Abolition of the Legis Actiones:** The legis actiones reached a high degree of unpopularity (*in odium venerunt*, says

---

[1] Festus, *condicere;* Gaius, 4, § 18.

[2] Cuq, *Institutions,* vol. i, pp. 667 *et seq.*

[3] Gaius, 4, § 20. Jobbé-Duval (*Histoire de la proc.*), pp. 110 *et seq.*, offers another explanation: The *condictio* should have been introduced by the lex Silia for the purpose of ameliorating the situation of the debtor. It is to be remarked, indeed, that the judex was appointed thirty days after the first appearance. This period of thirty days was a period of favor. — The introduction of the condictio is one of the phases of this evolution which tended to make of actions, originally wholly penal, actions *freed from the characteristic of penality.* Let us call attention to this quite striking observation of Jobbé-Duval: In the Talmud all actions are penal, except that which aims at the payment of a sum of money. Now the payment of a *certa credita pecunia* was the first objective aimed at by the condictio.

Gaius);[1] a lex Aebutia, the date of which is much disputed, but which should be placed,[2] according to the latest research, about 126 or perhaps even about 98 B. C., gave them a telling blow, without suppressing them, by authorizing the employment of a concurrent system already in use before certain courts (the formulary procedure); they were definitely abolished by two leges Julia of the time of Augustus or perhaps of Caesar.[3]

502. Even after its abolition, the procedure of *legis actiones* was employed before the centumviral court.[4]

CHAPTER II

THE FORMULARY PROCEDURE

SECTION I. — **Fundamental Idea of the System**

503. **The Formula:** The formulary procedure always admits of the distinction of magistrate and judge, judex (*ordo judiciorum*); but the magistrate, after the proceedings taking place before him (procedure *in jure*), draws up and delivers to the parties a short decree summarizing the suit, which decree is given by the litigants to the judex appointed to hear the case. The judex tries the questions laid down in the decree which is submitted to him and pronounces judgment without ever being able to go outside of the circle of questions submitted to him.

504. The decree under discussion is called the

[1] Gaius, 4, § 30.
[2] "About 170 B. C." Poste, *Gaius*, p. 487.
[3] Gaius, 4, § 30.   [4] *Ibid.* § 31.

formula. Sometimes the plaintiff (*actor*, he who brings the suit) selects one all drawn up on the *album* of the praetor; sometimes, no formula exactly fitting the suit, the praetor frames and draws up a formula on the statements of the parties (*actor*, the plaintiff, *reus*, the defendant, against whom the suit is brought) which discusses all the points of the case.[1] When the formula which has been drawn up is finally delivered by the plaintiff to the defendant, who accepts it, there is a *judicium acceptum;* then is produced the *litiscontestatio* (issue) which concludes the proceedings *in jure*.[2]

505. **How the System of Legis Actiones gave Way to the Formulary System:** The most accredited theory consists in asserting that the formulae were introduced by the praetor peregrinus for the benefit of persons coming under his jurisdiction who could not claim the right of owner or of creditor *ex jure quiritium*, a right which the terms of the ritual of the legis actiones insistently called to mind. The citizens of Rome, struck by the convenience of the procedure, would have finished by borrowing it for all suits which concerned them exclusively.

This view, largely held, is nevertheless very suspicious, for it is certain that the path of the Roman legis actio was not closed to peregrini. Girard thinks he sees in the introduction of the formulary procedure an imitation of foreign institutions, perhaps of what

[1] Roby, *Rom. Priv. Law*, vol. i, pp. 349, 350; Colquhoun, *A Summary of the Rom. Civ. Law*, §§ 2005–2014; Keller, *De procédure et actions chez les romains (die Römische Civilprocess und die Actionen summarischer Darstellung)*, pp. 221, 222, notes. — S.

[2] Girard, *Manuel*, p. 997, note 4.

governors already did in certain provinces by virtue of the local law maintained after the conquest.[1]

SECTION II. — **Composition of the Formula**

506. **Parts of the Formula:** The formula comprises usually three parts: (1) the *demonstratio*, summary statement of the suit; for example: "QUOD AULUS AGERIUS NUMERIO NEGIDIO HOMINEM VENDIDIT."[2]

(2) The *intentio* (essential part), wherein is formulated the claim of the plaintiff: "SI PARET NUMERIUM NEGIDIUM AULO AGERIO CENTUM SESTERTIA DARE OPORTERE."[3]

(3) The *condemnatio*, which orders the judex to condemn or acquit, according as he shall or shall not find the claim of the plaintiff well founded: "SI PARET JUDEX CONDEMNA, SI NON PARET ABSOLVE."[4]

Nothing more simple, in short: it is a set of questions analogous to what in our time the presidents of the *Cour d'assises* submit to the jury: our example puts on the stage a vendor, Aulus Agerius, and a vendee, Numerius Negidius (these two names were traditional among the Roman jurisconsults for designating the plaintiff and the defendant).

Aulus Agerius has sold a slave to Numerius Negidius for which he has not been paid. There is the case in a few words (*demonstratio*).

What does Aulus Agerius wish? to be paid the price of the slave sold. This is what he asks (*intendit*).

What has the judex to do? To condemn the defendant if the plaintiff is right (*si paret*), to acquit

---

[1] Girard, *Manuel*, p. 985 *et seq.*   [2] Gaius, 4, § 40. — S.
[3] *Ibid.* § 41. — S.   [4] *Ibid.* § 43. — S.

him if the plaintiff is wrong (*si non paret*). This is precisely what the magistrate orders the judex in the *condemnatio*.

507. The formula admits sometimes of a fourth part, the *adjudicatio*. We will speak of it when treating of the modes of acquiring ownership.[1]

508. There is, after all, in the formula but one absolutely essential part, the *intentio*; if I ask the judex to condemn my adversary to pay me five hundred francs, I will be able when pleading to tell him why; and if only to the 'intentio' is added the order to the judex to decide for or against me, according as my claim shall or shall not be well founded, the formula, although indifferently explicit, will be nevertheless "on its feet;" also, in certain suits where the magistrate did not see the necessity of explaining facts absolutely simple, the formula is reduced to the 'intentio' and the condemnatio.

509. It might even be restricted to the 'intentio' when the judgment of the judex should itself be reduced to a simple decision without a pecuniary condemnation.[2]

Let us take, for example, a suit in regard to the freedom of an individual: the question laid down will be: "SI PARET HOMINEM STICHUM LIBERUM ESSE;" the 'intentio' is sufficient without the need of adding anything.

510. **Exceptiones:** The formula delivered by the praetor is not made up solely of the recital of the claims of the plaintiff, it also presents certain grounds of defense alleged by the defendant (reus). These

---

[1] Gaius, 4, § 42. See *infra*, §§ 632 *et seq.*
[2] Gaius, 4, §§ 39, 44.

grounds of defense stated in the formula after the 'intentio' are called *exceptiones*.[1]

511. The *exceptio* must not be confounded with the defense properly speaking, or real defense. The defense denies the existence of the plaintiff's right. The 'exceptio' admits this right, but implies the allegation of a fact which renders it worthless. To Primus, who claims a sum of money from me, I answer: "I owe you nothing." This is a defense. — If I answer to Primus, "I owe you, but we made an agreement by the terms of which I am not to pay you within five years," I plead an 'exceptio,' and this 'exceptio' (technically *exceptio pacti*) will, upon my demand, be inserted in the formula after the 'intentio.'[2]

512. **Replicationes and Duplicationes:** The plaintiff is not left disarmed before the *exceptio;* he may oppose to it a *replicatio:* to the replicatio the defendant may answer by a *duplicatio*, to which there would be, if necessary, a reply by a *triplicatio;* and so on; the formula may, if necessary, constitute quite a dialogue *in jure*, the contradictory allegations of which the judex would have to try.[3]

Ex.: Primus has sold to Secundus a *res mancipi* and has delivered it to him by simple *traditio;* he has therefore retained,[4] as we shall see, the quiritary ownership. Primus retakes this property. Secundus sues him by an *actio Publiciana*. Primus answers by an *exceptio justi dominii:* — immediately Secundus pleads against it the *replicatio rei venditae et traditae;* — but Primus alleges in his turn that he sold to

---

[1] *Dig.* 44, 1–5 (Ulpian); Gaius, 4, 118, 119.
[2] Cf. Girard, *Manuel*, pp. 1015 *et seq.*
[3] *Inst.* 4, 14 pr. §§ 1, 2.   [4] See *infra*, § 638.

Secundus only under pressure of a threat of death and pleads a *duplicatio metus*. . . . All these points will be stated in order in the formula and will be tried by the judex.

513. **Praescriptiones**: The statement at the head of the formula (praescribere) of certain particulars which limit or define the suit, or which are pleaded against the condemnation of the defendant, is called praescriptio.[1]

514. In this subject are distinguished *praescriptiones ex parte actoris* and *praescriptiones ex parte rei*, inserted in the formula, the first at the request of the plaintiff, the second at the request of the defendant.

515. A. *Praescriptiones ex parte actoris:* [2] They have, we have said, for their purpose the limiting or defining of the suit. Ex.: arrears due on an annual income for life are sued for by the annuitant: he has simply put in the intentio of the formula: "if it appears that Aulus Agerius owes to Numerius Negidius an annual income for life of one hundred?" . . . If he thus claims, he will not be able to count on again bringing the same action in case other arrears should afterwards happen to be unpaid. He would be defeated by the *exceptio rei in judicium deductae*. "You have, would be said, already brought this action; *non bis de eadem re agitur*," and he would be dismissed from court.[3]

This is not all. In the first suit the judex would say to him: you claim an *annual income;* now there is due

[1] Gaius, 4, § 132.
[2] *Ibid.* §§ 130, 131.
[3] See *infra*, § 542.

to you only the *income for one year;* you claim too much, you shall have nothing.[1]

The unfortunate plaintiff, therefore, would irremediably compromise his right both in the present and in the future, unless he took the precaution to limit the suit to arrears due: which he will do by means of a praescriptio thus framed: *Ea res agatur cujus rei dies fuit,* "that he sues only for arrears already due."[2]

516. B. *Praescriptiones ex parte rei:* Praescriptiones ex parte rei are nothing but 'exceptions' which are inserted not after the 'intentio,' but at the head of the formula, doubtless because their examination is imposed before all study of the claim which they would avert by a sort of preliminary question if they are proved.[3]

517. One of these praescriptiones ex parte rei is well known. This is the *praescriptio longi temporis*[4] which we precisely call in French law "*la prescription.*"

518. **Actiones in Jus, Ficticiae, in Factum, Utiles:** It is seen by what precedes that the framing of the formula presents a great elasticity. There is nothing, says Cicero, which cannot be introduced into a formula.

It was not always so: the praetor commenced by transposing into the 'intentio' of the formula, by putting them in the third person, the very terms of the *legis*

[1] See what will be said of *plus petitio, infra,* §§ 531 *et seq.*
[2] Gaius, 4, § 131.
[3] *Ibid.* § 133. Gaius notes them in passing and says that they no longer existed in his time: should they be merged with the *exceptiones* ?
[4] See § 642, *infra.*

THE FORMULARY PROCEDURE 167

actiones: the formulae thus modeled on the terms of the legis actiones were called *conceptae in jus*.[1]

These formulae, restricted in number, could not suffice for the satisfaction of the legal needs which had increased proportionately as the aspects of transactions multiplied. The praetor provided for the deficiency by the creation of *actiones ficticiae*, and *actiones in factum*.[2]

519. *Actiones ficticiae:* In the actio ficticia, the praetor supposes a fact to have occurred which does not exist and commands the judex to decree as if this fact existed: thus the praetor grants to individuals who are not heirs according to the ' jus civile ' a sort of praetorian inheritance which is called *bonorum possessio*. If these bonorum possessores have need of bringing an action relative to the hereditas, the formula commands the judex to decree *as if they were heirs:* this is a *ficticious* formula.[3]

520. *Actiones in factum:* It sometimes happens that no fiction can remedy the gap in the statute (lex): then the praetor states, in a ' demonstratio ' which he manufactures throughout, the facts without analogy in the ' jus civile,' on account of which he judges it expedient to give an action, and commands the judex to pronounce condemnation if these facts are proved. This formula thus constructed throughout, without any fiction, without derivation from an *actio directa*,[4] is a

[1] Gaius, 4, § 45.
[2] *Ibid.* § 46.
[3] *Ibid.* §§ 34–38. See, also, *infra*, §§ 620 *et seq.*, and what will be said of the actio Publiciana.
[4] That is, *an action proceeding from the jus civile.* — S.

formula *in factum*, the *ultima ratio*, the last resource of the praetor.[1]

521. *Actiones utiles:* The actio utilis is not of a nature as essentially praetorian as the 'actiones ficticiae' and 'actiones in factum.' It is a civil or praetorian action given by the praetor outside of the limits for which it was made. Thus the *actio legis Aquiliae* for the reparation of damage caused was made only for the owner of the property destroyed; the praetor gives it, as an actio utilis, to a person who, without being owner of the property destroyed, nevertheless suffers from its destruction (for example, a creditor to whom the property was hypothecated). To the *actio utilis* is opposed the *actio directa*, that is, one which is given under the precise conditions provided by the legislator.[2]

SECTION III. —**Powers and Rôle of the Judex**

522. Powers of the Judex: The limits of the formula are, as is seen, quite large, and, without departing from them, — which is absolutely prohibited to him, — the judex seems to have some liberty of action. We are not going to hesitate to state that this liberty is quite relative.

523. First Restriction: Pecuniaria Condemnatio: A suit, in Roman law, can never end except in a pecuniary condemnation. If, in French law, we sue for the recovery of a thing belonging to us, the judge finding our claim proved will condemn our adversary to the surrender itself of this thing. *The Roman judex will never condemn except in damages.* Primus sues for the recovery of the slave Eros; the

---

[1] Gaius, 4, § 46.   [2] Girard, *Manuel*, p. 1004.

judex, in declaring that the slave Eros is the property of the plaintiff, will not condemn his adversary to surrender him, but rather to pay a certain sum of money.[1]

524. *Actiones arbitrariae:* This evident inconvenience of their system of procedure the Romans tried to avoid by means of actiones arbitrariae. In the actiones arbitrariae, which are numerous in Roman law, and noticeably embrace all real actions,[2] the judex renders successively two decisions. In the first, called *pronuntiatio,* he calls on the defendant to give to the plaintiff a satisfaction which he fixes (and which is moreover indicated by the praetor in the formula by a mention called *clausula arbitraria*).

If, for example, I sue for the recovery of the slave Eros, the 'pronuntiatio' (it is also called *jussus judicis* or *arbitratus judicis*) will call on the defendant to surrender to me the slave Eros; if I sue for the recovery of the fundus Cornelianus, the 'pronuntiatio' will call on me to surrender the fundus Cornelianus.

If the adversary complies with the 'jussus judicis,' the suit is ended. If he does not execute it, the judex condemns him in a sum of damages which the plaintiff himself fixes upon oath. Nevertheless the judex may tax these damages if he is fearful that the plaintiff puts them at too high a figure.[3]

As we see, the actio arbitraria, like all the rest, ends

[1] Gaius, 4, § 48.

[2] They comprise *all* real actions, and also quite a number of personal actions: actions *de dolo, quod metus causa, de eo quod certo loco, Pauliana,* etc. *Inst.* 4, 6, *de act.* 31.

[3] This *taxatio* occurs only when the defendant is *bonae fidei:* if he is *malae fidei,* he is condemned *in quantum adversarius in litem sine ulla taxatione in infinitum juraverit. Dig.* 6, 1, 68 (Ulpian).

in the second part only in a pecuniary condemnation, — there exists, nevertheless, a serious controversy on the question of knowing if the 'pronuntiatio' could be brought to a material execution, — but it gives the plaintiff the very satisfaction which he is pursuing provided the defendant, notified by the judex that he is going to lose his suit, shrinks from the weight of the damages with which he is menaced.

525. Litiscontestatio: This characteristic substitution of the obligation to pay a sum of money for the obligation existing before the suit is produced at the precise moment of the litiscontestatio, that is, at the moment when the defendant in the presence of the magistrate accepts the formula which the latter has just given to the plaintiff.[1]

It is the consequence of what is called the *extinctive effect* of litiscontestatio. The first obligation (to restore a piece of land or an object, to abstain from exercising a servitude, to execute an act agreed upon, etc.) no longer exists: *it is extinguished;* the *reus* is bound henceforth by one thing: to have himself judged (*condemnari oportere*), and when he shall be judged to execute the condemnation (*judicatum facere oportere*).[2]

526. (a) The right transformed by litiscontestatio is spoken of as *deducta in judicium:* it cannot revive under its ancient form; hence this consequence that whoever should allow to fall within the period of limitation (*expiratio judicii*[3]) the case started by him and brought to litiscontestatio, will not be able to establish in a new case his former right *which is extinguished.*

[1] Girard, *Manuel,* p. 997, note 4.
[2] Gaius, 4, § 180.   [3] See *infra,* §§ 541 *et seq.*

His claim will be defeated by the *exceptio rei in judicium deductae*.[1]

527. (b) Litiscontestatio produces a second effect: it determines the time at which the judex should place himself in order to appreciate the *existence* and the *extent* of the rights of the parties. The judex takes cognizance of only the formula, and so it is at the time of the delivery of the formula that he should place himself to study the question to be decided. He will acquit, if the right was not then established, even although it should afterward become so (and reciprocally). And he will return likewise to this time in order to determine the amount of the 'condemnatio.'[2]

528. Litiscontestatio has besides the effect: (1) of interrupting prescription; (2) of preventing the extinguishment of actions which cannot be brought only during a certain time, or which do not pass to the heirs of the plaintiff: *actiones quae tempore aut morte pereunt semel inclusae judicio salvae permanent.*[3]

529. Second. **Restriction of the Powers of the Judex Condemnationes certae et incertae. — Actiones stricti juris and bonae fidei:** moreover, to fix this amount, the judex will not always enjoy the same latitude: we know that he is confined within the terms of the formula: it is therefore

---

[1] Gaius, 4, §§ 107, 108. If the *judicium* is *legitimum* (see *infra*, § 540), it will not be necessary to write in the formula the *exceptio rei in judicium deductae;* extinction will be produced *ipso jure*. Extinction was produced *ipso jure* under the system of *legis actiones* (the exceptiones were not invented). Gaius, loc. cit.

[2] Girard, *Manuel*, p. 998.

[3] *Dig.* 50, 17, 139 (Gaius).

necessary to consider in what terms the *intentio* puts the question which he has to decide:

530. The *intentio* may be *certa* or *incerta;* that is, specify the sum demanded by the plaintiff, or leave the judge charged with estimating it.

"*Si paret N. Negidium A. Agerio centum dare oportere.*" There is an *intentio certa.*

"*Quidquid paret ob eam rem N. Negidium A. Agerio dare oportere.*" There is an *intentio incerta.*

531. (1) *Intentio certa:* The judex can reply only by yes or no. The defendant owes or does not owe one hundred to the plaintiff. *There is no middle ground.*

What then shall the judex do if the defendant instead of owing *one hundred* owes *fifty?* Shall he not at least condemn him to pay *fifty?*

No. The brutal logic of the jurisconsults forbade him. What did the magistrate say? "If N. Negidius owes one hundred, condemn him; if he does not owe it, acquit him." From the moment that N. Negidius owes but *fifty*, he does not owe *one hundred*, and the rigorous order for the judex is to acquit him.

It is the business of plaintiffs who claim a sum certain (certa) to calculate exactly the amount of their claims. Claiming a sestertium too much exposes them to losing the whole sum. This is what is called the penalty of *plus petitio*.[1]

532. *Plus petitio* may take place: (1) *re*, when suit is brought for a sum greater than that for which a person is creditor; (2) *tempore*, when payment of a debt before it is due is sued for; (3) *loco*, when suit is brought in one place for a debt payable in another

[1] Gaius, 4, § 53.

place; (4) *causa*, when a person is creditor under an alternative, as, for example, when Primus owes Secundus an ox or a horse at his option and payment of one of the things due is specifically claimed.

In all these cases there is a dismissal from court definitely, completely, for everything and forever. We shall see that these exigencies of the classic law disappeared with the formulary procedure.[1]

533. (2) *Intentio incerta:* The judex has a power, a function of estimation, — and 'plus petitio' is not possible, but the function of the judex varies greatly, according as the action with a formula 'incerta' is an *actio stricti juris* or an *actio bonae fidei:* — an important division which will be made the object of a profound study in the second year,[2] but which we can only mention here.

534. Every *actio certa* is *stricti juris*, but even an *actio incerta* may itself be *stricti juris;* in this event the judex has only the power of estimating, of appraising, so to speak, the object described by the intentio, according to its value at the time of 'litiscontestatio,' and without power to take into account any cause for increase or depreciation.

If there are 'actiones incertae stricti juris,' there are some of them which are called "*actions bonae fidei*," very recognizable from the words 'ex fide bona,' which the praetor inserted in their 'intentio.'[3]

In these actions, the judex enjoys a large power of determination which is denied him in the others. "He has the power to appreciate in accordance with good

---
[1] See *infra*, § 566 *in fine*.
[2] See Bernard, *la deuxième année de droit Romain.* — S.
[3] Cicero, *De Officiis*, 3, 17.†

faith the legal relation invoked by the plaintiff," and consequently of taking into account all the elements intrinsic in or connected with the suit which might moderate the 'condemnatio' or render it more severe.[1]

SECTION IV. — **Duration of Actions and of Proceedings**

535. **Duration of Actions:** Actions are *perpetuae* or *temporariae*, that is, some may be brought at any time, while others should be brought before the magistrate within the year which follows the creation of the right which they sanction.[2]

536. But the year in question here is what the Romans call an *annus utilis*,[3] *i. e.* three hundred and sixty-five days in which are not reckoned the days when it is not permissible to sue (*dies nefasti* and *dies comitiales*); it has been calculated that an 'annus utilis' is nearly equivalent to two years.[4]

537. It is generally said that civil actions[5] are 'perpetuae' and praetorian actions 'temporariae';[6] that is

---

[1] Gaius, 4, § 61; the text is mutilated, but the sense is not doubtful.

[2] *Inst.* 4, 12 pr.

[3] The *annus utilis* is contrasted with the *annus continuus* of three hundred and sixty-five days.

[4] According to a more recent doctrine adopted by Girard, by *annus utilis* should be meant an *annus utilis ratione initii*, and not an *annus utilis ratione cursus*, that is to say, a year which does not run so long as the plaintiff is prevented from suing (has not the *potestas experiundi*), but which, as soon as the plaintiff has had the *experiundi potestas*, continues then to run, whatever may happen. Girard, *Manuel*, p. 721.

[5] That is, *actions ex jure civili.* — S.

[6] *Dig.* 44, 7, 35 (Paulus).

not absolutely exact, for many praetorian actions are 'perpetuae,' and certain civil actions are 'temporariae.'

538. Theodosius the Younger reduced to thirty years the duration of actions which had been 'perpetuae' down to this time.[1] This provision passed into our law under the title of *prescription des actions*.[2]

538. *Cont.* The survival of actions, being connected with the subject of obligations, will be treated in the second year course.[3]

539. **Limitation of Proceedings (exspiratio judicii).** Prescription of actions must not be confounded with limitation of proceedings. The powers of the judex derived through a 'legis actio' lasted indefinitely; under the formulary procedure, they had only a limited duration.

540. There are distinguished, under the formulary procedure, the *judicia legitima*, organized at Rome or within the radius of a mile around Rome, before *unus judex*, a Roman citizen, between parties having all the qualities of Roman citizens.

All other suits were termed *imperio continentia*.[4]

541. In 'judicia imperio continentia' the powers of the judex expire with those of the magistrate who appointed him. — In 'judicia legitima' the powers of the judex expire at the end of eighteen months by virtue of an express provision of the *lex Julia judiciaria*.[5]

We should say in French law that "proceedings fail

---

[1] *Code,* 7, 39, 3 (Theodosius II and Honorius).
[2] That is, *limitation of actions*. — S.
[3] Bernard, *La deuxième année de droit romain,* §§ 590 *et seq.* — S.
[4] Gaius, 4, §§ 103–107.   [5] *Ibid.*

by limitation," in Roman law, "*judicium exspiravit*" is said.

542. But the 'exspiratio judicii' of the Roman has a more extended import than the limitation for bringing suit of the French law.

Nothing prevents the French plaintiff, who has allowed his proceedings to fail by limitation, from bringing a new suit. The Roman plaintiff who has, for want of continuing proceedings, allowed the *exspiratio judicii* to be accomplished, will, if he wishes again to begin the suit, be defeated by the *exceptio rei in judicium deductae*.[1]

The 'exspiratio judicii' therefore produces indirectly the extinction of the right of the plaintiff.

Section V. — Classification of Actions

543. **Principal Divisions of Actions:** We have not wished to interrupt by arid classifications the rational march of our description. In the course of our explanations we have been able, however, to perceive a certain number of divisions of actions which it is important to recall by a rapid synthesis.

We have distinguished, in passing: —

(1) *Actiones in jus* and *actiones in factum*.[2]
(2) Civil and praetorian actions.[3]
(3) *Actiones directae* and *actiones utiles*.[4]
(4) *Actiones certae* and *incertae*.[5]
(5) *Actiones arbitrariae* and *non arbitrariae*.[6]
(6) *Actiones stricti juris* and *bonae fidei*.[7]

[1] See *supra*, § 526. [2] See *supra*, §§ 518–521.
[3] Or more exactly *actiones civiles* and *actiones honoriae*.
[4] See *supra*, § 521. [5] See *supra*, § 529.
[6] See *supra*, § 524. [7] See *supra*, § 534.

(7) *Actiones perpetuae* and *temporariae*.¹

(8) *Judicia legitima* and *judicia imperio continentia*.²

544. This classification should be completed by the following divisions: —

(1) Actions *in rem* and actions *in personam* according as the action sanctions a real right or an obligatory right.³ The particulars of actions *in rem* will be shown later on,⁴ those of actions *in personam* belong to the second year course.⁵

545. (2) Actions *for the recovery of property* and actions *for the recovery of a penalty*, which have for their purpose, the first to obtain for the plaintiff what belongs to him or what is owed him, in a word to prevent the impoverishment of his property, and the second to have a penalty pronounced against the defendant. — This classification is completed by *actiones mixtae*, which are both for the recovery of property and for the recovery of a penalty.⁶

546. (3) Actions giving simple damages, which constitute the common law, — and actions giving double, triple, quadruple, which are one of the aspects of penal actions.⁷ The action is for double, triple, quadruple damages, when the condemnatio commands the judex to condemn the defendant for double, triple, quadruple the value stated in the intentio. The penalty is therefore a product of which the intentio is the multiplicand and the condemnatio the multiplier.⁸

---

¹ See *supra*, §§ 535–538.   ² See *supra*, §§ 540 *et seq.*
³ See *supra*, § 431.   ⁴ See *infra*, §§ 608–613.
⁵ See Bernard, *La deuxième année de droit romain.*
⁶ *Inst.* 4, 6, §§ 16–19.   ⁷ *Actiones poenae.* — S.
⁸ *Inst.* 4, 6, §§ 21–27.

547. The principal actions will be described at the same time with the rights which they sanction.

548. **Interdicts:** We should call attention to a group of actions which are of an entirely special type: we mean interdicts.

The interdict was a sort of decree rendered by the magistrate, upon demand of one party, to order or forbid something: "*Exhibeas — Restituas — Vim fieri veto.*"

Sometimes the interdict is called for by anybody in behalf of the public welfare, — interdict *ne quid in loco sacro fiat*, *ne quid in loco publico fiat*, — sometimes interdicts are demanded and pronounced for a private matter in urgent cases, noticeably in regard to possession.

If the person against whom the interdict had been granted was obedient to it, the case was ended; if he refused to obey, the matter became a legal proceeding which the magistrate sent before the judex.[1]

Section VI. — Sketch of a Lawsuit in the Formulary Era

549. We have given so far the spirit of the Roman lawsuit rather its material machinery: it is fitting to say something about this machinery before passing to the explanation of the system of *cognitiones extraordinariae* by which it was profoundly modified.

550. **Vocatio in Jus:** The vocatio in jus corresponds to what we call the summons to court; there were not, in old Rome, any officers corresponding to our officers to serve process. The summons to court was

[1] Gaius, 4, §§ 141–163.

THE FORMULARY PROCEDURE 179

made by the plaintiff himself, orally; if the defendant refused to present himself before the magistrate, his adversary could drag him there by force (*obtorto collo*).[1]

551. Representation in Court: In 'legis actiones,' the parties were obliged to appear in person, and could not be represented in court by an agent. *Nemo alieno nomine lege agere potest.*

This rule allowed but few exceptions admitted in matters of tutela (*pro tutela*), of a suit brought by a city (*pro populo*); also an action for theft could be brought, *ex lege Hostilia*, in the name of a citizen in captivity or absent in the service of the state.[2]

552. Representation in court was, on the contrary, permitted in the formulary era: the parties could intrust the defense of their interests in court either to a cognitor or a procurator.

553. (1) *The cognitor:* The cognitor is appointed before the magistrate, in formal words, all parties being present.[3] It is quite generally taught that the judgment is rendered — for or against the *dominus litis* (the party represented). Girard thinks, on the contrary, that, at least in the normal and early law, the judgment was rendered in behalf of the cognitor.[4]

But a point as to which there is accord is that the cognitor takes into court the right of the party repre-

---

[1] Gaius, 4, § 46; Plautus, *Curc.* 5, 2, 23, also *In. Pers.* 4, 9, 10; Aulus Gellius, *Noctes Atticae*, 20, 2.† —The Romans were not acquainted with procedure by default. When the defendant hid from legal process (*latitat*), the magistrate, to overcome his resistance, put the plaintiff in possession of his property. [Digest, 2, 4, 19. See, also, Roby, *Rom. Priv. Law*, vol. ii, pp. 333, 334.]

[2] *Inst.* 4, 10 pr. [3] Gaius, 4, § 83.

[4] Girard, *Manuel*, p. 1013.

sented, and that the latter cannot, disregarding the decision rendered, bring anew the suit without being defeated by the *exceptio rei judicium deductae*.[1]

554. (2) *The procurator:* The procurator derives his powers from an informal commission.[2] On principle, the *dominus litis* could disregard the judgment rendered against his procurator and begin the suit again.

So his adversary has to take precautions: precautions which consist in making the procurator furnish him security "*dominum rem ratam habiturum*," or, more briefly, the "*cautio de rato.*" That is, the procurator will have to assume the obligation secured by sureties[3] of paying to his adversary damages if the 'dominus litis' should have a fancy to bring the suit again.[4]

555. **The Rôle of the Magistrate:** The part of the 'legis actio' which takes place before the magistrate is less a trial than a ceremony. "The magistrate would believe himself too happy, Cicero humorously assures us, if he could say something of his own composition," — but the ritual forbade this.[5]

556. On the contrary, after the *lex Aebutia* had established the powers of the magistrate, the proceedings *in jure* became a real suit. Interrogatories (*interrogatio in jure*) may be employed before the magistrate in order to clarify the proceedings; and if the defendant's admission is obtained, the proceedings go no

---

[1] Gaius, 4, §§ 97, 98.   [2] *Mandatum actionis.*— S.
[3] *Fidejussores.* — S.   [4] Gaius, 4, § 101.
[5] Cicero, *Pro Murena*, 12.†

further, for the *confessus in jure* is in the identical situation of the *judicatus*.[1]

557. Moreover, the magistrate can oblige the parties to assume certain obligations and to give certain securities without which he would not consent to give the formula. These are the *praetorian stipulations*, upon which we cannot dwell here.

558. **Execution of Judgments:** It is a disputed point whether, in the time of the 'legis actiones,' execution *in ipsam rem* was possible or if suits did not necessarily end in a condemnation in damages. The seat of the controversy is in the Institutes of Gaius, IV, § 48. The opinion which seems to prevail to-day is that execution *in ipsam rem* did not exist any more under the régime of 'legis actiones' than in the time of the formulary procedure.

It was therefore only a matter, as in the classical era, of bringing to execution a money condemnation with the help of the means of constraint then in use.

559. The means of constraint in force at the time of the 'legis actiones' is the *manus injectio*. The creditor arrests his debtor, and, if he is not paid within thirty days he can sell him *peregre trans Tiberim*, or even kill him. The same coercion was employed against the *praedes*[2] whom the defendant had to furnish in certain suits.[3]

[1] At least if it is a matter of a *confessio certae pecuniae*, for the admission of the *principal* of a debt, the *quantum* of which is not determined or known, does not terminate anything; it is necessary to liquidate the amount of the debt. *Lex de Gallia Cisalpina*, c. 21; Girard, *Textes*, p. 74.

[2] *Praes*, kind of surety or, more exactly, *expromissor*.

[3] Arrest of the body in the time of the *legis actiones* would be

560. *Actio judicati:* Under the formulary procedure, execution on the person is always the regular means of execution. But the *judicatus* is no longer threatened with death or sale *trans Tiberim.* He is *addictus* by the magistrate to his creditor, shut up by the latter in his *ergastulum* (private prison), and fettered when necessary, until he shall be liberated by his work. But it is to be remarked that execution is preceded by a new action, the *actio judicati.* If the *judicatus* contests the existence or legality of the judgment rendered against him, a new trial takes place, and if the defendant loses in it, he is condemned *in duplum,* which shows us that this 'actio judicati,' a wholly Roman creation, without analogy in our law, is modeled on the *manus injectio judicati* of the 'legis actiones.'[1]

561. *Execution on the property (venditio bonorum):* According to the *lex Poetelia Papiria* (law of 326 B. C. on *nexum*), a new mode of execution is introduced, the *publicatio bonorum* or sale *en bloc* of the property of an insolvent debtor *(defraudator)* to an individual who takes the name of *bonorum emptor.* The property of the insolvent, after being advertised and a list of charges drawn up, is sold at auction to the person offering to the creditors the highest dividends. The purchaser *(bonorum emptor)* takes all the property and is obliged to pay the debts to the extent of the dividend promised.[2]

562. The *venditio bonorum* could be ordered only by the magistrates of Rome and not by municipal

employed against the *praedes* alone, if it is admitted that, even in a litigious matter, the *praes* obligates himself *in place of,* and not *along with,* the debtor for whom he is surety. See Girard, *Textes,* p. 796.

[1] See *supra,* § 491.   [2] Gaius, 3, §§ 77–80.

magistrates, which proves that execution on the person is the means of coercion of the common law.[1]

563. *Distractio bonorum:* The 'venditio' or 'publicatio bonorum' involved infamy. That persons of high rank (senators, for example) might avoid the stigma, we see introduced from the time of the first Antonines the *distractio bonorum*, that is, the sale *en détail* made for the benefit of the creditors themselves by a curator. This institution, very analogous to our *saisie*[2] of to-day, was to bring about the disappearance of the old 'bonorum venditio.'[3]

CHAPTER III

THE EXTRAORDINARY PROCEDURE

564. Character of the Extraordinary Procedure: The essential character of the extraordinary porcedure (*cognitio extraordinaria*), is the disappearance of the distinction between *jus* and *judicium*, between magistrate and judex. The magistrate no longer contents himself with organizing the suit: he decides it himself.

565. Under what Conditions and at what Time is the Extraordinary Procedure established? It is quite generally taught that the extraordinary procedure was substituted for the *ordo judiciorum* by a constitution of Diocletian of 294 A. D. The truth is that Diocletian only declared a state of facts which already existed. The extraordinary pro-

[1] *Lex de Gallia Cisalp.* c. 22, *in fine;* Girard, *Textes*, p. 76.
[2] That is, *seizure* or *levy.* — S.
[3] *Dig.* 27, 10, 5 (Gaius); *ibid.* 9 (Neratius).

cedure was in operation, from the beginning of the empire, for administrative suits, and had been applied, in private causes, in several instances. Thus the *praetor fideicommissarius*, the *praetor tutelaris*, the *praetor de liberalibus causis* used to judge *extra ordinem* in suits coming under their jurisdiction.

The judicial praetors themselves (praetor urbanus and praetor peregrinus) used to judge *extra ordinem*, questions of *honoraria*[1] which interested doctors, lawyers, and nurses. The provincial governors (praesides provinciarum) used to judge in person or have decided by their deputies, who must not be confused with the 'judices,' a great number of cases.[2]

The work of Diocletian simply consisted in making universal a practice which was already very general.[3]

566. **Principal Details of the Extraordinary Procedure:** The suppression of the *ordo judiciorum* characterizes the last state of the procedure.

But the latter underwent many other modifications: (1) The *vocatio in jus* is no longer the work of the plaintiff himself, but of an *apparitor*, a sort of officer to serve process, charged with delivering a *libellus conventionis*. — (2) Cases are judged no longer publicly *pro tribunali*, but in the *sectarium* where only a privileged public penetrates. — (3) Furthermore, the chief innovation, the judge no longer pronounces money condemnations exclusively: he can condemn the defendant *in ipsam rem*, that is, to the material fulfillment of the obligation when it is possible, and the judgment is

---

[1] That is, *fees, remuneration for services*. — S.

[2] See the judgment rendered by Blaesius Marianus, prefect of the first cohort of Cilician knights. Girard, *Textes*, pp. 838 *et seq*.

[3] *Code*, 3, 3, 2.

THE EXTRAORDINARY PROCEDURE 185

brought to execution by military force (*manu militari*). (4) Finally, the penalty for *plus petitio* ceased to exist in actions *stricti juris*, and the judge could reduce the amount of the judgment, instead of dismissing entirely an exaggerated claim.[1]

[1] Girard, *Manuel*, pp. 1052–1064.

BOOK V

OWNERSHIP

TITLE I

ATTRIBUTES OF EVOLUTION AND OWNERSHIP

567. Definition and Elements of Ownership: Ownership is the right which a person has of using a thing, of enjoying the fruits, and of having control over it, which is expressed in Latin by the words: *jus utendi fruendi, et abutendi*.

568. Primitive peoples do not attain all at once to this conception of individual ownership, the need of which does not obtrude itself until after men have passed from the pastoral and nomadic state to the agricultural and settled state.

569. The people who were to be called the Roman people had to pass, like all others, through the phases of this evolution; but Rome, even in legendary times, appears to us only with a population of agriculturists already familiarized with the notion of individual ownership.

570. Several terms of the legal language give rise, however, to the suspicion of a remote period of family co-ownership (the term *suus heres*, own heir, for in-

stance).¹ But at the period when we commence to know with exactness, namely, at the time of the law of the XII Tables, Roman ownership presents an individual character clearly established.

¹ See *infra*, § 802. Cf. Roby, *Rom. Priv. Law*, vol. i, p. 188. — S.

TITLE II

POSSESSION

CHAPTER I

ELEMENTS, ACQUISITION, LOSS OF POSSESSION

571. Possession: Ownership, that is to say, the right of using, enjoying the fruits, and having control over property, is externally revealed by the fact of use, enjoyment of the fruits, and control over property. The whole of these facts constitute possession, as the whole of the rights with which they correspond constitute ownership. Hence this excellent definition of possession by Ihering: "*Possession is the externality of ownership.*"

Nevertheless, it may happen that these external manifestations do not correspond with a right: the thief performs all the acts whereby ownership is revealed, and yet he is not owner; let us add that, if he is not owner, he *wishes to be such*, and that surely there cannot be denied him the *claim of ownership* (*affectus rem sibi habendi, animus dominantis*, or, in Greek, ψυχὴ δεσπόζοντος).

572. The exercise of the *jus utendi*, of the *jus fruendi*, may even, in certain cases, imply no claim to ownership. Thus the enjoyment of a tenant may present the external aspect of ownership, and yet he who exercises this enjoyment has neither ownership nor the claim of acting as owner.

573. **Degrees of Possession:** Starting from these observations, a doctrine which seems to plunge its roots most deeply into the past has distinguished two kinds of possession: (1) nuda detentio; (2) protected possession or possessio ad interdicta.

574. *Detention and possession:* Nuda detentio indicates no claim to personal appropriation of the thing.

575. *Possessio ad interdicta* admits of, generally at least,[1] the *animus domini* (or, better, *dominantis*), and public authority intervenes to protect it by means of decrees to which the name of *interdicta* was attached.

576. *Possessio ad usucapionem:* Finally, to these two terms, *nuda detentio* and *protected possession*, a complementary creation has added a third: 'possessio ad usucapionem;' when possession is prolonged for a certain time, it comes to be considered as establishing *the right of ownership*. We will return to this point when studying 'usucapio.'[2]

It is sufficient now to bear in mind that the doctrine of possession, when reaching its complete development, distinguishes: (1) nuda detentio; (2) possessio ad interdicta; (3) possessio ad usucapionem.

577. **Elements of Possession:** Possession, properly speaking, implies two elements: corpus and animus.

Corpus is the material element: the effective control over the thing (*detentio usus rei*).

---

[1] We say "*generally at least*" because certain detainers without *animus domini*, as the holder of a *precarium* [Colquhoun, *A Summary of the Rom. Civ. Law*, § 1562], and the pledgee, have the possessory interdicts.

[2] See *infra*, §§ 640 *et seq*.

Animus is the intent to act toward the thing as owner (*affectus rem sibi habendi*).[1]

578. Acquisition of Possession: Possession is acquired *animo et corpore;* there is no difficulty concerning acquisition by one's self.[2]

579. As to acquisition through another person, the rule is on principle we can indeed acquire *corpore alieno*, but that acquisition can take place only *animo nostro:* — or, if we wish, that acquisition admits of agency as to the *corpus*, but not as to the *animus*.

Still the rule that possession may be acquired *corpore alieno* is not established at once. The ancient law admits at first only the acquisition of possession by the intermediate agency of *persons* under the power of the paterfamilias: thus the head of a family used to become possessor through his children or his slaves; the taking made by the latter was made for him and as if by him.

In classical law it is stated that possession can be acquired *per extraneam personam*. This theory, slowly elaborated, must have been accepted first for procurators charged with the general administration of the property of a person (these general agencies as to the property of a person were not rare, and were intrusted to former slaves who had become stewards for their masters), then it was allowed for tutors, curators, and finally for special agents and *negotiorum gestores*.[3]

580. As to the *animus*, on principle no agency is

---

[1] Mühlenbruch.†   [2] Paulus, *Sent.* 5, 2, § 1.

[3] The stages of the elaboration of this theory may be followed in the following texts: *Dig.* 41, 1, 13 (Neratius) (general agents and tutors); *Code*, 7, 32, 1 (Severus and Caracalla) (special agents and *negotiorum gestores*).

possible, but exceptions are admitted as to tutors, and curators who may acquire possession for the benefit of persons under guardianship (tutela) or curatorship *even without the knowledge of these latter*.[1]

Let us add that the paterfamilias and the master acquire by a sort of preventitive *animus* the possession of things acquired *peculiariter* by a slave or a filiusfamilias.[2]

581. Loss of Possession: Possession is incontestably lost where both the 'animus' and the 'corpus' together disappear.

But is it lost when one of its elements is wanting? In other words, can possession be retained *corpore tantum* or *animo tantum*?

Corpore tantum? We do not perceive how the loss of the 'animus' can be shown so long as substantial detention exists. The loss of the 'animus' is a mental secret. We do not see how any effectiveness can be given to an *intention to no longer possess* which escapes all investigation.*[3]

582. *Animo tantum?* It has taken a long time to admit that possession can be retained *animo tantum*. This was first admitted as to *saltus aestivi hibernique*,

[1] *Dig.* 41, 1, 13 (Neratius).
[2] Girard, *Manuel*, p. 269, note 4, and p. 270, note 2.

*[3] There exists, however, a case where possession is lost *animo tantum*; it is the case of *constitutum possessorium*, namely, the case where the possessor *animo domini* agrees to possess hereafter for a third person, *constituit se possessurum*. For example: Primus, possessor *animo domini* of the fundus Cornelianus, sells it to Secundus and agrees to hold from him the title of tenant. The *corpus* of the possession has not changed, but the *animus* has passed from Primus to Secundus. [See Roby, *Rom. Priv. Law*, vol. i, p. 458.]

that is, for pasture lands occupied only for a season: still later the doctrine was made general as to immovables; and to every owner who found a third person installed in his property during his absence was given the right to bring against this intruder a simple possessory interdict, without having to furnish proof of ownership.[1]

583. Rule: Nemo potest sibi causam possessionis mutare: Will it be optional to a holder to change the nature of his possession and to claim of his own authority the *animus domini?* Thus, could a tenant say: "It does not please me to possess for my proprietor: starting from to-day, I wish to possess for myself?"

No, since the real possessor, for whom the tenant is but an instrument for holding, retains possession *animo tantum.*[2]

584. Such was possession at the outset, such it remains in the hands of the holder; this is what is expressed by the rule "*nemo potest sibi causam possessionis mutare*," result of the doctrine just explained in the preceding paragraph.[3]

CHAPTER II

POSSESSORY PROTECTION

585. Of Possession opposed to Non-possession: The ideas just explained are indispensable

[1] *Dig.* 41, 2, 27; *ibid.* 45 and 46.
[2] *Dig.* 41, 3, 33, § 1 (Julian); *Dig.* 41, 5, 2 (Julian); *Dig.* 41, 2, 19, § 1 (Marcellus).
[3] See *supra*, § 583.

to a knowledge of the doctrine of possessory protection.

The *possessor* being protected against the *non-possessor*, it is important to determine first of all who is the possessor and who is not, when possession commences, when it ends, consequently how it is acquired, is lost and retained.

586. Although possession is but a state of fact, it procures for him who proves it some very important legal advantages.

Suppose two persons dispute about a thing without either of them being able to prove ownership: which one will triumph? The possessor. For there is no reason to take away the thing from him to give it to the other. "*In pari causa melior est causa possidentis.*"

587. **Of Possession opposed to Ownership:** Suppose, on the contrary, *possession is opposed to ownership*, possession will succumb and the possessor will have to yield before owner. But the latter will be obliged to pay the part of plaintiff in revindication (*rei vindicatio*), and hence of proving his right of ownership. The possessor will consequently find himself in a more advantageous situation.

The possessor is therefore protected *absolutely* against the non-possessor who is not an owner, and protected *provisionally* against the owner who is not possessor.

588. **Foundation of Possessory Protection:** Why does the law protect possession which is a *fact* and not a *right*? There are on this point two celebrated doctrines: that of Savigny and that of Ihering.[1]

[1] Girard, *Manuel*, p. 266. — S.

589. The doctrine of Savigny makes possessory protection rest on the public peace. If possession were not protected, men would pass their time in despoiling one another. It is therefore a powerful advantage to society to maintain actual conditions so long as these are not worsted by proof of a contrary right.

590. The doctrine of Ihering rests on this idea, that the law, in the person of the possessor, sees the owner (which generally will be true to reality), and, if it protects the possession which is the *appearance* of ownership it is in order to more effectively protect ownership itself. So we should bear in mind, along with the statement already quoted of Ihering, this other metaphorical statement and, with that, the more impressive one of Girard: "*possession is the outwork of ownership.*" [1]

We would say, if it were allowed us to express a personal opinion, that each of the rival doctrines is partly true. The doctrine of Ihering better justifies the interdicts *retinendae possessionis:* that of Savigny explains in a more satisfactory fashion the interdicts *recuperandae possessionis.*

591. **Actions which protect Possession:** Possession is protected by the possessory interdicts which are divided into two principal groups: (1) The interdicts 'retinendae possessionis causa,' the object of which is to maintain the possessor in possession; (2) the interdicts 'recuperandae possessionis causa,' which have for their object to recover for him a possession substantially lost.[2]

592. *Interdicts Retinendae Possessionis:* There are

---

[1] Girard, *Manuel*, p. 267.   [2] *Inst.* 4, 15, § 4.

two of these: the interdict 'utrubi' for movables, the interdict 'uti possidetis' for immovables.[1]

(1) *Interdict UTRUBI:* Of two persons who both lay claim to the possession of a movable, the interdict utrubi causes him to triumph who has possessed the movable the longest time during the preceding year.

(2) *Interdict UTI POSSIDETIS:* This interdict awards possession of the immovable to that of the two parties who possess it at the time they appear in court.

593. It is not useless to make here the remark that the French law has followed absolutely the reverse of the Roman policy. In case of conflict as to the possession of an *immovable*, the party who obtains it in French law is the one who proves a prolonged possession (possession for a year). On the contrary, as to movables, actual possession not only causes him who proves it to triumph, but it is equivalent for him to a title of ownership. " In matter of movables possession is equivalent to title." [2]

594. *Interdicts RECUPERANDAE POSSESSIONIS:* (1) The interdict *unde vi* which is applicable only to immovables, and which is given to the *dejectus* (he who has been dispossessed by violence of an immovable) against the *dejiciens*. It was on the application of this interdict that Cicero delivered his oration *pro Caecina.*

595. (2) The interdict *de precario* given to him who made a revocable grant called *precarium*, in order to retake the thing granted.

[1] His possession must not be bad, that is, that he does not possess *nec vi, nec clam, nec precario.*

[2] Art. 2279, *Code civil* of France.

596. (3) Under the Republic the existence is admitted of an interdict *de clandestina possessione*, symmetrical to the interdict *unde vi* and given on the occasion of clandestine occupation of property temporarily deserted. The doctrine of the retention of possession *animo tantum* would have caused this interdict to fall into disuse. It was necessary merely to bring, in this case, the interdict *uti possidetis* (*retinendae possessionis*).

TITLE III

DIFFERENT KINDS OF OWNERSHIP

597. **Quiritary Ownership:** The law of the XII Tables recognized but one kind of ownership: quiritary ownership (*dominium ex jure quiritium*), which presumes a Roman owner and a Roman object (res).[1]

Peregrini and non-Roman soil (unless this soil had the benefit of the grant of the *jus Italicum*) are excluded from it.

598. **Its Object:** Roman ownership, limited at first to *res mancipi*, commenced by being extended to *res nec mancipi* acquired by citizens by simple delivery, but always left alone things which, by their nature, were not susceptible of quiritary ownership: noticeably provincial land. The soil of the provinces is not indeed within the ownership of individuals; it belongs to the Roman people; it can therefore be made the object only of a sort of perpetual grant, the difference between which and dominium is established by the tax (*stipendium* or *tributum*) which provincial soil pays and from which Italian soil is freed.[2]

599. **Bonitary Ownership:** Subsequently jurisprudence introduced, along with 'dominium ex

---

[1] "*Quo jure etiam populus Romanus olim utebatur: aut enim ex jure Quiritium unusquisque dominus erat, aut non intelligebatur dominus.*" Gaius, 2, § 40.

[2] *Ibid.* § 21.

jure quiritium,' a right less complete, a sort of ownership according to the jus gentium, the holder of which is called by Theophilus, in his paraphrase of the Institutes, δεσπότης βονιτάριος: whence the expression *bonitary ownership* employed by the commentators, but perfectly foreign to the Roman legal language. The Roman jurisconsults indeed speak of having this ownership of inferior order, "*in bonis habere,*" but they never conceived of any adjective corresponding with this idea.[1]

600. Objects of Bonitary Ownership: We can have *in bonis* either objects susceptible of quiritary ownership, but over which this ownership is not yet acquired; — or objects which could never be made the subject of 'dominium ex jure quiritium.' This distinction, which often passes unperceived, is to be borne in mind, for the sanction of the law is not absolutely the same in the two cases (*actio Publiciana* in the first, *vindicatio utilis* in the second).

601. Bonitary Ownership and the Praetorian Law: Bonitary ownership (we will continue to call it thus for want of a more appropriate expression) was covered by the praetorian law with an effective protection, and "the distinction ends by existing more in words than in reality."[2]

602. Ownership under Justinian: Under Justinian 'dominium ex jure quiritium' exists no longer in fact: "It remains only as an enigma serving as a bugbear in the study of law. The emperor abolishes it. Just as in ancient times, only one ownership was recog-

---

[1] Gaius, 2, § 40.
[2] *Ibid.;* Ortolan, *gén. du droit romain.*†

nized; but instead of ownership ex jure quiritium, exclusively peculiar to the Romans, it is ownership open to all and over all territories: the jus civile has yielded to the jus gentium." [1]

[1] Ortolan, *gén. du droit romain.*†

TITLE IV

SANCTION FOR THE RIGHT OF OWNERSHIP

CHAPTER I

GENERALITIES

603. Actions which protect Ownership: Quiritary ownership is protected by the *rei vindicatio*, — bonitary ownership susceptible of being transformed into quiritary ownership (for the benefit of the possessor *in causa usucapiendi*) by the *actio Publiciana*; — bonitary ownership not susceptible of being transformed into quiritary ownership either because the thing possessed cannot be the object, or because the possessor cannot be the subject of the *jus quiritium* (for example, a 'fundus provincialis' or a 'peregrinus possessor') by a *rei vindicatio utilis*.

CHAPTER II

REI VINDICATIO [1]

604. Rei Vindicatio under the Régime of Legis Actiones: In the time of the 'legis actiones,' revindication of quiritary ownership is made by means of the *legis actio sacramenti*.

[1] A real action; action for the recovery of ownership: see Poste, *Gaii Institutiones Iuris Civilis*, pp. 456 *et seq.*; Roby, *Rom. Priv. Law*, vol. i, p. 438. — S.

The parties bring before the magistrate the subject of the suit, a slave, a beast of burden; if it is a matter as to land, or a house, they will bring a piece of the thing, a clod of earth or a tile. The plaintiff touches the thing with his rod and says: "*Hunc ago hominem*" (we will suppose that it is a matter as to a slave) *meum esse aio ex jure quiritium secundum suam causam; sicut dixi esse tibi vindictam imposui.* This is the *vindicatio.*

The defendant, touching in his turn with his *vindicta* the object in litigation, repeats the same statement; this is the *contravindicatio.*

The two parties thus feign a kind of combat which is called *manuum consertio.*

"*Mittite ambo hominem*" (or *rem*) says the praetor; the parties let go of the object in litigation and the dialogue is continued: —

Primus: "I ask you why you have claimed?"

Secundus: "*Jus peregi sicut vindictam imposui.*"

Primus: "As you have claimed unjustly I challenge you by the *sacramentum* of five hundred *as* (*quando tu injuria vindicavisti, D aeris sacramento te provoco*)."

Secundus: "And I likewise" (*similiter ego te*).[1]

605. Then the praetor commenced by giving the provisional possession of the object in litigation to one of the two parties whom he chose at his pleasure, but in return he obligated this party to furnish sureties to secure in case of loss, the restitution of the thing and the profits (*praedes litis ac vindiciarum*).[2]

---

[1] Gaius, 4, § 16.

[2] *Contra,* Cuq, *Institutions,* p. 411, note 1; yet the text of Gaius, 4, § 16, seems to us conclusive of this acceptation: "*Postea praetor secundum alterum eorum vindicias dicebat, id est interim ali-*

The *sacramentum* was at first deposited: later they contented themselves with securing payment by means of sureties (*praedes sacramenti*).[1]

606. These formalities accomplished, the parties took for witnesses the persons present by saying "*testes estote.*" That was the end of the proceedings in jure (the *litiscontestatio*): the magistrate had only to send the trial before the judex, and we recall that, when it is a question of ownership, the judex is the court of the *centumviri*.

607. The court declares *justum* the *sacramentum* of the party for whom it gives a decision, *injustum* the *sacramentum* of him who loses his suit. This award evidently does not end litigation, if the party who obtained provisional possession is not declared owner. It is necessary, furthermore, to have determined the amount of restitution to which the party unjustly dispossessed has a right. This determination is made by 'arbitri' (*arbitrium liti aestumandae*),[2] and the recovery of the damages thus determined is pursued by means of arrest of the body (*manus injectio*) against the *praedes litis ac vindiciarum*.

608. **Rei Vindicatio in the Time of the Formulary Procedure:** In the time of the formulae, the action for the recovery of ownership

quem possessorem constituebat." Cf. Girard, *Manuel*, pp. 334, 335; Jobbé-Duval, *opus cit.*, pp. 320–328.

[1] Gaius, 4, § 16.

[2] Valerius Probus, *Notae*, Girard, *Textes*, p. 195; lex *Acilia repetundarum*, line 58, Girard, *Textes*, p. 41; but, as Girard says, this *arbitrium* will be generally superfluous; the plaintiff condemned will not suffer the execution of *manus injectio* against his *praedes*. Girard, *Manuel*, pp. 334–335.

may appear in two aspects: the plaintiff sues either per sponsionem, or per formulam arbitrariam.

609. *Procedure PER SPONSIONEM:* This is evidently a reminder of the 'sacramentum'; perhaps a transition procedure.

By means of reciprocal obligations entered into before the magistrate (*sponsio* and *restipulatio*), the parties make a sort of wager as to ownership. He who loses his wager loses his suit. That is only an artifice of procedure: for the loser does not pay even the amount of his wager. Which the Roman jurisconsults express by saying that the 'sponsio' and 'restipulatio' of the action for the recovery of ownership are *praejudiciales* and not *penal*.[1]

610. *Procedure PER FORMULAM ARBITRARIAM* (it is also called *per formulam petitoriam*): The formula, very simple, casts on the judex the question of ownership.

"*Si paret fundum Cornelianum Auli Agerii esse ex jure quiritium.*"

This *intentio* is immediately followed by an *arbitratus judicis* (we have said in effect that all actions *in rem* are *arbitrariae*):

"*Neque is fundus arbitratu tuo restituatur.*"

Then comes the *condemnatio:* "*judex, quanti ea res erit, tantam pecuniam Numerium Negidium Aulo Agerio condemna:* si non paret absolve."

" Judex, condemn N. N. to pay to A. A. a sum equal to the amount in litigation: if the claim does not appear to you to have a foundation, acquit."

611. We find here the application of all the principles which we have laid down in the subject of the

[1] Gaius, 4, § 94.

'actio arbitraria,'[1] the previous *pronuntiatio* of the judex, and where the defendant does not submit to the 'pronuntiatio,' a money judgment: (let us add that the amount of this judgment will be fixed by the oath of the plaintiff, without taxation by the judex).

612. **Interdict quem fundum:** There is no place in the procedure *per formulam arbitrariam* for the provisional grant of possession by the magistrate. Possession is retained of right by the defendant: however this situation may become modified. The defendant should furnish before the magistrate security for the amount of the condemnation to come: this is the *cautio judicatum solvi*, evident transformation of the ancient obligation of the *praedes litis ac vindiciarum*. If the defendant does not furnish sureties (fidejussores) the praetor, by an interdict (the interdict *quem fundum*),*[2] awards possession to the plaintiff on condition by the latter of himself furnishing the 'cautio judicatum solvi.' The rôles are then reversed, and with them the burden of proof.

613. The necessity for the possessor of furnishing the 'cautio judicatum solvi' is special to actions *in rem* and causes the great superiority of rights *in rem* over obligatory rights.

614. **Extent of Satisfaction given to the Plaintiff in the Matter of Rei Vindicatio:** It is again necessary to place ourselves successively in the time of the 'legis actiones' and the era of the formulary procedure.

[1] See *supra*, §§ 524 *et seq.*
*[2] *Quem fundum*, if it is a matter of land; *quem hominem*, if it is a matter of a slave; *quam hereditatem* in a *petitio hereditatis*. Inst. of Ulpian, fr. iv.; Girard, *Textes*, p. 467.

REI VINDICATIO

615. In the time of the 'legis actiones,' did the *arbitrium liti aestumandae* include all the fruits obtained by the defendant before litiscontestatio? We have in order to solve this question only a mutilated text of Festus [1] which declares as to the law of the XII Tables:

"*Si vindiciam falsam tulit . . . tor tres arbitros dato fructuum duplione decidito.*"

Which would appear to declare: "If a possessor is condemned . . . the praetor chooses three arbitri: — that the proceeding is decided by the awarding of double the fruits."

But Esmein thinks that it is a matter here of only fruits obtained since litiscontestatio;[2] and that restoration of the fruits should be demanded by a separate action. What might be this action? A *condictio furtiva* according to Ihering, a *condictio sine causa* according to Esmein, — condictio which, whatever may be its character, could be brought, as we shall presently see, only against the possessor in bad faith.[3]

616. In the time of the formulae, the question is simplified in this sense that it is not doubtful that the *satisfactio* imposed by the judex on the plaintiff should include the fruits, and that in the condemnatio he will be held accountable for the value of these fruits; what is owed by the possessor who is condemned is the value of the fruits *cum omni causa*.[4] But this restitution of the fruits is subjected to these different rules according as the defendant is a possessor *mala fide*, or a possessor *bona fide*.

[1] See *Vindiciae*, Bruns. *Fontes juris*, part ii, p. 48 — S.
[2] Esmein, *Mélanges*, p. 192.
[3] *Ibid.*
[4] *Dig.* 6, 1, 20 (Gaius).

617. Acquisition of the Fruits by the Possessor Bona Fide: There is no need of distinguishing between the possessor *bona fide* and the possessor *mala fide* as to fruits gathered since litiscontestatio; these fruits are always restorable: indeed, the possessor notified by a suit can no longer maintain a full confidence in his right: he ceases to be completely *bonae fidei*.

618. As to fruits gathered before litiscontestatio, the situation of the possessor *bona fide* and that of the possessor *mala fide* become very different.

The possessor *male fide* is accountable for all the fruits, consumed or not consumed, for those which he neglected to gather as well as for those which he gathered. There is no difficulty on this point.*[1]

619. The possessor *bona fide* is held, according to the texts of the Digest, to restore only the *fructus extantes*: he should, it seems, be held to restore the fruits gathered in good faith but not yet consumed.

That this is so at the time of Justinian is not doubtful. But was it really so in the classical era? There are texts even in the Digest laying down the principle that the *bona fide* possessor acquires the fruits (*makes the fruits his own* according to the consecrated phrase) by *perceptio*, that is, before having consumed them.[2]

---

*[1] That results *a contrario* from all the texts which limit the obligation of the possessor in good faith, — from *Code*, 3, 32, 22 (Diocl. and Maxim.), interpolated on another point by Justinian. — Yet the restitution of the fruits which the possessor in bad faith neglected to gather should date, according to Girard (*Manuel*, p. 342, note 2), only from a constitution of Valentinian and Valens of 362 A. D. (*Cod. Theod.* 4, 18, 1).

[2] *Dig.* 41, 1, 48; 22, 1, 25.

A certain number of texts from classic writers inserted in the Digest seem suspected of alteration,[1] and it used to be a very debated question among Romanists of knowing if in the classical era the fructus were acquired for the *bona fide* possessor by perceptio or solely by consumption as the suspected texts appear to declare. This controversy has come to an end. A constitution of the Theodosian Code (*de fructibus*[2]), which had passed unperceived, has been noticed in recent times by a German jurist, de Czilarz:[3] this constitution plainly says that the *bona fide* possessor acquires the fructus by *perceptio*. As the Theodosian Code stands between the texts of the Digest and the time of Justinian, it results therefrom that acquisition of the fruits by *consumption*, which has for a consequence the restoration of the fructus extantes, was established by Justinian, and that this emperor audaciously altered the texts of the classical jurisconsults, to which he caused to be given as admitted since their time a solution which is of his own invention.

We should therefore lay down the principle that in the classical era the *bona fide* possessor sued in an action for revindication ought to be held to account to the plaintiff only for the fruits obtained since litis-contestatio.

[1] *Dig.* 41, 3, 4, § 19 (Paulus). See, also, *Code*, 3, 32, 22.
[2] *Cod. Theod.* 4, 18, 1.
[3] *Institutionen des Römisches Rechts.* — S.

CHAPTER III

THE ACTIO PUBLICIANA

620. Principle of the Action: We shall see a little later[1] that when a thing susceptible of quiritary ownership has been possessed for a certain time (one year for movables, two years for immovables) by a person who is able to become 'dominus ex jure quiritium,' the *bonitary* ownership is transformed into quiritary ownership for the benefit of the possessor by means of 'usucapio.'[2]

A praetor by the name of Publicius, of uncertain date, conceived the idea of anticipating the period of time for 'usucapio' by giving to him who is *in causa usucapiendi*, in the case where he is going to be dispossessed by a third person, an *anticipated rei vindicatio*, which from the name of its inventor took the name of actio Publiciana.[3]

621. The "Publiciana" is a very plain type of the *actio ficticia*.[4] The praetor orders the judex to consider as completed an 'usucapio' in course of being completed.

622. Exceptio Justi Dominii: The actio Publiciana, effectual against all possessors, is powerless, however, against the owner 'ex jure quiritium.' It will be, in such case, defeated by the 'exceptio justi dominii.'[5]

623. Replicatio Rei Venditae et Traditae:

[1] See *infra*, § 644.
[2] See *infra*, §§ 640 *et seq*.
[3] *Dig.* 6, 2 pr. (Ulpian).
[4] See *supra*, § 519.
[5] *Dig.* 6, 2, 16 (Papinian).

There is nevertheless a case where the 'dominus ex jure quiritium' cannot prevail against the possessor *in causa usucapiendi:* it is where the 'dominus ex jure quiritium' is the originator of the possession *in causa usucapiendi*.

Suppose that Primus has sold and delivered to Secundus a *res mancipi*. Primus has reserved the 'dominium ex jure quiritium,' and Secundus has acquired only the bonitary ownership.

By reason of any circumstance whatever, Primus reënters upon possession of the thing. Secundus brings against him the actio Publiciana. Without doubt Primus will be justified in opposing him by the *exceptio justi dominii*, in making this statement to him: "You have the object *in bonis*, but I myself am owner of it *ex jure quiritium*, and your right is effaced before a superior right." — To which Secundus will reply: "You are wrong in contesting my right, for you yourself sold and delivered to me the object in litigation." Condensed in the formula, this objection will constitute what is called the *replicatio rei venditae et traditae*.[1]

CHAPTER IV

OTHER ACTIONS PROTECTING OWNERSHIP

624. **Vindicationes Utiles:** In order to bring the actio Publiciana it (the *res*) must be in causa usucapiendi, and for that two things are necessary: (1) that the object in litigation can be usucapted; (2) that the possessor can usucapt.

The first of these conditions would be wanting if

[1] *Dig.* 21, 3, 1 (Ulpian); *ibid.* 3 (Hermogenianus).

the object in litigation was a 'fundus provincialis;' the second, if the possessor was a 'peregrinus.'

In place of the actio Publiciana, impossible in the cases supposed, the praetor gives a vindicatio utilis.[1] This vindicatio utilis is likely to be a little confused with the *actio Publiciana directa,* as there is an *actio Publiciana utilis* in which the praetor anticipates, not the *usucapio,* but the *praescriptio longi temporis.* The composition of this "Publiciana utilis" has not come down to us.[2]

625. Actio Rescissoria: We shall not speak here of the actio rescissoria or *the opposite of the Publiciana* of which certain commentators treat. It is but a badly qualified form of the *restitutio in integrum.*

626. Actio ad exhibendum: The actio ad exhibendum is the auxiliary and sometimes the preface of the *rei vindicatio.* This action, which is made, without proof, moreover, to date from the XII Tables, "enforces the obligation laid on him who has something in his possession to produce it, exhibit it on the request of whosoever wishes to bring an action relative to this thing."[3]

If we suppose an owner dispossessed before an adversary who claims not to have the thing in his possession, this owner will bring the actio ad exhibendum.

Suppose he proves that the defendant refused *mala fide* to exhibit the thing? The defendant will be con-

---

[1] See *supra,* § 221. — Gaius, 4, § 37, gives an idea of the fictions which might be in such case introduced in the formula.

[2] *Dig.* 6, 2, 12, § 2 (Paulus).

[3] Girard, *Manuel,* p. 629; Cuq. *Institutions,* vol. i, p. 508.

demned for double the value of this thing. Suppose he obtains, on the 'pronuntiatio' of the judex (the action indeed is *arbitraria*), the production which he calls for? He then can bring *rei vindicatio*.

TITLE V

MODES OF ACQUIRING OWNERSHIP

DIVISION

627. Original and Derivative Modes: The modes of acquiring ownership are at first divided into *original* and *derivative modes:* the *original mode* is when ownership is created for the first time in the person of an individual (for example, game which is secured in hunting belongs to him who takes it by virtue of an original mode); the *derivative mode* is when ownership is transferred from one individual to another.

628. Modes of Acquisition of the Jus Civile and the Jus Naturale: From another point of view modes of acquiring property are divided into modes of the 'jus civile' and modes of the 'jus naturale.' The modes of the jus civile are mancipation, *in jure cessio, adjudicatio, usucapio,* and *lege.* . . . We add quite usually *traditio,* which may pass as belonging to the jus naturale as well as the jus civile.[1]

The modes of acquisition of the jus naturale are occupation and accession.

[1] Ulpian, *Reg.* 19, § 2 and § 7.

CHAPTER I

MODES OF THE JUS CIVILE

629. Mancipation: Mancipation is not applicable for the transference of all things, but only for the transference of *res mancipi*.[1] Mancipation is a formal mode of acquisition requiring the presence of five witnesses and a 'libripens' (carrying the scales), all Roman citizens and 'puberes.' — However 'peregrini' could figure in it when they have the 'jus commercii.'[2]

In the presence of the witnesses and the libripens, the purchaser, touching the object, or at least something representing the object (for instance a tile for a house), utters these words: "*Hunc ego hominem* (suppose that it is a slave) *meum esse aio ex jure quiritiumisque mihi emptus esto hoc aere aeneaque libra.*" And having said this, he strikes the scales with the piece of bronze which he holds in his hand.

630. This ceremony, in the last state of the law, is purely symbolical: it is explained historically. Mancipation has indeed passed through three periods: the period of *aes rude*, of *aes signatum*, and of money.

At the time when the Romans were not acquainted at all with money, the representative token used in transactions consisted of copper ingots; the scales really served to weigh the quantity of copper necessary to make up the purchase price, and the purchaser who made the ingots resound on the dish of the scales did nothing else than verify by the sound the quality of the metal. This metal, indeed, was not stamped; this is *aes rude*.

[1] Ulpian, *Reg.* 19, § 3.   [2] *Ibid.* §§ 4, 5.

Later, the state stamped the ingots; it was always necessary to weigh them, but these were not made to resound except to carry out the ritual: this is the period of *aes signatum* (aes signatum is not money, as some commentators have believed, but a stamped ingot).

When money was coined by the state (about 349 B. C.) there was no need any longer of weighing the pieces: it was sufficient to count them. From this time on the ceremony of mancipation became purely symbolical.[1]

631. In Jure Cessio: *In jure cessio* is a simulated suit occurring before the magistrate before whom the vendor and the purchaser present themselves together: the purchaser, touching the object with his rod, utters these words: "*Hunc ego hominem meum esse aio ex jure quiritium et ecce ei vindictam imposui.*" The vendor instead of making likewise a contrary claim lowers his rod (*vindicta*), and says "*Cedo*" (I do not resist), and the magistrate declares that the ownership is (*addicit*) his who claimed it without contradiction.[2]

632. Adjudicatio: The third civil mode of acquisition is adjudicatio. It is the awarding (and not the declaration as in the *in jure cessio*) of ownership made by the judex. It is manifested in three actions: the actions *familiae eciscundae* (dividing an inheritance), *communi dividundo* (dividing common property), *finium regundorum* (fixing boundaries).[3]

633. In these three actions the judex, besides the

[1] Girard, *Manuel*, p. 284; Cuq, *Institutions*, vol. i, pp. 253, 259; Gaius, 1, §§ 119, 122.

[2] Gaius, 2, § 24; Ulpian, *Reg.* 19, § 9. The *in jure cessio* is applicable to *res mancipi* and *nec mancipi* (Ulpian, *loc. cit.*).

[3] Ulpian, *Reg.* 19, § 16.

power of delivering money judgments which the 'condemnatio' of the formula conferred on him, had the power of awarding the ownership, which was put into the clause of the particular formula for the three actions above mentioned, the clause which bore with precision the name of *adjudicatio*.

634. Adjudicatio therefore designates both the clause of the formula which gives to the judex some special powers and the exercise of those powers.

635. **Traditio** is the material delivery without formality of the possession of a thing by the vendor to the purchaser, or at least the putting of the thing at the disposal of the purchaser (as, for instance, the delivery to the purchaser of the keys of the granary which contains the grain sold). It presents this peculiarity; that is, it is both a mode of acquisition of natural law and a mode of acquisition of civil law. If its character evidently attaches it to the natural law, the civil law has made of it a regular mode of transferring the ownership of *res nec mancipi*.[1]

636. *Justa causa:* Every traditio, however, does not transfer ownership: traditio, by itself, is an act with several endings: I make a traditio of my property as well to the borrower to whom I lend it, to the bailee to whom I intrust it, to the lessee to whom I let it, as to the vendor or donee whom I intend to make owner.

Traditio is therefore characterized only by the intention which is attached to it: it will not transfer ownership only as often as the *tradens* shall have had the intention to transfer the ownership, and the *accipiens* the intention to acquire it. It is this intention

[1] Ulpian, *Reg.* 19, § 7.

to *transfer the ownership* which the Roman law calls *justa causa*.[1]

637. It is *traditio cum justa causa* which operates the displacement of the *dominium*; and the Roman law has pushed this theory so far that, in sales for cash, the vendor who, contrary to his intention, does not receive the price, does not cease to be owner. He had not, by imprudently delivering his thing, the intention of losing the ownership thereof without obtaining payment: the 'traditio' is not deemed to have been made *cum justa causa*.[2]

638. Applied to a *res nec mancipi* 'traditio cum justa causa' operates the displacement of the ownership: applied to a *res mancipi*, in the civil law, it should not produce any effect; but the praetor tempered the rigor of the civil law by establishing that he who should have acquired by simple 'traditio' a *res mancipi* would have this thing *in bonis*.

639. *Praetorian ownership or bonitary ownership* is far from being deprived of effect: it presents almost all the advantages of ownership: (1) it is transformed into *civil* or *quiritary ownership* by *usucapio*; (2) to the bonitary owner is given, for want of civil vindication, the praetorian vindication, or *actio Publiciana*, which was scarcely less efficacious.[3]

640. **Usucapio:** Usucapio is the acquisition of ownership by possession continued for a time fixed by

---

[1] Ulpian, *Reg.* 19, § 7; *Dig.* 41, 1, 31 pr. (Paulus).

[2] *Inst.* 2, 1, § 41. Justinian makes this rule date from the law of the XII Tables.

[3] See *supra*, §§ 599, 420 *et seq.*

law (one year for movables, two years for immovables, according to the law of the XII Tables).[1]

641. Usucapio exists when: (1) a quiritary ownership has been transferred by a non-quiritary mode (when a res mancipi has been transferred by simple traditio);[2] (2) when anything has been delivered *a non domino*, that is by an individual who was not the owner thereof. In the first case, the *accipiens* acquires only the bonitary ownership; in the second, he does not acquire either quiritary ownership or bonitary ownership, for "*nemo plus juris ad alium transferre potest quam ipse habet.*"

Usucapio is the means for attaining in both cases quiritary ownership of the object acquired.

642. *Praescriptio longi temporis:* Usucapio was applicable, consequently, only to objects susceptible of quiritary ownership, and for the benefit of those who could become quiritary owners; it did not protect the acquisition of things not susceptible of Roman ownership, as provincial land, for example; it could not furthermore be invoked by 'peregrini' who cannot become owners 'ex jure quiritium.'

The 'jus honorarium' provided for this deficiency by establishing the *possessio* or *praescriptio longi temporis*, which is not a civil mode of acquiring ownership, which is not even strictly speaking a mode of acquiring ownership, but of which we here treat on account of the comparison which obtrudes between it and 'usucapio.'

[1] Ulpian, *Reg.* 19, § 8.
[2] Gaius, 2, § 26 (passage mutilated, the sense of which may be completed by connecting it with Ulpian, *Reg.* 19, 4 *et seq.*).

So long as any individual possesses a 'fundus provincialis,' or a 'peregrinus' possesses a *res mancipi*, the ownership strictly speaking will not be acquired: but is this a reason why the holder of this fundus or of this thing should live forever exposed to being dispossessed?[1] The *praetor peregrinus* and the *praesides* recognize that after a period of time, which was fixed at ten or twenty years, according to circumstances, the possessor shall be able to defend himself against the vindication of the real owner.[2]

643. This defense is made forceful by means of an *exceptio* which the magistrate inserted at the head of the formula and which from this fact was called *praescriptio*.[3] The appointed judex tried first the question of *possessio longi temporis*, and, if he found in favor of the possessor, it was not necessary to pass to the trial of the right of ownership of the plaintiff. The *vindicatio* of the latter was therefore defeated.

644. *Parallel between USUCAPIO and PRAE-SCRIPTIO LONGI TEMPORIS:* Prescription presents some notable differences from usucapio. (1) Usucapio was established by the law of the XII Tables; praescriptio longi temporis is a creation of the jus honorarium.[4]

645. (2) *Usucapio* engenders an actio and an exceptio: *praescriptio longi temporis* engenders only an

---

[1] This dispossession might, when it was a matter of a *fundus provincialis*, be produced by means of a *vindicatio utilis*. (See *supra*, § 624.)

[2] This owner is, in the present case, only a *bonitary* owner.

[3] See *supra*, 519.

[4] The most ancient document making allusion is a constitution of Severus and Caracalla of 199 A. D. (papyrus at Berlin).

exceptio;[1] in other words, whoever has usucapted can not only victoriously defend himself against everybody who should bring against him an action in vindication, but he himself can, if he is dispossessed, bring *rei vindicatio* in order to have declared that the usucapted thing belongs to him. On the contrary, whoever can invoke only the *longi temporis praescriptio* can indeed defend himself, so long as he is possessor, against the revindication of a third person, but if he becomes dispossessed, he cannot bring an action in revindication in order to have his right of ownership recognized for his benefit. "Long time prescription" is, therefore, from this point of view, less advantageous than usucapio.

646. (3) From another point of view, *praescriptio longi temporis* presents more advantages than *usucapio:* for indeed usucapio operates "*salvo jure servitutis vel hypothecae;*" prescription operates, on the contrary, both against the owner and against all those who would have acquired from preceding owners a real right over the thing: so, at the end of ten years, whoever becomes owner by *usucapio* can hold only an ownership burdened with servitudes or hypothecs, while whoever benefits by *praescriptio longi temporis* has, at the expiration of the period, an *unencumbered ownership.*[*2]

[1] *Code,* 7, 31, 1 (Justinian).

[*2] This theory generally taught is absolutely exact only when the mortgage creditor (*hypothecarius*) and the *dominus* are found in the same conditions of presence or absence, and prescription has commenced to run at the same time against both. There is not indeed *one prescription* running against the *dominus* and the mortgage creditor, but *two parallel prescriptions* which may have different points of departure and different periods of limitation.

647. (4) On the other hand, *praescriptio longi temporis* is interrupted by *rei vindicatio*, while *usucapio* can be accomplished *inter moras litis*.

This will not at all prevent the defendant from being condemned, for the judex, in order to understand the situation of the parties, is bound to go back to the time of litiscontestatio;[1] but, in his 'pronuntiatio,' the judex will order the defendant not only to deliver possession of the thing to the plaintiff, but to re-transfer the ownership thereof.

648. *Periods of time for praescriptio longi temporis:* We have spoken until now, without explaining it, of this period of ten to twenty years whereby 'praescriptio longi temporis' is accomplished. The period was ten years between persons not absent, and twenty years between absent persons. *By not absent*, must be understood the possessor and owner domiciled in the same province; *by absent*, the same persons domiciled in different provinces; but the meaning of these expressions does not appear to have been definitely fixed until the time of Justinian.[2]

649. *Justus titulus and bona fides:* It is quite probable that the XII Tables required for the accomplishment of usucapio only a single condition: *the requisite time.*[3] The exceptional usucapiones of which we will speak later[4] are probably simple survivals from this time.

650. But, at quite a remote era, three conditions are

---

[1] See *supra*, § 527.
[2] *Code*, 7, 33, 12 (Justinian).
[3] Esmein, *Mélanges*, pp. 171 *et seq*.
[4] See *supra*, §§ 657–660.

required in order that usucapio may take place: (1) the time fixed by law; (2) justus titulus; (3) bona fides.

651. *Justus titulus:* Is a fact which implies, in acquisitions by a derivative mode, the reciprocal intention of alienating and of acquiring ownership, — or, in acquisitions by an original mode, the lawful intention to acquire. — We may speak more briefly: justus titulus is a juridical fact which explains possession (sale, inheritance, dos, etc.)[1] (what is called *titulus putativus* is the belief in the existence of a juridical fact which does not exist: *titulus putativus* is not sufficient in order to found usucapio.)*[2]

652. *Bona fides:* Is ignorance of the defect in the title on which possession is reposed. Primus has bought the slave of Secundus, whom he wrongly believed to be owner of this slave: the sale constitutes the justus titulus of Primus (who possesses *pro emptore*): his ignorance of the non-ownership of Secundus constitutes his bona fides.

653. It belongs to him who invokes a justus titulus to prove its existence. — Bona fides is, on the contrary, presumed, and it belongs to him who contests it to prove mala fides.

[1] For the principle, see the terms of the Edict concerning the actio Publiciana: *ex justa causa petit.*

*[2] The Roman jurisconsults show little harmony on this point. See, in the sense indicated in the text, *Dig.* 41, 4, 2 (Paulus); *Dig.* 41, 8, 2, *ibid.* 3 (Papinian); *Dig.* 41, 3, 27 (Celsus) cited by Ulpian; — and in a less rigorous sense, *Dig.* 41, 10, 5 (Neratius); *Dig.* 41, 4, 11 (Africanus), who admits the possibility of usucapio when there is *justus* and *probabilis error.*

The most rigorous view seemed to have triumphed in the time of Justinian: "*Error falsae causae usucapionem non parit,*" the *Institutes* say, 2, 6, § 11.

654. *Joining and continuation of possession:* It is not necessary, moreover, that the possessor who claims usucapio has possessed by himself during the whole of the period; he obligatorily continues the possession of its originator (with its initial character of good or bad faith which his personal good or bad faith can change in no respect) if he has succeeded to the said originator by universal title (*successio in possessionem* of the testamentary heir or heir *ab intestato*).[1]

655. If he is a successor by singular title (singular legatee, donee, purchaser, etc.) he begins a new possession of good or bad faith according as he himself has good or bad faith,[2] but he may (he is not obliged to), in order to arrive more quickly at the expiration of the period of time, join to his possession that of its originator (*accessio possessionum*).

656. *Things which cannot be usucapted:* Stolen property (*res furtivae*) cannot be usucapted according to a prohibition of the law of the XII Tables renewed later by a lex Atinia.[3] Furthermore, property possessed by violence (*vi possessae*) cannot be usucapted, according to a lex Julia and Plautia. The vice of *res furtivae*, and *res possessae* is purged if, after the theft or violent dispossession, they are returned to the ' dominus.'

657. *Usucapiones lucrativae or improbae:* We have noticed above [4] the existence of usucapiones which are accomplished without justus titulus or bona fides,

---

[1] *Inst.* 2, 6, § 12.
[2] *Dig.* 41, 4, 2, §§ 17, 20, 21 (Paulus).
[3] Aulus Gellius, *Noctes Atticae*, 17, 7.† It is the same of *res fisci* (*Inst.* 2, 6, § 9), and of the *fundus dotalis* (*Dig.* 23, 5, 16).
[4] *Supra*, § 649.

and which Esmein considers, rightly in our opinion, as survivals from the primitive régime of the XII Tables.[1]

These usucapiones which the texts call usucapiones lucrativae or improbae are three in number.

658. (1) *Usucapio lucrativa pro herede:* In order to prevent successions from remaining vacant, and for the evident purpose of hastening the *aditio hereditatis* of *heredes extranei*, the Roman law, when a succession was not devolved on the *heredes sui*, authorized usucapio, without justus titulus or bona fides, of objects of the inheritance by the first comer. The period of time of this usucapio was only a year, even for immovables.[2]

The progress of customs caused the disappearance of this usucapio, which was abolished under Hadrian.[3] Marcus Aurelius went farther, and we find under his reign the existence of an action by the state (*judicium publicum*) against the spoliator of an *hereditas vacans* (*crimen expilatae hereditatis*).

659. (2) *Usureceptio:* It operated for the benefit of the pledgor who had recovered his property. Usureceptio is explained by this consideration that pledge formerly operated by means of an alienation of the ownership of the thing pledged, accompanied by a contract of fiducia by the terms of which the creditor was obliged, when once paid, to re-transfer the ownership of the thing pledged to his former debtor. If the creditor, in place of re-transferring the ownership to the debtor (which necessitated a mancipation if the thing

[1] Esmein, *Mélanges*, pp. 171 *et seq.*
[2] Gaius, 2, §§ 52–58.   [3] *Ibid*

pledged was a *res mancipi*), contented himself with returning to him the object, or if the debtor was contented to retake his property, an irregular situation resulted therefrom. The debtor re-became possessor, but not owner; and he was *malae fidei*, not in this sense that his possession was stained with unscrupulousness, but by this fact alone that he knew he had not acquired the ownership, — which suffices to constitute *mala fides*, in the legal sense of the word. Usureceptio remedied this irregularity by fixing, at the end of a year, ownership in the person of the debtor reëntered into possession of the thing pledged.[1]

660. (3) *Usureceptio ex praediatura:* The passage of Gaius is not very clear on this point. It is a matter of things sold by the *fiscus* and which reënter the possession of the debtor who suffered the execution: the latter, according to the text, re-becomes owner by usucapio without justus titulus or bona fides, which is accomplished at the end of two years.[2]

661. *Reforms of Justinian:* Justinian merged, under the name of usucapio, usucapio and praescriptio longi temporis, — reforms which had all the more *raison d'être* as the distinctions between civil ownership and praetorian ownership, between citizens and peregrini had disappeared at the time of Justinian.

From the praescriptio longi temporis Justinian borrowed the period of ten and twenty years: but at the expiration of the period, the possessor acquires not only an 'exceptio' but also the action in vindication.

Usucapio of movables is accomplished after three years.[3]

[1] Gaius, 2, § 59.   [2] *Ibid.* § 61.
[3] *Code*, 7, 31, 1 (Justinian).

662. *Praescriptiones longi et longissimi temporis:* Justinian required for *usucapio* justus titulus and bona fides, but along with the new usucapio he had already admitted a *praescriptio longi temporis* which was accomplished after thirty years without justus titulus or bona fides.[1]

There was since Theodosius II a *praescriptio longissimi temporis* which was accomplished after thirty years, and allowed the possessor after this period to repulse the *vindicatio* of the owner even when the possession was without justus titulus or bona fides.

This is this praescriptio longissimi temporis which Justinian makes his own in 528, by attaching to it not only an exceptio but an action, and which the general policy of 531 is to complete.

Only he calls it by a wrong name: it is termed the *praescriptio longi temporis.*

The name of *praescriptio longissimi temporis* is reserved for a prescription of forty years, which is applicable as to the right of ownership of religious establishments and hypothecs.

663. **Acquisition Lege:** Acquisition *lege* occurs when the law itself furnishes a person with an action in vindication of a given thing: so of *legacies per vindicationem;*[2] so again of *caduca,*[3] the vindication of which expired, so to speak, automatically, *vi legis*, for heirs or legatees favored by the leges Julia and Pappia Poppea.[4]

[1] *Code*, 7, 39, 8, § 1 (528 A. D., three years before the constitutio *de usuc. transformanda* — *Code*, 7, 31).
[2] See *infra*, § 869.
[3] See *infra*, § 899.
[4] Ulpian, *Reg.* 19, § 17.

CHAPTER II

MODES OF THE NATURAL LAW

664. The modes of acquiring ownership of the natural law are *occupation* and *accession*.

665. **Occupation:** Is the taking of possession of an object which does not as yet belong to any one, or which has ceased to belong to any one. It is by occupation that we acquire the ownership of wild animals which are hunted, of wild fruits which are gathered; of abandoned objects, in a word of *res nullius*.*[1]

666. **Accession:** Accession is a mode of acquisition based on the principle that "the accessorial thing should follow the fortune of the principal thing: *accessio cedat principali*."

It is by accession that the riparian owner along a stream becomes owner: (1) of the imperceptible increase which the material deposited by the waters add to his bank (*alluvio*).

(2) Of the island formed in a river; but in the present case the rights of the two riparian owners are concurrent: the centre of the stream is laid out and the line following which the island is divided by this centre marks the boundaries of the rights of the riparian owners; all the portion of the island on the left of the centre belongs to the riparian owner of the left bank,

---

*[1] Treasure trove should be included in this category and belong exclusively to the finder. According to a constitution of Hadrian the principle of which is preserved even in our Code, treasure trove in the land of another is shared between the finder and the owner of the soil.

all the portion on the right of the centre to the riparian owner of the right bank. If the island is entirely on one side of the centre, it belongs to the owner of the bank near which it is formed.

(3) Of the bed abandoned by a stream (*alveus derelictus*).[1]

667. *Specificatio, adjunctio, confusio, commixtio*: With acquisition by accession is connected: (1) *specificatio*, which is the making of an object with the material of another, for example, a statue with the marble of another.

668. (2) *Adjunctio*: Incorporation of an accessorial object which preserves its nature with a principal object (for example, a precious stone with a ring).

669. (3) *Commixtio*: That is commingling, for example, the union of two piles of grain.

670. (4) *Confusio*: Commingling of two liquids: for example, of red and white wine.

671. This whole subject is dominated by the rule "*accessio cedat principali*." Ownership is acquired, by the owner of the principal thing, subject to the awarding to the owner of the accessorial thing of an indemnity which is sued for, according to the cases, by an action in vindication or an *actio ad exhibendum ;* when the accessorial thing has preserved a distinct existence and can be separated from the principal object, either by the actions for theft [2] if there was a theft, or by

[1] Compare the more complicated solution of Art. 563 of the *Code civil* of France.

[2] *Actiones furti ; condictio furtiva.* See Roby, *Rom. Priv. Law*, vol. ii, p. 201; *ibid*. p. 82. — S.

actions for partition.¹ We indicate rapidly the general principles, but we cannot stop for the solutions of cases obligingly enumerated by Justinian in his Institutes.²

672. *Rule "QUIDQUID SOLO IN AEDIFICATUR SOLO CEDIT:"* We will, however, call attention as to the application of the principle of accession which makes the owner of the soil acquire the ownership of every edifice or structure erected on his land.

A peculiarity to be noticed in the subject of edifices: where the owner of land has built thereon edifices with the materials of another, the *actio ad exhibendum* is not given, although it were possible, to the owner of the materials "*ne ruinis urbs de deformetur.*" The Romans had such a horror of demolishing that special laws prohibited the taking down of old buildings.³ It was therefore necessary to substitute for the *actio ad exhibendum*, which is *arbitraria*, a special action for indemnity which is not: the *actio de tigno juncto*.

---

¹ *Judicia divisoria; actio communi dividundo; familiae erciscundae; finium regundorum.* See Roby, *Rom. Priv. Law*, vol. ii, p. 135; *ibid.* vol. i, p. 287; *ibid.* vol. i, p. 449. — S.

² We refer in a general way in regard to this whole matter of *accessio* to Gaius, 2, §§ 70–79, and to the *Institutes*, book 2, title 1.

³ *SC. Hosidianum*, under Claudius, Girard, *Textes*, p. 124. — *SC. Volusianum*, under Nero, Girard, *Textes*, pp. 124, 125.

TITLE VI

EXTINCTION OF THE RIGHT OF OWNERSHIP

673. Destruction of the Thing: Ownership is, from its nature, a perpetual right (consequently it cannot be transferred *ad tempus*).[1]

It is extinguished only by the destruction of the thing: *Extinctae res vindicari non possunt.*[2]

To the destruction of the thing is assimilated the putting of it out of commerce (for example, if it becomes *divini juris*).

674. Abandonment: Is ownership lost by abandonment of the thing? The Proculians and the Sabinians differed on this point. According to the Proculians, ownership was lost only when a third person became possessed of the thing: the Sabinians held that the abandoned thing became *res nullius* from the moment of the *derelictio*. Their opinion has prevailed.

[1] *Frag. Vat.* 283 (Diocletian and Maxim.).
[2] *Inst.* 2, 1, § 26.

TITLE VII

CIVIL AND PRAETORIAN DISMEMBERMENTS OF THE RIGHT OF OWNERSHIP

675. The civil dismemberments of ownership are the personal and praedial servitudes; the praetorian dismemberments, the right of superficies, emphyteusis, and hypotheca.

CHAPTER I

CIVIL DISMEMBERMENTS OF OWNERSHIP

SECTION I. — **Praedial Servitudes**

§ I. Character and Divisions of Praedial Servitudes

676. **Definition:** A praedial servitude is a burden created on one piece of land (*fundus*) for the advantage and utility of another piece of land.

The land which suffers the servitude is called the *servient* land: that which benefits therefrom, the *dominant* land.

677. A servitude, which is a *real* right, actively follows the dominant land and passively the servient land into whatever hands it passes; that is, all the successive owners of the dominant land will forever exercise the servitude against all the successive owners of the servient land.

678. **Division of Servitudes:** Roman law divides praedial servitudes into urban and rural servi-

tudes. — But what distinguishes a rural servitude from an urban servitude? The Roman doctrines are not clear on this point.

If we refer to the Institutes of Justinian, rural servitudes would be those the creation of which does not imply the existence of buildings (*quae in solo consistunt*); urban, servitudes which can have meaning only by recognizing the existence of land with buildings (*quae in aedibus consistunt*). Thus, a right of way for the benefit of one fundus over another fundus would constitute a rural servitude, for it does not imply in the least the idea of land with buildings; on the contrary, the servitude "*ne luminibus officiatur*" (prohibition on blocking up or obstructing windows) would be an urban servitude, since it cannot be conceived of without the existence of a building.[1]

679. This very logical division (of but little importance indeed) was not, however, that of the classical jurisconsults: from the texts which have come down to us it plainly appears that the 'prudentes' of the great era distinguished urban and rural servitudes according to the character of the dominant land: thus, a right of way could be urban or rural according as it was exercised for the benefit of land with buildings or land without buildings.[2]

680. The Roman jurisconsults caught sight of, without formulating it, a more logical and practical division of servitudes: which distinguishes *positive* servitudes (*servitutes in habendo vel in faciendo*) and *negative* servitudes (*servitutes in prohibendo*). — Fundamentally all their decisions rest on this distinction, but no text

[1] *Inst.* 2, 3, § 1.   [2] Girard, *Manuel*, pp. 353, 354, 358.

with which we are acquainted allows us to declare that they plainly had knowledge of this.

681. *Positive* servitudes are those which permit the owner of the dominant land either to build (*S. in habendo*), or to exercise a positive right (*S. in faciendo*), on the servient land. Thus a house situated on the edge of the land of an individual and projecting its roof or a balcony over the adjoining land is an affirmative servitude, *in habendo;* — a right of way is an affirmative servitude, *in faciendo*.

682. A *negative* servitude (*S. in prohibendo*) consists, on the contrary, in the right, for the dominant land, of prohibiting the owner of the servient land from doing anything on his own land; for example, the servitude *altius non tollendi;* the owner of the dominant land has the right of preventing the owner of the servient land from increasing the height of buildings on his own land. This is a negative servitude.

683. **Importance of the Division of Servitudes:** This rational division of servitudes (positive and negative) was felt and understood, but not adopted, by the Roman jurisconsults; their official division is the division into rural and urban servitudes based on the nature of the dominant fundus.

And this division has a very serious importance.

In reality *rural servitudes of fundi Italici* are *res mancipi:* it follows that they can be established by mancipation, — the rest cannot.[1] . . .

Furthermore, from the point of view of extinguishment, rural servitudes are extinguished by non-user and urban servitudes only by *usucapio libertatis*.[2]

[1] Gaius, 2, § 29.
[2] Paulus, *Sent.* 1, 17; *Dig.* 8, 2, 6 (Gaius). See *infra*, § 702.

CIVIL DISMEMBERMENTS

684. Principal Servitudes: Servitudes are very many in number; we will instance: —

(a) *Servitudes in faciendo:* (1) Rights of way are three in number: *iter, actus, via.* — **a** *Iter*, right to pass on foot; — **b** *Actus*, right to pass while driving cattle or chariots; — **c** *Via*, which embraces *iter* and *actus*: *via* admits of width of four feet where it is straight and eight feet at the turning.

(2) Right to draw water (*aquaehaustus hauriendae*).

(3) Right to drive cattle to water (*pecoris ad aquam adpulsus*).

(4) Right to dig sand (*arenae fodiendae*).

(5) Right to burn lime (*S. calcis coquendae*), etc.

685. (b) *Servitudes in habendo:* (1) *S. protegendi* or *S. projiciendi:* the right to project a roof or a balcony over adjoining land.

(2) *S. Aquaeductus* (of conducting water).

(3) *S. cloacae* (of sewer).

(4) *S. tigni immitendi* (right to place beams in an adjoining wall).

(5) *S. oneris ferendi* (right to support houses on an adjoining wall).

686. (c) *Servitudes in prohibendo:* (1) *S. altius non tollendi*, right to prevent the owner of adjoining land from erecting houses, or of building, above a certain height, opposite to which is the *S. altius tollendi*.[1]

(2) *S. ne luminibus* (right to daylight).

(3) *S. prospectus* (right of prospect).

687. *S. altius tollendi:* This servitude as well as the *S. luminibus officiendi* and the *S. stillicidii non avertendi* raises a difficulty. The most accepted theory

[1] See *infra*, § 687.

is that which presumes the existence of local regulations governing the height of buildings and prohibiting the obstruction of a prospect, or turning water on land of a neighbor: freedom from these regulations was possible by obtaining from the owners of the adjoining land rights *altius tollendi* (of erecting buildings above the the height fixed by the local regulation), or *luminibus officiendi* (obstructing a prospect), or *stillicidii non avertendi* (of turning water on a neighbor's land).[1]

688. **Effects of Servitudes:** A servitude creates on principle a purely passive state for the servient land, the owner of which cannot be obliged to do anything but simply to suffer or not do so.[2]

689. An exception to the principle, however, is presented by the *S. oneris ferendi:* in derogation to the general principles (a derogation probably of customary origin) the owner of the servient land is obliged to maintain his wall in a state to support the buildings of his neighbor.[3]

690. **Indivisibility of Servitudes:** Servitudes are indivisible: that is they can neither be acquired, exercised, or lost in part. This very difficult doctrine receives its practical application when the dominant or servient land belongs either originally, or subsequently to the creation of the servitude, to several owners. The most important consequences of this doctrine are: (1) that upon a fundus which belongs in common to several co-owners, a passive servitude is created only when all the co-owners of the servi-

---

[1] Girard, *Manuel*, p. 357, note 6.
[2] *Dig.* 8, 1, 15, § 1 (Pomponius).
[3] *Dig.* 8, 3, 33.

ent fundus proceeded to create it; (2) that a servitude for the benefit of a fundus which belongs to several owners, or which, originally owned by a sole owner, is divided among several successors of his, is extinguished by non-user only when all the owners of the dominant fundi (parts of the former sole dominant fundus) have neglected to use it. The exercise of the right by *one alone* of the owners would preserve the servitude for the benefit of all the others.

Suppose there is right of way for the benefit of the fundus Cornelianus. This fundus, on the death of the sole owner, is divided among three heirs, Primus, Secundus, and Tertius; if the right of way is exercised by Primus alone, it will be none the less preserved for the benefit of Secundus and Tertius.

§ 2. Acquisition of Praedial Servitudes

691. Distinction: It is necessary to distinguish between rural servitudes for the benefit of Italian land which are *res mancipi* and other servitudes.[1]

692. Mancipatio: Rural servitudes for the benefit of fundi Italici can alone be created *directly* by means of mancipatio; but mancipatio can be employed to *indirectly* arrive at the creation of urban servitude.

There are indeed two modes of acquiring a servitude in land by means of mancipatio: *translatio servitutis* and *deductio servitutis*: the first proceeding consists in conveying (mancipating) the servitude itself; "*jus eundi per fundum Cornelianum meum esse aio, etc.,*" and can be applicable of course only to a servitude which is a *res mancipi:* the second proceeding consists in conveying a fundus, but retaining for the

[1] Gaius, 2, § 29.

benefit of another fundus the servitude it is desired to create, and this servitude cannot be a *res mancipi*, for it is not this, but the land which is conveyed. For example: I convey the fundus Cornelianus, but retain for the benefit of my house which is contiguous a *servitude ne luminibus officiatur* (an urban servitude and consequently *res nec mancipi*).[1]

693. But how to do so, if I should wish to create an urban servitude precisely on the fundus which I hold? I would convey *without reservation* this fundus to the owner of the fundus which I wished to render dominant, and this owner reconveys it to me *deducta servitute*, that is, retaining the servitude which was intended to be acquired.[2]

694. **In Jure Cessio and Adjudicatio of Praedial Servitudes:** The general proceeding for the creation of servitudes was *in jure cessio* which is, in the present case, a simulation of the *actio confessoria*.[3]

695. Frequently also the creation was by *adjudicatio*: the judex charged with a partition in proceeding to the allotment, equalized the value of the lots by creating servitudes for the benefit of some over the rest; if he divides, for example, into two parts a fundus a part of which will be without access to the public highway, he will reëstablish the equilibrium of values by awarding with the inclosed part a right of way over the part which borders on the highway.[4]

[1] *Dig.* 8, 4, 6 pr. (Ulpian).   [2] *Frag. Vat.* 51.
[3] Gaius, 2, § 29; Ulpian, *Reg.* 19, 11. See *infra*, § 727, *supra*, § 631.
[4] *Frag. Vat.* 47.

696. Usucapio: Rural servitudes were originally acquired by usucapio (doubtless through a confusion between the servitude and the seat of the servitude of the incorporeal right with reference to the object over which it is exercised); but the usucapio of servitudes was abolished by a lex Scribonia, the uncertain date of which is placed by some commentators (without proof also) about 50 B. C.[1]

697. *Diuturnus usus:* But, on the other hand, the praetor recognized (1) that if servitudes could not be made the object of possession strictly speaking, incompatible with their character of incorporeal objects, they could be made the object of a *quasi-possession* resulting from *usus* and *patientia* (*usus*, exercise of the servitude by the owner of the dominant land, *patientia*, sufferance of the owner of the servient land); (2) that a servitude could be acquired in praetorian law and subsist *tuitione praetoris* (under the protection of the praetor), if this quasi-possession was prolonged (*diuturnus usus*) for a period of time which the praetor first reserved for himself to determine according to the case, but which he finally fixed at ten and twenty years as for the *longi temporis praescriptio*.[2]

698. We believe that the *diuturnus usus*, the prolonging of the *quasi-possessio*, can cause to be acquired only servitudes susceptible of *quasi-possessio*: and as it seems impossible to us to quasi-possess a negative servitude (by what acts would *quasi-possessio* be delivered?) we therefore conclude that acquisition

---

[1] The usucapion of servitudes is however mentioned by Cicero *pro Caecina*, 26. See *Dig.* 41, 3, 4, § 28. Cf. Cuq, *Institutions*, vol. i, pp. 251, 273.

[2] Paulus, *Sent.* 5, 5a, § 8; *Dig.* 8, 5, 10 (Ulpian).

by *diuturnus usus* is applicable only to positive servitudes (*S. in habendo* or *faciendo*).

699. Pacts and Stipulations: In jure cessio and adjudicatio were inapplicable to servitudes of provincial land and non-obtainable by peregrini. The praetors, or rather the praesides, conceived the creation of servitudes *pactis et stipulationibus*, that is, by agreements which were fortified by the addition of a penal stipulation in case there should be a contravention of the agreement and the putting of restraint on the exercise of the servitude.

This proceeding was applied in Italy, by the praetors to urban servitudes; it became, under Justinian, the normal mode of creating servitudes.[1]

700. It had long been generally held that pacts and stipulations did not suffice to create a servitude, and that it was always necessary to add a *quasi-traditio* resulting from *usus* and *patientia*.[2] This doctrine of *quasi-traditio* has now suffered a breach, and tends to be abandoned: not one text indicates the necessity of this *quasi-traditio*: it is the commentators alone who proclaim it.

They say "it is by deliveries and not by mere pacts that the ownership of things is transferred (*traditionibus non nudis pactis dominia rerum transferuntur*), and that consequently the simple pact is powerless to create a servitude which is a real right, a dismemberment of ownership." To this it may be replied that, if this principle is incontestable in the civil law, it does not belong to the praetorian law, and that it is the praetorian law which conceived the creation of servi-

[1] *Inst.* 2, 3, § 4. Cf. Theophilus, *paraph. eod. loc.*
[2] See *supra*, § 697.

CIVIL DISMEMBERMENTS 239

tudes by means of pacts and stipulations. The proof that in the praetorian law a real right can be created without delivery is that there is no necessity of any delivery to create the real right of hypotheca which is of praetorian invention. If the praetorian pact of hypotheca suffices for the creation of the real praetorian right of hypotheca, why would not the praetorian pact of servitude suffice for the creation of a real praetorian right of servitude? *[1]

§ 3. **Extinguishment of Praedial Servitudes**

701. **Modes of extinguishing Praedial Servitudes**: Praedial servitudes are extinguished:—

(1) By *confusion*, that is, by the union of the dominant and servient lands in the hands of the same owner (which can happen when the owner of one fundus buys the other fundus or becomes heir of its owner): nobody, in fact, can have a servitude on his own property "*nemini res sua servit.*" [2]

(2) By renunciation of the owner of the dominant fundus.

(3) By annulment of the right of the grantor: dismemberments of ownership are, like ownership itself, subjected to the rule "*resoluto jure dantis, resolvitur jus accipientis.*" [3]

(4) By destruction of one of the fundi, dominant or servient.

(5) By non-user, to which we give a special consideration.

*[1] Girard, *Manuel*, p. 371, text and note 3. This doctrine is, however, very much disputed.

[2] *Dig.* 8, 6, 1 (Gaius); *Inst.* 2, 4, 3; *Dig.* 8, 2, 30 pr. and § 1.

[3] *Dig.* 8, 6, 14 (Javolenus).

702. **Non-user and Usucapio Libertatis:**
Non-user is understandable without difficulty when it is a question of a servitude *in faciendo:* the owner of land A had a right of way over land B: he ceases to pass over it: here is non-user; it is not understandable, furthermore, when it is a question of a negative servitude. Suppose Primus has on the land of Secundus a servitude *altius non-tollendi:* how can non-user of this servitude be conceived of? in order that non-user be conceived of it is necessary that an encroachment against the servitude has been made on the servient land, and that the owner of the dominant land has allowed this encroachment to pass without protesting: we then say that there is a *usucapio libertatis,* for the benefit of the servient land;[1] it is necessary that the owner of the servient land have raised buildings beyond the height fixed by the servitude, and that this new condition of the premises contrary to his right was endured by the owner of the dominant land for a determinate time.

The servitude *in habendo* requires, like the servitude *in prohibendo,* an act creative of a new condition of the premises in order to serve as a point of departure for *usucapio libertatis.* Thus the period of time for *usucapio libertatis* against a servitude *luminum* (right to a window) will commence to run from the day when the window shall have been obstructed either by the owner of the dominant land, or by the owner of the servient land.

703. This doctrine, which is rational only if it is based on the antithesis of negative servitudes and positive servitude, is founded by the texts of the Ro-

[1] *Dig.* 8, 2, 6 (Gaius).

man jurisconsults on the meaningless distinction between *urban* servitudes and *rural* servitudes. According to them, *rural* servitudes are those which are extinguished by mere non-user; the extinguishment of *urban* servitudes requires in addition *usucapio libertatis*.[1]

This is the consequence of the disturbed view of the Roman jurisconsults which we have already noticed. *Urban* servitudes are generally negative, *rural* servitudes positive: therefore the 'prudentes' identified, somewhat unconsciously, negative servitudes with urban servitudes, positive servitudes with rural servitudes.

704. The period of time for non-user and *usucapio libertatis* was two years (*biennium*), down to Justinian. Justinian raised it to ten years between non-absent persons and twenty years between absent persons.[2]

Section II. — Personal Servitudes

705. Personal servitudes are not established over one fundus for the benefit of another fundus, but *over a thing for the benefit of a person*. Of these four principal ones are recognized which are: *usufructus, usus, habitatio, operae servi* (*vel alterius animalis*, according to one text).

§ 1. Usufructus

706. **Definition:** Usufructus is the right to make use of a thing the ownership of which belongs to another and of gathering the fruits but without altering its substance: *jus utendi fruendi, salva rerum substantia*.[3]

707. **Modes of Creation:** Usufruct can be

[1] *Dig.* 8, 2, 6 (Gaius). [2] *Code*, 3, 34, 13 (Justinian).
[3] *Inst.* 2, 4 pr.

created either *mortis causa*, by will; — or *inter vivos* by the civil modes already indicated for praedial servitudes; *in jure cessio*,[1] *adjudicatio* and *mancipatio*.

Mancipatio can cause the creation of usufruct only by way of a reservation, *deductio* (conveyance of a fundus *deducto usufructu*) and not by way of a *translatio*.[2]

708. Usufruct can also be established over provincial fundi by pacts and stipulation: Primus and Secundus make an agreement (a pact) by the terms of which Secundus will have the enjoyment of a 'fundus provincialis' belonging to Primus; and, in order to assure the execution of this pact, Secundus stipulates in these terms from Primus: "If you obstruct my enjoyment, do you promise me one hundred as a penalty?"

709. As to the question of knowing if the usufruct could be acquired by *longi temporis praescriptio*, it is very much controverted.

710. **Rights of the Usufructuary:** *division of the fruits*. The usufructuary has the *jus utendi*, the *jus fruendi*, but he does not have the *jus abutendi*. By *fruits* is meant all the periodical products of the things; *natural fruits*, spontaneous products; industrial fruits, obtained by cultivation; *civil fruits*, revenue from houses and rural property, interest on capital, etc.[3]

711. The young of animals are considered as fruits, but not the offspring of a female slave.

712. The products of mines and quarries are

---

[1] This is the normal mode. Gaius, 2, § 30.
[2] *Frag. Vat.* 47 (Paul.).
[3] *Dig.* 7, 1, 12, § 2 ; Paulus, *Sent.* 3, 6, §§ 27, 28.

assigned to the usufructuary only so far as the mines and quarries were being worked at the commencement of the usufruct.

713. How the Usufructuary obtains the Fruits: This question amounts to asking at what time and on what conditions the fruits become the property of the usufructuary.

It is necessary to distinguish between natural fruits and civil fruits. The usufructuary becomes owner of the fruits by reason of and at the time of their collection made by him or for him.[1]

714. Civil fruits are acquired for him, in Roman law, according to a distinction which has not passed into French law: among us, civil fruits are acquired *per diem* without any distinction between the rents from houses and the rents from rural property; that is, if, in the course of a year, the usufructuary has lived for 250 days and died after this period, the civil fruits will be shared between the heirs of the usufructuary and the naked owner at the pro rata of 250/365 for the former and of 115/365 for the latter.

The Roman law distinguishes: as to the rents from houses it applies the acquisition *per diem* which has passed into French law: as to the renting of rural property, it examines to see if the crop was harvested by the lessee in the lifetime of the usufructuary or after his death: if the crop was harvested in the lifetime of the usufructuary, the rent is due to his heirs; if the

---

[1] The thief who takes the fruit on the tree does not act relatively to the usufructuary. Consequently the usufructuary does not have the *condictio furtiva* against the thief: the fruit stolen did not belong to him. Gérardin, *Nouv. rev. histor.* 1884, pp. 626 and 627.†

crop was harvested after the decease of the usufructuary, the rent is due to the naked owner.[1]

715. Transfer of Usufruct: The usufructuary can alienate his right by means of a *cessio in jure;* usufruct is therefore not non-transferable in the strict sense of the word, but it is rather the exercise, the emolument of the right which is transferred in such case rather than the right itself: for the right remains fixed in the person of the usufructuary and is extinguished by his death or *capitis deminutio.* — Furthermore, it is the usufructuary alone who ever after the transfer can exercise the *actio confessoria*.[2]

716. Obligations of the Usufructuary: The usufructuary is held to enjoy as a good paterfamilias and to restore the thing not deteriorated by his fault at the expiration of the usufruct.

In order to assure the performance of this obligation the edict compelled the usufructuary (not on principle however) to furnish security.[3]

717. *Repairs:* The usufructuary ought to make repairs for maintenance; the larger repairs fall upon the owner.

718. *Care of the fruits:* The usufructuary is held for all the expenses of cultivation and of maintenance of the property. (*Fructus non intelliguntur nisi deductis impensis.*)

719. *Usufruct of a flock:* The usufructuary is held by

[1] Gérardin, *Nouv. rev. histor.* 1884, pp. 626, 627; *Dig.* 7, 1, 58, § 1 (Scaevola).

[2] *Dig.* 7, 1, 12, § 2. See *infra*, § 727.

[3] *Ususfructuarius quemadmodum caveat, Dig.* 7, 9; Praetor's Edict, c. 45, *de stip.* § 7; Girard, *Textes*, p. 157.

a special obligation to maintain the flock by the help of the increase; he does not profit until he has replaced those which have died.[1]

720. Obligations of the Naked Owner: The rôle of owner is on principle purely passive; he is compelled only to suffer and not to be active; *pati, uti, frui.* This is what differentiates the rôle of the naked owner towards usufructuary from the rôle of a lessor towards a lessee: the lessor is held to procure the enjoyment for the lessee, *praestare, uti, frui.*

721. Extinguishment of Usufruct: Usufruct is extinguished: —

(1) By expiration of the period of time when it was created for a limited time.[2]

(2) By the death of the usufructuary.[3]

(3) Where it was created *for the life of a third person*, by the death of this third person.

(4) By the three *capitis deminutiones* of the usufructuary.[4]

(5) By the loss of the thing subjected to the usufruct.[5]

(6) By *consolidation*, that is, by the union in the same person of the qualities of owner and usufructuary.[6]

(7) Finally, by *non-usus*[7] for a year as to movables, for two years as to immovables.

722. Of Quasi-usufructus: It would seem that things fungible by their nature, as money, provisions, cannot be made the subject of a usufruct, since

---

[1] *Inst.* 2, 1, § 38.　　[2] Paulus, *Sent.* 3, 6, § 33.
[3] *Ibid.*　　[4] *Ibid.* § 29.　　[5] *Ibid.* § 31.
[6] *Ibid.* § 32; *Inst.* 2, 4, § 3.　　[7] Paulus, *Sent.* 3, 6, § 30.

it would be impossible for the usufructuary to make use of them without consuming them and consequently to return the substance at the expiration of the usufruct.[1] However, under the reign of Tiberius, a senatusconsultum instituted not the usufruct of fungible things, but a *quasi-usufruct* of fungible things. The quasiusufructuary of fungible things does not have, of course, to return, at the expiration of the usufruct, the same things *in specie*, but he will restore a like quantity of things of the same nature, value, and excellence.

The restoration *in genere* of the things over which a usufruct was established is secured by a *satisdatio* (security by fidejussors) required by the same senatusconsultum which created the institution.

§ 2. Usus, habitatio, operae

723. Of Usus: To take this word in its exact sense, usus should be but a ususfruct which would lack the *jus fruendi* and which would be reduced to the *jus utendi*. Thus he who should have the usus of a flock could indeed make use of its manure (*ad stercorandum argum*), but he could not take either the milk or the wool.[2]

Such is the rigor of the principle: but it is departed from by allowing the holder of the usus to take a small quantity of milk and wool for his personal needs. Thus altered, usus is no more than a *restricted usufruct*. It was often created by masters for the benefit of old freedmen, old servants.

[1] The usufruct of things fungible was rejected from the time of Cicero, *Topica*, iii.† See *Dig.* 7, 5, *de usuf. earum rerum quae usu consumuntur vel minuuntur.*

[2] *Inst.* 2, 5, § 4.

CIVIL DISMEMBERMENTS

Usus, differing from usufructus, is non-transferable;[1] it is created and extinguished like usufructus.[2]

724. Of Habitatio: Habitatio is in short but the usus of a house; he who was favored with it had the right to occupy the immovables with his family, but not to let it. This right was allowed him by Justinian.[3]

725. Non-transferable like usus, habitatio differs from it only in this sense that it is acquired *per singulos dies.* The right of habitatio is extinguished and renewed each day; this is not so, so far as can be believed, a caprice of a subtle legislator; thanks to this fiction, the Roman legislator made habitatio protected from extinguishment by *capitis deminutio.*[4] The right, in being renewed each day, takes the beneficiary in the condition where he is found, it is perpetuated without undergoing attack.

726. Of Operae: We thus call the real right of profiting from the services of a slave, and even according to fr. 5, § 3 of the Digest, *ususfructus quem ad modum*[5] . . . of the services of an animal. These operae could be let out, and according to a text of Papinian would be transmissible to the heir of the legatee.[6]

Section III. — Actions relative to Servitudes

727. Actio Confessoria: Servitudes, personal as well as praedial, are protected by the actio confessoria: this action is given to him who wishes to

---

[1] *Inst.* 2, 5, § 4.   [2] *Ibid.*
[3] *Code,* 3, 33, 13 (Justinian).
[4] *Dig.* 7, 8, 10 pr.   [5] *Dig.* 7, 9.
[6] *Dig.* 33, 2, 2 : *Quia legatarius fructuarius non est, ad heredem suum operarum legatum transmittit.*

show the existence of a servitude in himself or in his land.[1]

728. Actio Negatoria: The actio negatoria, on the contrary, is given to him who wishes to establish the freedom of his land as against his adversary who claims that it is incumbered with a servitude for his benefit.[2]

729. There is, on the subject of proof in the actio negatoria, an old and celebrated controversy. According to one view, it would be sufficient for the plaintiff in the actio negatoria to prove his ownership: the ownership being presumed unincumbered, it will be for the defendant to prove the servitude claimed by him: this will be, therefore, the inversion of the rule "*actori incumbit onus probandi.*" In favor of this view is invoked this consideration, that to place upon the plaintiff in the actio negatoria the duty of proving the non-existence of the servitude would be to ask him "to furnish proof of a negative fact," which is deemed to be an almost impossible task.

Another view holds: that proof of the non-existence of the servitude is not impossible if only the praetor, as is his right, limits the proceedings by an *interrogatio in jure* in which the defendant shall be called upon to explain upon what he bases his alleged servitude; and that no text authorizes him to depart in this matter from the fundamental rule as to proof, — that the plaintiff shall therefore, conformably to the common law, have to prove not only his ownership, but the *libertas*[3] of his land.[4]

[1] *Inst.* 4, 6, § 2.   [2] *Ibid.*
[3] That is, *freedom from incumbrance.* See § 702 *supra.* — S.
[4] Cf. Girard, *Manuel*, p. 346, text and note 4, and p. 347.

CIVIL DISMEMBERMENTS

730. The actiones confessoria and negatoria are *arbitrariae;* but in this matter is seen, not so much as in the action in vindication, the nature of the material satisfaction which can be determined by the *pronuntiato* of the judex. It consists, doubtless, in a *cautio de non amplius turbando,* engagement secured by fidejussors not to trouble the neighboring owner, which the defendant was obliged to undertake, on penalty of incurring the pecuniary condemnation in which all actions ended.[1]

731. **Interdicts in the Matter of Servitudes:** Possessory protection does not exist for all praedial servitudes: it exists, as to rural praedial servitudes, only in water rights and rights of way, and then is made the object of special interdicts (*de itinere actuque privato, de itinere reficiendo, de aqua, de rivis, de fonte*).

732. It is a controverted question to know if the interdicts which protect servitudes usually rural are applicable to those servitudes rendered urban by the character of the dominant land.

733. As to servitudes usually urban, some texts grant the interdict *uti possidetis.* It is not doubtful that this interdict is applicable to *positive* servitudes, but we do not think that it can be applied to *negative* servitudes. *Possessory protection* cannot indeed exist where *possession* cannot exist.[2]

734. Personal servitudes are protected by the interdicts *uti possidetis, utrubi, unde vi* and *de precario.*[3]

[1] Girard, *Manuel,* pp. 346, 377.

[2] *Ibid.* p. 374, text and note 5. See *supra,* § 697.

[3] *Frag. Vat.* 90, 91 ; *Dig.* 43, 1, 1 pr. (Ulpian). See, also, Praetor's Edict, ch. 43, *de interdictis,* Girard, *Textes,* pp. 152, 154, 155 ; Gaius, 4, §§ 150, 160. — S.

CHAPTER II

PRAETORIAN DISMEMBERMENTS OF THE RIGHT OF OWNERSHIP

735. **Superficies:** When one person has built on the land of another with the permission of the owner, in the rigor of the civil law the buildings belong to the owner of the land (*superficies solo cedit*); but according to a usage which originated in the relations of the state and the cities with the builders who had erected buildings on their land, the enjoyment of these buildings was left in perpetuity to those who had constructed them in consideration of the payment of a rent (*solarium*).[1]

736. That which was on principle only a long term lease the praetor made a real right, by first granting to the builder, in order that he might defend himself against those who troubled him in the exercise of his right, a special interdict *de superficie*, analogous to the interdict *uti possidetis*, then some *actiones in factum* based on the *vindicatio*, the *actio confessoria* and the *actio negatoria*.[2]

737. **Emphyteusis:** Emphyteusis is, also, an imitation of a perpetual lease which the cities were accustomed to grant to those who were charged with cultivating and especially with clearing their domains.

---

[1] Petition of Adrastus. Girard, *Textes*, p. 795.

[2] Edict. praetor. cap. 43, *de interd.* Girard, *Textes*, pp. 152, 153 : *De superficiebus : Uti ex lege locationis sive conductionis q. d. a. nec vi, nec clam, nec pr. alter ab altero fruimini, V. f. v. . . . Si qua alia actio de superficie postulabitur causa cognita dabo.* (*Dig.* 43, 18, 1 pr.).

Individuals resorted to the same proceeding in order to improve the immense estates which were called *latifundia*. The lessee could sell his right, transmit to his heirs, acquire the fruits by mere separation before any gathering. He had to pay to the owner of the soil a rent (*vectigal* if land granted by a city, *pensio, canon, reditus* where the agreement took place between mere individuals), and his right could be declared forfeited if he failed for two years to pay this rent.

738. The praetor, in granting to the lessee a real action (*actio vectigalis*) modeled upon the *vindicatio*, seems indeed to have recognized for his benefit the existence of a real right. However, the character of the contract was controverted [1] down to the reign of the emperor Zeno, who declared that it ought to be considered neither a *locatio* nor a sale, but a special contract, the contract of emphyteusis.[2]

739. **Hypotheca**: In order to understand what the praetorian real right of hypotheca is, it is necessary to take a look at the transformations through which the contract of pledge passed, in Roman law.

Pledge, as we shall see in studying obligations, is a contract by which a debtor delivers to his creditor something as a security for his debt.

It is necessary, in the history of pledge, to distinguish three periods: (1) the period of fiducia; (2) the period of pignus; (3) the period of hypotheca.

740. (*a*) On principle, in order to safeguard the interest of the creditor, nothing better was conceived of than to transfer to him the ownership of the property which it was proposed to give him as security, binding

[1] Gaius, 3, § 145. [2] *Inst.* 3, 24, § 3.

him, by a contract of *fiducia*, to retransfer the ownership of this property to the debtor as soon as the debt should be paid;[1] the debtor found himself placed in quite a dangerous situation, for the creditor, having become owner of the property given him as security, could lawfully alienate it.

741. (*b*) In the second period, that of *pignus*, instead of transferring the ownership to the creditor, it was sufficient to deliver to him the possession. The debtor retook his property when he had paid his debt, and found himself in the same position as prior to the establishing the pledge, without there being any necessity, on the part of the creditor who was paid, of a re-transfer of ownership.

The debtor evidently ran less risk than at the time of the fiducia, since he retained the ownership, but he was deprived of the possession.[2]

742. (*c*) A last step was taken with the praetorian institution of *hypotheca* which already existed in the time of Cicero,[3] but of which the primary idea and the antecedents could be found even in the formulas of Cato.[4] The first example of pledging without delivery of possession consists of the right of pledge, which, by virtue of mere agreement, was granted to the lessor of a farm over the things stocking the property (*invecta et illata.*)[5] If the lessor was not paid his rent when it was due, he obtained from the praetor an interdict, the

[1] Gaius, 2, 60. — *Formula Baetica*, Girard, *Textes*, p. 786; *Mancipation fiduciaire de Pompei*, Girard, *Textes*, p. 783.
[2] *Inst.* 3, 14, § 4 ; *Dig.* 50, 16, 238, § 2.
[3] Cicero, *Epist. ad Familiares*, 13, 56.†
[4] Cato, *De Re Rustica*, 46.†
[5] Colquhoun, *A Summary, etc.* § 1469. — S.

interdictum Salvianum, by means of which he could obtain the delivery of possession of the property pledged as security for his debt.[1]

743. Later, instead of the interdictum Salvianum (which did not disappear, however), the lessor obtained an action, the *actio Serviana*, which pursued the same end, and allowed him to bring suit, in order to obtain the delivery of possession of his pledge, not only against the lessee, but against all third persons who are detainers.[2]

744. Some subsequent praetors generalized the institution by extending the action, under the name of *actio quasi-Serviana* or *hypothecaria* to all creditors who should have with their debtors an analogous agreement.[3]

745. *The actio quasi Serviana* was given not only against him who had pledged his property, but against third persons who are detainers; it therefore sanctioned a *right of pursuit*.

Furthermore, the creditor who employed the actio quasi-Serviana enjoyed, in regard to the things upon which the agreement bore, a *right of preference* over the other creditors.

In a right which is analyzable into a right of preference and a right of pursuit, it is easy to recognize a real right, in other words, a *dismemberment of ownership*, a *praetorian* dismemberment, since it is of praetorian creation and sanctioned by actions invented by the praetor.

[1] Gaius, 4, § 147.
[2] *Inst.* 4, 6, § 7 ; Edict. praetor. cap. 43, Girard, *Textes*, p. 150.
[3] *Inst.* 4, 6, § 7.

746. When once the creditor, by means of the actio *hypothecaria*, has delivered to him the things which were made the security for his debt, he has the right of preserving them in pledge (*jus possidendi*), but the hypotheca itself underwent some successive transformations; and after the right of having delivered to him the hypothecated property was awarded to the creditor, to him was afterward granted the right to sell it and pay himself out of the price; this is what is called the *jus distrahendi*.[1]

[1] Gaius, 2, § 64 ; Paulus, *Sent.* 2, 5, 1.

BOOK VI

SUCCESSIONS

TITLE I

SUCCESSION IN GENERAL — INSTITUTION OF THE HEIR

747. Definitions: Succession is defined in French law as the transmission of the property and rights of a deceased person. In Roman law, it would be more exact to say: the transmission of the *personality* of a deceased individual to one or more persons who bear the name of heirs.

In effect the deceased is deemed to survive with his domestic cult, with all his rights and obligations in the person of the heir, or heirs.[1]

748. Testamentary Succession; — ab intestato: The succession (we also say *inheritance*) may be testamentary, or *ab intestato*.[2] Testamentary, when the continuator of the personality of the deceased is nominated by the deceased himself; *ab intestato*, when, in default of a manifestation of the last will of the *cujus*, the law is charged with appointing the continuator or the continuators of his person. In French law succession *ab intestato* has all the preferences of

[1] Cuq, *Institutions*, vol. i, p. 279 ; Paulus, *Sent.* 4, 8, § 6.
[2] Gaius, 2, § 99.

the legislator; it is not the same in Roman law.[1] The Romans attached a great importance to not dying intestate, and considered the non-existence or the loss of a will as a grave misfortune.

749. Institution of an Heir: Other differences: the provisions of a will, in French law, are not connected one to another; certain ones may be valid when others would be void.

In Roman law, every will depends on the validity of the institution of an heir (*caput et fundamentum totius testamenti*): if this institution fails, all the provisions of the will fail also.[2]

750. Partial Institution: Finally, in French law, it is possible to die partly testate, partly intestate; that is, to regulate the distribution of part of one's estate and leave the law to provide for the rest. In Roman law, "*Nemo paganus partim testatus partim intestatus decedere potest.*" *Paganus*, the non-military individual, "the civilian," is here contrasted with the soldier, who, by a special privilege, can die partly testate, partly intestate.[3]

751. Plurality of Heirs: Furthermore, the testator may institute several heirs, each one appointed to receive but a part of the inheritance, provided that the sum of these parts makes up the whole of the inheritance.[4]

752. Calculation of the Share of the

[1] That results from the expression itself of the XII Tables on the vesting of the succession *ab intestato*, "*Si intestato moritur....*"
[2] Gaius, 2, § 229.
[3] *Inst.* 2, 14, § 5 ; *Dig.* 50, 17, 7 (Pomponius).
[4] *Inst.* 2, 14, § 4.

Heirs: A. If the testator has not designated the share of each of the heirs, they share equally: Primus, Secundus, and Tertius, instituted without their shares being designated, will each take a third.[1]

B. If the deceased designated the shares of all the heirs, there will not be any further difficulty. Titius and Seius are instituted, Titius for *two*, Seius for *three*: Titius will take two fifths, Seius, three fifths.[2]

C. The deceased designated shares to certain heirs: "I give," he said, "four to Primus, three to Secundus, the remainder to Tertius." What will be the share of each? The language of the testator, a veritable enigma to us, is clear to a Roman. The *hereditas*, according to Roman practices, is considered as a unit, an *as*, which is divided into twelve *unciae:* Primus will have four *unciae*, Secundus three *unciae*, and "the remainder" belonging to Tertius will be valued at five *unciae* $(4+3+5=12)$.

Sometimes the testator, in his distributions,[3] exceeds the figure 12: he will have given five to one, six to another, two to a third, the remainder to a fourth. Suppose that he wished to calculate the inheritance as two *asses*, making it two units (*dupondius*). Has he disposed of 13 *unciae?* There still remain 11 of them which he can dispose of $(13+11=24$, or twice 12 *unciae)*. — If there are many heirs, the testator can make three units, *tripondius*, and calculate his hereditas as three *asses* or 36 *unciae*.[4]

---

[1] *Inst.* 2, 14, § 6.

[2] *Ibid.*

[3] On this topic of distribution, see Roby, *Rom. Priv. Law*, vol. i, p. 201; *Inst.* 2, 14, § 5. — S.

[4] *Inst.* 2, 14, § 8.

753. **Right of Accretion:**[1] Each heir, even when his share has been designated, is called to the entire inheritance. Even though I should have said: "I institute Primus my heir for one half, Secundus, for the other half:" if by reason of predecease, incapacity, repudiation, Secundus happens not to receive his share of the inheritance, the entire inheritance will be devolved on Primus. This is what is called the right of accretion (*jus adcrescendi*).[2]

754. If several heirs are appointed to receive the share of an heir who has failed to take, they will divide this share proportionally to the respective shares which they were appointed to receive in the succession, let Primus be instituted for two, Secundus for four, Tertius for six: if Tertius happens to fail to take, the share designated for him will be divided between Primus and Secundus in proportion to their respective portions, that is, Secundus, instituted for four, will take four parts of this against two given to Primus, instituted for two.

755. **Jus Caduca Vindicandi:** Such was the rule down to the leges Julia and Papia Poppaea; such it was to become in the last state of the law; but the right of accretion, replaced by the *jus caduca vindicandi*, suffered a long eclipse from Augustus to Justinian.

The civil wars had depopulated the empire: the corruption of morals diminished the birth-rate: people no longer married, no longer had children: Augustus

---

[1] Or "*Right of survivorship,*" Colquhoun, *A Summary of the Rom. Civ. Law,* § 1177.

[2] Paulus, *Sent.* 4, 8, § 26 [Colquhoun, *A Summary*, etc. vol. ii, § 1274.

conceived the idea of bestowing favors on marriage and fruitfulness, of punishing sterility and celibacy: this was the work of the leges Julia and Papia Poppaea.

The *coelibes* (bachelors or widowers not remarrying) appointed to an inheritance lost the *jus capiendi*, that is, the right to receive it, the *orbi* (people married but childless) lost only a half of it: such was the penalty.

But what became of these portions escaping from heirs incapacitated by law? (They were called *caduca*, from *cadere* to fall, and the laws which had created the incapacities bore the name of *leges caduciariae*). They were given, by way of favor (*proemia patrum*), to heirs who are 'patres'; in default of these to the legatees who are 'patres'; in a word, to those who "*liberos habent in testamento;*" and if no person nominated in the will satisfies the required conditions, the *pars caduca* is devolved on the *fiscus*.[1]

This is the policy of the *jus caduca vindicandi* which, for five hundred years, replaced the right of accretion. It was abolished piecemeal under the Christian emperors, and Justinian caused the last fragments of it to disappear.[2]

Certain persons were exempted from the application of the *leges caduciariae:* these were ascendants and descendants to the third degree; it was said of these that they enjoyed the *jus antiquum*.

756. **Substitutions:** Resulting from the unlimited importance which the Romans attached to not dying intestate, they became ingenious to avoid by every means that their succession, by means of prede-

[1] Gaius, 2, §§ 144, 206 ; *Dig.* 50, 16, 142 (Paulus) ; *fragm. de jure fisci*, 1, 3 (Girard, *Textes*, p. 470).
[2] *Code*, 6, 51, 1 (Justinian).

cease, repudiation, incapacity of the heir, should become vacant: here is the motive for the creation of substitutions.

757. A. *Ordinary substitution*: [1] Nothing is more simple than ordinary substitution. I institute Primus, and, in case he should not succeed me, I substitute for him Secundus; it is possible to make a long series of substitutions, and at the end, to institute a slave as *heres necessarius*. Ordinary substitution is, therefore, a conditional institution in the second (or third, fourth, etc.) degree in case the person originally instituted should happen not to receive the inheritance.[2]

758. B. *Pupillary substitution*: [3] Pupillary substitution is more original. It is not his hereditas with which the testator is preoccupied, but the hereditas of his impubes child, in case this child, dying before puberty, should die intestate of necessity, since he must be pubes in order to make a will.

The paterfamilias is not contented with nominating his heir, but he also nominates the heir of such and such of his children, in case this child shculd die impubes: this is pupillary substitution.[4]

759. C. *Quasi-pupillary or exemplary substitution*: [5] Exemplary substitution is, as its name indicates, only an imitation of the preceding. It is no longer an impubes son with whom the paterfamilias is preoccupied, but a son, who is a *furiosus*: and exemplary substitu-

---

[1] *Substitutio vulgaris.*

[2] *Inst.* 2, 15 pr. [Roby, *Rom. Priv. Law*, vol. i, p. 188].

[3] *Substitutio pupillaris.*

[4] *Inst.* 2, 16 pr. and § 3 ; Cicero, *De Oratore*, 1, 39, 180, etc. [Roby, *opus cit.* vol. i, pp. 202, 204].

[5] *Substitutio quasi-pupillaris or exemplaris.*

tion is nothing else than the nomination of an heir by the paterfamilias for the *furiosus* in case he should die without recovering his reason.[1]

760. D. *Fideicommissary substitution:* or gradual fideicommissum: This provision belongs less to the subject of substitutions, with which its name connects it, than to the subject of fideicommissa. This is the provision whereby a testator institutes for his heir a person whom he charges with holding his property for life and handing it over at his death to a second person who is designated.

This provision is prohibited in French law under the abridged name of "*substitution.*"

[1] Justinian made this substitution a regular institution, *Code*, 6, 26, 9. — Decisions along the same line of ideas (for instance as to a *filius mutus*) are noticed by Paulus as acts of imperial good pleasure, *Dig.* 28, 6, 43. [See, also, Colquhoun, *A Summary of the Rom. Civ. Law*, vol. ii, § 1291.]

TITLE II

CONDITIONS FOR THE VALIDITY OF WILLS

CHAPTER I

FORMS OF WILLS

761. **First Period:** *Will CALATIS COMITIIS:* In the old Roman law, a will is made *calatis comitiis*, that is, in an assembly of the comitia curiata, which could not help being disadvantageous, for the comitia curiata met but twice a year, and death could not wait for them. The will *calatis comitiis* is a real law enacted by the curiae, which sanctions the intention of the testator.[1]

762. *Cont. Will PER AES ET LIBRAM:* From the early times of Rome is seen to appear, along with the patrician form of the will *calatis comitiis*, the will *per aes et libram*, which is in short but a mancipation of the hereditas.

763. On principle the testator really and directly conveyed his hereditas to the heir whom he wished to institute, which offered a double inconvenience; the heir was known: his appointment was irrevocable. Later, the *familiae emptor* was nothing more than a figurehead charged with handing over the hereditas to an unknown successor whom the testator had appointed in the *sealed tabulae* of his will.

After accomplishing the ceremonies of mancipation

[1] Gaius, 2, § 101.

the testator made a declaration thus framed: "*Haec ita ut in ceris tabulisque scripta sunt, ita volo, ita rogo, ita testor.*" This formal attestation was called the *nuncupatio*. *Nuncupare*, says Festus, is "*palam nominare*," to appoint publicly. The will *per aes et libram* still existed during the first centuries of the empire.[1]

764. *Will in procinctu*: Soldiers during this early period make their wills *in procinctu*, before the army, in battle array: "*procinctus est armatus expeditusque exercitus.*" Thus five cohorts of the army of Metellus made their wills before going up to assault Contrebia.[2]

765. *Nuncupative will*: The purely nuncupative will consists in a simple verbal declaration before seven witnesses. This is the will of men at the point of death. By a similar will the poet Horace instituted Augustus his heir.[3]

766. **Second Period:** *Praetorian will*: The praetor had adopted the practice of holding as valid the will shown by the testator to seven witnesses who place thereon their seals (*obsignatio*) with their names opposite (*praescriptio*): it is a deformation of the will *per aes et libram*, by means of which the *familiae emptor* and the *libripens* become simple witnesses. This will, much more simple, became daily employed.[4]

(The *nuncupative* will still exists.)

[1] Gaius, 2, §§ 102, 104.

[2] Gaius, 2, 101 ; Velleius Paterculus, 2, 5. — By virtue of various privileges given by Julius Caesar, Titus, Domitian, Nerva, Trajan, the last will of a soldier would be carried out under whatever form he expressed it. See *Inst. de milit. testam.* book 2, tit. 11.

[3] Suetonius, *Deperd. libr. reliquiae.*†

[4] Ulpian, *Reg.* 28, § 6 ; Gaius, 2, § 119.

767. Third Period: *Wills of the Later Empire:* We find under the Later Empire the nuncupative will still in existence. — The special form in this period is the *tripartite will*, a written will, which the testator shows to the witnesses, and which bears the signatures of these witnesses at the end of the provisions (which the testator moreover might conceal by folding the part of the parchment or papyrus containing these). This will is called *tripartite* because it borrows: (1) from the civil law the assembling of the witnesses and the *unitas actus*. By *unitas actus* is meant the duty of accomplishing at one time and without interruption all the formalities of the will; — (2) from the praetorian law, the affixing of the seals of the seven witnesses (*obsignatio* and *praescriptio*) on the outside of the tabulae, or on the external part of the papyrus used more in this period; — (3) from the imperial constitutions, the *subscriptio*, that is, the internal signature before the sealing by the witnesses and by the testator himself in the presence of the witnesses. When the testator does not know how to write and has to resort to the pen of a third person, the presence of one more witness is required.[1]

768. Appointment of the Heir: The formula for appointing an heir is constant, whatever be the form of the will. It is "*Titius heres esto*" or "*Titium heredem esse volo* (or *jubeo*)." — The words of the institution reduced to three or four models were formal down to Constantine.[2]

[1] *Inst.* 2, 10, § 13.
[2] Gaius, 2, §§ 116, 117 ; Ulpian, *Reg.* 21 ; *Code*, 6, 23, 15.

CHAPTER II

CONDITIONS FUNDAMENTAL TO THE VALIDITY OF WILLS

769. The condition fundamental to the validity of a will is the *testamenti factio* of the *cujus* and of the heir. It is necessary to distinguish in this matter: (1) on the one hand, active testamenti factio (capacity to make a will) and passive testamenti factio (capacity to take); (2) on the other hand absolute testamenti factio and relative testamenti factio.

770. **Active Testamenti Factio:** (or capacity of the testator): A. Those alone have on principle active testamenti factio in whom the law recognizes the right to hold property. — This excludes slaves,[1] 'peregrini,' persons in *patria potestate*. This rigor is diminished in course of time. The capacity to make a will has been granted: (1) to public slaves as to half of their 'peculium.'[2]

(2) To 'peregrini' who had received the 'jus commercii.'

(3) To filiifamilias as to their 'peculium castrense.'

771. B. Certain incapacities to make a will might probably be connected with the ancient form of will, *calatis comitiis*, for example, that of a woman, which did not disappear until under Hadrian.[3]

---

[1] Except persons in captivity, the application of the *lex Cornelia*.

[2] Ulpian, *Reg.* 20, § 16.

[3] This did not prevent the woman from making a will *per aes et libram*, and yet we know that the freedwoman alone can make a will: hence the *coëmptio testamenti faciendi gratia* (see *supra*, § 251). Ulpian, *Reg.* 20, 15.

772. C. Others are founded on a lack of intel'-gence: that of the *impubes*, the *furiosus* (except he is in a lucid interval), the spendthrift: those could not disappear, and were maintained.

773. D. Finally testamenti factio is withdrawn by operation of law: anciently from persons who are *improbi intestabilesque*, later; from Latini Juniani and dediticii.[1]

774. **Passive Testamenti Factio** (or capacity to inherit): these did not have the capacity to take.

(1) Persons who are *intestabiles*.[2]

(2) 'Peregrini' not favored with the 'jus commercii;' and consequently those who have lost the right of citizenship.[3]

(3) Women by virtue of the lex Voconia (269 B. C.). (It is only by persons belonging to the first class of the census, having therefore more than 100,000 *asses*, that women cannot be instituted.)[4]

(4) Persons who are *incerti*: however, it was permitted to institute in advance a postumus.[5]

775. It is necessary to remark that slaves might be instituted either by their masters or by third persons. By their masters, with express freedom; but in the last state of the law, institution itself is equivalent to implied freedom. — By third persons: they inherit for their master. It is necessary in this case that relative testa-

---

[1] Ulpian, *Reg.* 20, § 14.

[2] See Girard, *Manuel*, p. 195.   [3] *Dig.* 28, 1, 8 (Gaius).

[4] Prohibition fallen quite rapidly into disuse: see Cicero, *Verr.* 40, 43, 104, 111†; and the will of Dasumius (108 A. D.), Girard, *Textes*, p. 767. — Aulus Gellius, 20, 1.†

[5] Ulpian, *Reg.* 22, 4; Aulus Gellius, 216.† — The jus honorarium extended this favor to the *postumi alieni* (*Inst.* 3, 9 pr.).

menti factio, of which we are now going to speak, exist between the testator and the master of the instituted slave.[1]

776. Relative Testamenti Factio: By relative testamenti factio must be understood the capacity, for two given persons, who enjoy absolute testamenti factio, of being instituted one to the other. Save for some exceptions in the last state of the law relative to incestuous children, to the second husband's wife, to natural children, all Romans, and their slaves for them, have testamenti factio.

777. Active testamenti factio should exist with the testator at the time of the making of his will and at the time of his death; — passive testamenti factio with the heir at the time of the making of the will, at the time of the opening of the succession, and at the time of the 'aditio hereditatis' (*tria tempora inspici debent*). — An incapacity coming upon the heir between the making of the will and the death of the testator is of no effect if at the time of the death the heir has recovered his capacity (*media tempora non nocent*).[2]

CHAPTER III

INVALIDATION OF WILLS

778. Causes of the Invalidation of Wills: A will is without effect: (1) when it is *nullum ab initio;* that is, when it shows a nullity of form, or the absence of a fundamental condition.

779. (2) When, valid on principle, it is *ruptum*.

[1] *Inst.* 2, 14 pr.   [2] *Dig.* 28, 5, 60, 4 (Celsus).

A will is broken (ruptum) when it is revoked by a later will;[1] it is equally ruptum by the birth of a postumus not disinherited.[2]

780. (3) When it is *irritum:* the will is irritum when the testator is, at the time of his death, *capite minutus.*[3]

781. (4) When it is annulled because it is *inofficiosum.*[4]

782. (5) When it is *destitutum,* that is, when the instituted heir refuses the succession. This subject will be studied a little later.[5]

CHAPTER IV

FREEDOM TO MAKE A WILL AND ITS RESTRICTIONS

783. **Law of the XII Tables:** The freedom of the paterfamilias to make a will perhaps did not always exist among the Romans, and it is not impossible that at a remote era it might have met an obstacle in family ownership. But it appeared complete at the time of the XII Tables: "*Uti legassit super pecunia suae rei ita jus esto.*"[6] Let us notice, however, the opposite opinion of Cuq, who, distinguishing in the estate of the paterfamilias two parts, the *familia* composed of *res mancipi* and the *pecunia,* mass of *res nec mancipi,* supposes that the freedom to make a will proclaimed by the law of the XII Tables affected only the pecunia.[7]

---

[1] Gaius, 2, § 144.   [2] See *infra,* § 796.
[3] Gaius, 2, § 145. See, however, the fiction of the *lex Cornelia,* § 123, *supra.*
[4] See *infra,* § 789.   [5] See *infra,* §§ 800 *et seq.*
[6] *Lex XII Tab.* v, 3.   [7] Cuq, *Institutions,* vol. i, p. 282.

784. **Reaction:** Subsequently [1] a reaction is produced which opposes to the freedom of the paterfamilias the right of his children. The stages of this reaction are: (1) the doctrine of disinherison; (2) the praetorian extension given to this doctrine; the *querela inofficiosi testamenti;* the doctrine of the statutory share.[2]

785. (2) **Disinherison:**[3] The law obliges a father who does not leave the succession to his *sui heredes* to disinherit them by a formal declaration and *designation* in regard to sons. Daughters and grandsons can be disinherited in general terms, *inter caeteros:* "*Titius heres esto, caeteri exheredes sunto*," or by omission. For want of proper disinherison of *sui heredes* the will was void.[4]

786. *Postumi:* But as it is possible to institute or disinherit only living persons, it follows from this that the birth of a *suus heres* after the making of a will broke the will, possible to be repaired if the testator was still in a condition to change his provisions, impossible to be repaired if the testator no longer was in existence. To obviate this inconvenience the law and also a positive statute, the lex Junia Vellaea (or Velleia) permitted the disinherison of postumi in advance; and by this word are designated not only *sui heredes* who are born after the death of the testator (*postumi legitimi*), but those who are born after the making of the

---

[1] Girard admits, on the contrary, that the necessity of *exheredatio* is not subsequent to the XII Tables. *Manuel,* pp. 844, 845.

[2] *Legitima pars: quarta e lege Falcidia, Code,* 3, 28, 31. See, also, § 880, *infra; Inst.* 2, 17, § 3 ; *Inst.* 2, 22 pr. and § 1. — S.

[3] *Exheredatio.*

[4] Gaius, 2, § 123.

will. The disinherison of the latter was permitted by the lex Velleia, and these are called *postumi Velleiani*.[1]

787. But it is possible not to be born a *suus heres*, not to be such at the time of the making of the will, and to afterwards become such: for example, a grandson whose father was in existence when the grandfather made his will, and is already dead at the time of the death of the latter, becomes *suus heres* only between the making of the will and the death of the testator. Events of this nature were provided for either by the lex Velleia, or by the *prudentes* who established or recognized the disinherison of all those *sui heredes* born or qualified since the making of a will under the name of *quasi-postumi Velleiani*, *postumi Aquiliani* (the invention of Aquillius Gallus), *postumi Juliani* (the invention of Salvius Julianus).[2]

788. *Praetorian extension of the doctrine of exheredatio:* (1) The praetor required the disinheriting of emancipated children who have ceased to be *sui heredes*.

(2) He required disinherison *nominatim* of all the descendants of the male sex, grandsons as well as sons.[3]

789. *Querela inofficiosi testamenti:* The querela inofficiosi testamenti is a creation of customary origin, and appears to have been adopted towards the beginning of the Empire in the law of the *centumviri*. This court caused the annulment even of wills in which *sui*

---

[1] *Inst.* 2, 13, § 1 ; *Dig.* 28, 2, 29, §§ 11–13.

[2] *Dig.* 28, 2, 29, §§ 13–15. There may likewise be agnation of a postumous after the making of a will by the *coëmptio* of the testator with his wife. Gaius, 2, 139, and *Laudatio funebris Turiae*, lines 13 et seq., Girard, *Textes*, p. 777.

[3] *Dig.* 37, 4 ; *Inst.* 2, 13, § 7 ; Gaius, 2, § 125.

heredes were properly disinherited, when the disinherison of these heirs appeared to it to be unjust, "*non ex officio pietatis conscriptum;*" it pretended to believe, in such a case, that the testator did not enjoy his full reason. The action by which the *suus heres* caused the will to fail was called *querela inofficiosi testamenti*.[1]

The question was at this time between the entire confirmation of the will or its complete nullity, even when the testator had left something to his disinherited *suus heres*.[2]

790. **Actio ad Supplendum:** Under the Byzantine law, we notice the creation of the actio ad supplendum, which, while letting the will stand, causes the *suus heres* to obtain his full *pars legitima*[3] fixed at one fourth his rights of succession. Thus is established the doctrine of the *statutory share* which will be found later in our *droit coutumier*[4] and which has passed

---

[1] Paulus, *Sent.* 4, 5; Cicero, *in Verrem*, 1, 42; Cicero, *De Oratore*, 1, 38, 57.†

[2] *Dig.* 5, 2, 6; *ibid.* 8, § 16 (Ulpian).

[3] *Code*, 3, 28, 30-36. Cf. Paulus, *Sent.* 4, 5, § 10; *Code*, 3, 28, 4. — S.

[4] France was anciently divided into the *pays de coutumes* (country of the customary law) and the *pays de droit écrit* (country of the written law). This is clearly manifest from the commencement of the thirteenth century and subsisted down to the Revolution of 1789 and even to the promulgation of the *Code civil*, Esmein, *Cours élémentaire d'histoire de droit français*, p. 712. The unwritten or customary law borrowed its general principles from law of Germanic origin, while the written law derived its general principles from the Roman law. The South of France followed the principles of the Roman law, called and developed under the name of the *written law* (*droit écrit*). In the north the local laws of the *usus* and *consuetudines* of the time of the Carolingians, modified by the effect of time and local

into the Code civil under the name of the "*théorie de la réserve.*" ¹

conditions, give birth to the *customary law (droit coutumier)*. *Livre du centenaire du Code civil*, vol. i, pp. 29 *et seq.* — S.

¹ *Cod. Theod.* 16, 7, 28 (Theodosius II and Valentinian III) ; *Majoriani aug. legum novell.* tit. 8, *de sanctimonialibus et viduis* ; *Code* 3, 28, 28 and 30, 31.

TITLE III

INTESTATE SUCCESSION

791. Opening of the Succession ab Intestato: When there is no will, or the will is void, or, for any reason whatever it is without effect, the succession *ab intestato* is opened. — The succession *ab intestato* is opened when it becomes certain that there will not be any testamentary succession. It is to this time, which may be very posterior to the death, that we must go back in order to know who are called as heirs.[1]

792. Systems of Succession ab Intestato: Three systems of succession were established at different times: the system of pure civil law, the system of the praetorian law, lastly the system of the imperial law.

793. System of Pure Civil Law: The law of the XII Tables calls in the first rank to the succession the *sui heredes*, in the second rank the *agnates*, in the third rank the *gentiles*.[2]

When there are no heirs of the first class, the nearest agnates receive the succession: *adgnatus proximus familiam habeto;* if there are several agnates in the same degree they share *per capita*.[3]

---

[1] *Inst.* 3, 1, § 7.   [2] *Lex. XII Tab.* v, 3.

[3] *Succession of freedmen:* The freedman has no agnates other than his patronus and his agnatic posterity. The second class of heirs is therefore represented, for freedmen, by the patronus and his children. Ulpian, *Reg.* 27, §§ 1, 4.

In default of agnates the succession passes to the gentiles: *gentiles familiam nancitor:* the early desuetude of the succession of gentiles has deprived us of every kind of information as to its operation.

794. System of the Praetorian Law: The praetor did not offer the hereditas, strictly speaking, but he granted *bonorum possessio* or the praetorian succession, and the order of devolution which he adopted defeated the order of succession of the civil law.

The praetorian succession is especially founded on the natural ties. The most important *bonorum possessiones* granted by the praetor are shown in the following order: —

(1) *Possessio unde liberi:* the praetor granted it to children gone out of the family by emancipation as well as to children who were *sui heredes.*

(2) *Possessio unde legitimi,* which corresponds to the succession of the agnates.

(3) *Possessio unde cognati:* a wholly praetorian creation which calls to the succession the members of the natural family to the sixth degree, and even to the seventh degree for children of own cousins. This innovation of the praetors contributed not a little to make the succession of the gentiles disappear.[1]

(4) *Possessio unde vir et uxor:* Succession between husband and wife. According to the civil law, the wife *in manu* inherited from her husband because she was *loco filiæ;* but there was no succession between husband and wife in a marriage *sine manu.* This succession, therefore, was introduced by the praetorian law.[2]

---

[1] Gaius, 3, §§ 25–31 ; *ibid.* 2, § 137 ; Ulpian, *Reg.* 8, 28 ; *Dig.* 38, 11.

[2] *Dig.* 38, 11.

795. *Possessio cum re or sine re:* Civil succession and praetorian succession are found, as can be seen, often in conflict. In certain cases the praetor, while maintaining his system, permitted its application to be deflected before superior rights conferred by the civil law; the heir of the civil law keeps the estate to the detriment of the bonorum possessor: *bonorum possessio* is then said to be given by the praetor *sine re*. In other cases the system of the praetor comes into collision with the system of the civil law, where if it is contrary to the civil law the praetor makes it prevail notwithstanding: possession is said to be given *cum re*.[1]

796. Collatio Bonorum: The son gone out of his family by emancipation whom the praetor calls to share in the paternal succession by *bonorum possessio unde liberi* is obliged to put in the estate to be divided the property which he has acquired since his emancipation. — This is what is called *collatio bonorum*.[2]

797. Innovations of the Imperial Law: The movement of reaction for the benefit of the natural family against the ancient privileges of the agnatic family continues under the empire. The senatusconsultum Tertullianum, passed under Hadrian, calls the mother to the succession of her children, and the senatusconsultum Orphitionum, passed under Marcus Aurelius, calls children to the succession of their mother.[3]

798. System of Succession of Justinian:

---

[1] Gaius, 3, § 35; Ulpian, *Reg.* 28, § 13.

[2] The restricted dimensions of this work do not permit us to treat of the *collatio dotis* and the *collatio emancipati*.

[3] See *Institutes* of Justinian, 3, 3 de *Sc. Tertull.*; *ibid.* 3, 4 *De Sc. Orphit.*

Novels 118 and 123 of Justinian introduced a system of succession the development of which cannot find room here, but which definitely established the rights of the natural family, and the principal features of which are again found in our French law of successions. Justinian recognized three classes of heirs: (1) descendants; (2) ascendants; (3) collaterals.

TITLE IV

ACCEPTANCE AND DISCLAIMER[1] OF THE INHERITANCE

799. Qualities and Differences of Heirs: Concerning the acquisition of the hereditas three kinds of heirs must be distinguished: (1) *heredes necessarii;* (2) *sui heredes* (also termed *heredes sui et necessarii*); (3) *heredes extranei.*[2]

800. (1) **Heredes Necessarii:** The heres necessarius is encountered only in testamentary successions: he is a slave whom the testator has instituted as a last resort in order that his hereditas may not become vacant when it is insolvent, and to avoid that, after his death, his memory should incur infamy from a *bonorum venditio.* The slave thus instituted becomes free, and will be heir willingly or unwillingly: it is in his name that the *bonorum publicatio* will be made: it is he who will incur infamy.[3]

801. But the praetor diminishes the inconveniences of this situation by granting to the heres necessarius the *benefit* of *separatio bonorum,*[4] that is, the advantage of not being able to be sued by the creditors of the hereditas for the property which he should subsequently acquire.[5]

802. (2) **Sui Heredes:** (children who are found in the power of the testator at the time of his death,

[1] *Repudiatio.* [2] *Inst.* 2, 19 pr.
[3] Gaius, 2, § 154. [4] Girard, *Manuel,* pp. 883, 884, 917.
[5] Gaius, 2, § 155.

including the wife *in manu*). — It makes little difference whether they come to the succession by will or *ab intestato*. In both cases they are heirs at law. But they can escape the burdens of the succession by exercising the *jus abstinendi* (also created by the praetor), namely by avoiding every act of taking the estate, all meddling with its assets.[1]

803. (3) **Heredes Extranei**: This title is applied to all instituted heirs as well as heirs *ab intestato* who are neither *heredes necessarii* nor *heredes sui*: it is applied, in successions *ab intestato*, to the agnates: the name of *extranei* therefore does not necessarily imply the idea of not belonging to the family.[2]

804. The *heres extraneus* is not heir in full right: he will become heir only if he wishes to, by an acceptance which is called in Roman law *aditio hereditatis*.[3]

805. *Forms of acceptance. Cretio: Aditio hereditatis* may be express or implied; it is made: (1) by an express declaration and acceptance called *cretio* (from *cernere* to decide);[4] (2) by acts of meddling in the management of the estate, *pro herede gerendo* (which we call to-day acting as heir);[5] (3) *nuda voluntate*, by taking the title of heir in a transaction.[6]

806. But as, if he makes an *aditio hereditatis*, the *heres extraneus* will become responsible for the debts not only to the extent of the property of the succession, but out of his own property, it is clear that the hereditas is liable to become vacant if it is insolvent or simply suspected of insolvency.

[1] *Inst.* 2, 19, § 2; Paulus, *Sent.* 4, 8, § 5; Gaius, 2, § 159; *Dig.* 29, 2, 57 pr. (Gaius); Girard, *Manuel*, pp. 834, 835.
[2] *Inst.* 2, 19, §§ 3 and 5.   [3] *Ibid.*
[4] Gaius, 2, §§ 164–178.   [5] *Inst.* 2, 19, § 7.   [6] *Ibid.*

ACCEPTANCE OF INHERITANCE

Hence, the *period of time for cretio*, and the *jus deliberandi* introduced by the praetor. The time for cretio is a period of one hundred days, during which the heir deliberates on the course to take (exercises the 'jus deliberandi'). If, at the expiration of the time the heir has not accepted the inheritance, the creditors are put in possession of the hereditas.[1]

807. Justinian maintained the 'jus deliberandi:' he even extended the time to nine months, if it was given by the magistrate, to one year if granted by the emperor; and, furthermore, he created the *beneficium inventarii*, that is, the right of the *heres extraneus* who has taken an inventory of the property of the hereditas before *tabelliones*,[2] to be held for the debts of the hereditas only to the extent of the assets. This is also the system of acceptance under benefit of inventory of our law of to-day.[3]

808. The benefit of inventory and the 'jus deliberandi' are not cumulative: the heir who has asked and obtained the 'jus deliberandi' cannot also subsequently invoke the benefit of inventory: he must accept or refuse the hereditas absolutely and unconditionally.[4]

809. (4) **Praetorian Heirs:** Praetorian heirs (*bonorum possessores*) become heirs only by demanding of the praetor *bonorum possessio*, and consequently only if they so desire.

810. **Consequences of Acquiring the Hereditas: Confusio:** The acquisition of the hereditas,

[1] Gaius, 2, § 167; *Dig.* 28, 8, 1, § 1 (Ulpian).

[2] Or *notaries*.

[3] *Beneficium inventarii*, see Colquhoun, *A Summary of the Rom. Civ. Law*, § 1273. — S.; *Code*, 6, 30, 22.

[4] *Code*, 6, 30, 22, § 14.

which results from an *aditio hereditatis* or some other act, has for its consequence the mingling of the estates, the assets and debts, of the testator and the heir.[1]

This *confusio* may be prejudicial either to the heir if he is solvent, and if the hereditas is burdened with debts greater than its assets, or to the creditors of the hereditas if, the hereditas being good, the heir is involved in debt; they are indeed obliged to share with the creditors of the heir the assets of the hereditas.

811. **Separatio Bonorum:** The law remedied the inconvenience of the confusio of estates by the system of separation of the property: we are already acquainted with two types of separating the property: that granted to a slave who is *heres necessarius*, that resulting from the benefit of inventory.

812. There is a third, symmetrical with the benefit of inventory, but of much earlier creation. This is the *separatio bonorum* granted on demand by the praetor to creditors of the hereditas. The creditors who obtained it are paid out of property of the hereditas to the exclusion of the creditors of the heir; but they cannot, on the contrary, share with the latter the property of the heir; nor even lay claim to this property, after payment of the personal creditors of the heir (*recesserunt a persona heredis*). (Papinian, however, expressed a contrary opinion.[2])

[1] Gaius, 3, § 81; Girard, *Manuel*, pp. 879, 883.
[2] *Dig.* 42, 6, 1, §§ 1, 2 (Ulpian); *ibid.* 1, § 17 (Ulpian); *ibid.* 3, § 2 (Papinian).

TITLE V

FIDEICOMMISSA HEREDITATIS[1]

813. **Of Fideicommissa in General:** A fideicommissum is a bequest intrusted, as its name indicates, to the good faith of the heir or legatee who is charged with handing over to a third person a particular thing, — or if an heir is concerned, a part or even the whole of the succession. The person charged with handing it over is called the *fiduciary*, he who receives from the fiduciary is called the *beneficiary*.

814. These bequests framed in *precatory terms*[2] are not on principle binding on the heir: in order to compel him to carry out the wishes of the testator there was only a sense of honor, and *the scrupulousness of honorable men*, the power of which was strong among the Romans.[3]

Augustus, on the opinion of a committee of jurisconsults whom he had assembled for this purpose, made fideicommissa obligatory and intrusted the surveillance of their protection to the administrative jurisdiction of the consuls.

Under Marcus Aurelius there was created to take cognizance of actions relative to fideicommissa a

---

[1] Or *testamentary trusts.* See Roby, *Rom. Priv. Law*, i, 356; Morey, *Outlines of Roman Law*, p. 335. — S.

[2] *Verbis precativis.* — S.

[3] See Cuq, *Institutions*, vol. i, pp. 487 *et seq.;* Ulpian, *Reg.* 25, § 1. — S.

special magistrate, the *praetor fideicommissarius*, who decided *extra ordinem*.

815. Fideicommissa Hereditatis: We have to do here only with testamentary trusts. When the fideicommissum had for its object the whole or part of the hereditas, the *heres fiduciarius* found himself in a very dangerous situation; for, obliged to hand over to the beneficiary all or part of the assets of the hereditas, he remained, nevertheless, chargeable with the *entire* burden of the debts of the hereditas, although he binds the beneficiary by a verbal contract (*stipulatio emptae et venditae hereditatis, stipulatio partis et pro parte*) to reimburse him for what he had been obliged to pay to the creditors of the hereditas, — insufficient remedy if the beneficiary was insolvent.

816. Senatusconsultum Trebellianum: A senatusconsultum of the reign of Nero, the senatusconsultum Trebellianum, ameliorated this situation by deciding that the heir who should have handed over all or part of the hereditas to the beneficiary would be, for the whole or this part, released from the burden of the debts. The creditors, in such case, to the extent of a fraction corresponding to the amount of the part handed over ($\frac{1}{2}$, $\frac{1}{3}$, $\frac{1}{4}$, if the restitution was $\frac{1}{2}$, $\frac{1}{3}$, $\frac{1}{4}$ of the hereditas), no longer had an action against the heir, and could sue only the beneficiary.[1]

817. Senatusconsultum Pegasianum: Henceforth acceptance became not dangerous, but offered no advantage to the fiduciary; nothing influenced him to accept: hence a second senatusconsultum, the senatusconsultum Pegasianum (of the reign

[1] Paulus, *Sent.* 4, 3, § 2; *ibid.* 4, 2.

of Vespasian), which allowed the heir to hand over to the beneficiary only three quarters of the hereditas, and to keep one quarter for himself (*the quarta Pegasiana*).[1]

817. *Cont.*—*Option of the heir:* But, in this case, it was the *heres fiduciarius* who was responsible for the debts due the creditors of the hereditas, but with a recourse against the beneficiary. The heir could choose between the Trebellian restitution and the Pegasian restitution, and he used to choose the one or the other according as the hereditas was more or less burdened and the beneficiary more or less solvent.[2]

818. **System of Justinian:** Justinian merged the two senatusconsulta: he authorized the heir to keep in all cases the Pegasian fourth, but released him, conformably to the senatusconsultum Trebellianum, from the part of the debts corresponding to the part of the assets which he had handed over to the beneficiary.[3]

[1] *Inst.* 2, 23, § 5.   [2] *Ibid.* § 6.   [3] *Ibid.* § 7.

TITLE VI

ACTIONS CONCERNING THE HEREDITAS

819. Petitio Hereditatis: The rights of the heres civilis are sanctioned by *hereditatis petitio* (*vindicatio generalis*). This is a real action which is successively brought by the *sacramentum in rem*, in the time of the *legis actiones*; later, by the *sponsio*, and by a petitory formula.[1]

820. This action is given to him who claims to be heir, or against a detainer of the hereditas who claims to be heir himself, or against the detainer of objects of the hereditas, who, without claiming to be heir, denies the quality of heir for the plaintiff. Viewed under this last aspect, *petitio hereditatis* is no longer a *vindicatio generalis*, but a *vindicatio singularis* in which the contention rests, nevertheless, on the existence or non-existence of the quality of heres for the plaintiff.[2]

821. Senatusconsultum Juventianum: Let us consider *petitio hereditatis* in its most interesting aspect, namely, in case of a conflict between two persons both claiming to be heirs. What will be the measure of the obligation of the losing party? He will have to hand over the estate, if he complies with the 'pronuntiatio' of the judex; the value of the hereditas, if he allows himself to be condemned. This is very well

---

[1] Cf. §§ 608, 609, *supra*.
[2] *Dig.* 5, 3, 9 (*Ulpian*), 10 (*Gaius*), 11, 12, 13 (*Ulpian*).

in theory: but what must be comprised in the valuation of the hereditas? It is precisely this question which the senatusconsultum Juventianum (under Hadrian, in 129 A. D., in the consulship of the celebrated jurisconsult Juventius Celsus) proposes to solve.

The senatusconsultum distinguishes between the *male fide possessor* and the *bona fide possessor*: the *mala fide possessor* is held to hand over to the heir *all that is wanting*. The *bona fide possessor* is held to restore only *whatever has enriched him*: consequently he has not to hand over either that which has perished through accident, or amounts wrongly paid to alleged creditors of the hereditas,[1] or the value of the fruits which he has neglected to obtain.

But, on the other hand, he will restore whatever has enriched him, not excepting the *fructus* which are still in existence, and even those which he obtained if he has sold them (*fructus naturales*) or invested (*fructus civiles*). — So, then, we cannot apply, in the matter of *petitio hereditatis*, the rule according to which "*the bona fide possessor makes the fruits his own.*" The principles we have just explained are condensed in the celebrated satirical phrase, "*fructus augent hereditatem.*"[2]

822. **Interdict Quorum Bonorum:** The praetorian heir (*bonorum possessor*) had, for the purpose of causing the corporeal things of the hereditas to be handed over to him, an interdict *adipiscendae possessionis*: the interdict *quorum bonorum*.[3]

---

[1] But he should relinquish in this event to the heres the *condictio indebiti* which belongs to him.

[2] *Dig.* 5, 3, 20, § 6 (Ulpian); Girard, *Manuel*, p. 893.

[3] *Inst.* 4, 15, § 3; *Dig.* 43, 2, 1 pr.

823. **Petitio Hereditatis Possessoria:** The interdict *quorum bonorum*, being applicable only to corporeal objects,[1] was insufficient; the praetor, becoming bold in this matter as in all those which he first touched but reservedly, gave to the *bonorum possessor* an *actio ficticia* based on *petitio hereditatis*, the *petitio hereditatis possessoria, actio ficticia* symmetrical with the civil *petitio hereditatis*.[2]

[1] *Dig.* 43, 2, 2 (Paulus).
[2] Gaius, 4, § 34; *ibid.* 3, § 81.

BOOK VII

DONATIONES INTER VIVOS AND MORTIS CAUSA

DIVISION

824. **Definition**: By *donatio* is meant a *gratuitous act*,[1] every act by which one person procures a benefit from another person without returning any advantage.[2]

825. **Division**: *Donationes* are divided into *donationes inter vivos* and *donationes mortis causa;* *donationes mortis causa* themselves comprise gifts *mortis causa* and legacies: so the Romanists often unite these last two kinds of *donatio* under the common title of *mortis causa capiones*.

[1] "*Acte à titre gratuit.*"
[2] *Dig.* 39, 5, 29 pr. (Papinian).

TITLE I

DONATIONES INTER VIVOS

CHAPTER I

GIFTS INTER VIVOS

SECTION I. — **Gifts in General**

826. **What is a Gift:** A gift *inter vivos* is not, whatever the Institutes of Justinian may say of it, a special mode of acquisition (*genus adquisitionis*). It is an act which has for its essential characteristics: (1) of causing the diminution of one estate and the enrichment of another; (2) of accomplishing to the injury of the donor an *actual and irrevocable* divestment.

827. **Its Form:** Besides, it borrows for its realization the most varied forms: mancipation,[1] *traditio*, if it has for its object a *res nec mancipi*, obligation by a verbal contract, *cessio bonorum*,[2] discharge of a debt[3] under the civil form of *acceptilatio* or under the praetorian form of *pactum de non petendo*.[4]

828. **Pactum Donationis:** Under the reign of Antoninus Pius the *pactum donationis* between

[1] Donationes of Artemidorus, Julia Monime, Statia Irene, Syntrophus (Girard, *Textes*, pp. 788 *et seq.*). — Mancipation is made in such case *nummo uno* (for a *sestertius*, or 0 fr. 20).

[2] *Frag. Vat.* 263. See Colquhoun, *A Summary of the Rom. Civ. Law*, § 1419; Roby, *Rom. Priv. Law*, vol. ii, p. 438. — S.

[3] See Roby, *opus cit.* vol. ii, p. 55. — S.

[4] *Dig.* 39, 5, 17 (Ulpian).

GIFTS INTER VIVOS

ascendants and descendants had already been raised to the rank of *pactum vestitum* and sanctioned by an action, the *condictio ex lege*.[1] Justinian generalized this measure, and applied it to all gifts; but this is not a reason for saying that gift is a *genus adquisitionis*; it is only a *causa adquisitionis*, like sale; and the emperor confuses the creation of the obligation with the transmission of ownership.

829. **Lex Cincia:** Gifts *inter vivos* were regarded unfavorably by the Romans. Free on principle, they became in 204 B. C. the object of a restrictive law, the *lex Cincia de donis et muneribus*. This law, the first provision of which prohibited lawyers from receiving fees *ad causam orandam*, limited, in the following provisions, gifts *inter vivos* to a fixed amount (*modus Cinciae*) which has not come down to us.[2]

830. What is known is: (1) that a gift *supra modum Cinciae* was void not only for the excess, but for the whole amount.

831. (2) That the lex Cincia was a *lex imperfecta*, namely, that it granted to the donor the means of escape from the executing of his gift in so far as this execution was not complete, but that it did not give him any means of recovering the gift when the donee had acquired full ownership of it.[3]

832. (3) That the lex Cincia did not always affect all gifts, nor, especially, all donees; that there were *personae exceptae* (ascendants, descendants, husband

---

[1] *Cod. Theod.* 8, 12, 4; *Cod. Just.* 8, 53, 35, § 5 (Justinian).

[2] Tacit. *Annales*, 11, 5.†

[3] Ulpian, *Reg.* 1 (text is mutilated); Girard, *Manuel*, p. 928, note 5.

and wife, relatives to the degree of own cousins, and even the son or daughter of the own cousin of the donor).[1]

833. (4) That the donor alone could invoke the benefit of the lex Cincia, and that the gift became absolute at his death (*morte Cincia removetur*).[2]

834. **Insinuatio:** Five centuries later, — the lex Cincia had become obsolete, — Constans Chlorus Cæsar of Gaul established, or, more exactly, made obligatory, for it was already introduced in practice,[3] the formality of insinuatio. Gifts of a certain amount were henceforth valid only on condition of being transcribed (*insinuatae*) on a public registry of the clerk of courts.[4]

Gifts under two hundred *solidi* were exempted from insinuatio. Justinian did not require insinuatio only when over five hundred *solidi*.[5]

835. In default of insinuatio, the gift was void only for that in excess of amount fixed by law. On the other hand, the nullity of the gift was enforced by an action for the benefit of the donor. The system of insinuatio, therefore, did not show the same deficiency as the system of the lex Cincia.[6]

836. **Revocation of Gifts Inter Vivos:** Gifts *inter vivos* are, on principle, absolutely irrevocable: except that they can be revoked for non-fulfill-

[1] *Frag. Vat.* 298–309 (Paulus).
[2] *Frag. Vat.* 259 (Papinian).
[3] See, indeed, *Frag. Vat.* 266 : the *professio apud acta* was already known under Alexander Severus in 229 A. D.
[4] *Cod. Theod.* 3, 5, 13 (Constantine); Girard, *Manuel*, p. 932.
[5] *Inst.* 2, 7, § 2; *Code*, 8, 53, 36, 3.
[6] *Code*, 8, 53, 54 pr. (Justinian) ; *ibid.* 36, 3.

ment of conditions, subsequent birth of children,[1] ingratitude; but it is necessary to remark that if, in French law, these three causes of revocation affect all gifts, in Roman law, revocations for *the subsequent birth of children to the donor*,[2] *or for ingratitude*, affect only gifts made by a patronus to his freedman.*[3] Revocation for non-fulfillment of conditions imposed alone has a general import.

837. *Gift SUB MODO:* Revocation for non-fulfillment of conditions imposed is applicable to a gift which is called, at Rome, gift *sub modo*. The *modus* is a provision which obliges the donee to do certain acts imposed by the donor as the condition of his gift; if the donee avoids these obligations, the donor will be able to compel him, by means of a *condictio*, to retransfer the ownership of the things given. Some jurisconsults, Marcellus and Ulpian noticeably, have gone so far as to hold that the very fact of non-fulfillment of conditions imposed authorized the donor to exercise *vindicatio* (less doubtless by reason of the return of the owner than because the donor is considered in delivering the thing to alienate the ownership only so far as the conditions of the gift (*modus*) should be fulfilled). This controversy of a most delicate nature should find no place here.[4]

[1] See Colquhoun, *A Summary of the Rom. Civ. Law*, § 1065. — S.

[2] *Code*, 8, 55, 8 (Constantine and Constans).

*[3] A constitution of Theodosius II and Valentinian III extends the revocation on account of ingratitude to gifts made by ascendants to descendants. This cause for revocation was generalized by Justinian, *Code*, 8, 55, 10.

[4] Consult in respect to this, Girard, *Manuel*, p. 936 and note 2; page 447, notes 1 and 2.

SECTION II. — Gifts between Husband and Wife

838. History of Gifts between Husband and Wife: Gifts between husband and wife, gifts *during* marriage, have passed through three well-marked phases: (1) at the time of the lex Cincia, 204 B. C., and prior to this law, they were unrestricted, since the lex Cincia enumerates husband and wife among the *personae exceptae* who may make gifts *ultra modum*.[1]

839. (2) Subsequently, we find gifts between husband and wife forbidden by usage, "*moribus*," says Ulpian.[2] Fears were entertained as to the outbursts of feeling which are regretted after the honeymoon, or the besiegings of an interested tenderness.

840. (3) A senatusconsultum proposed by Antoninus Caracalla (under the reign of Severus and Caracalla), *oratio Antonini,* decided that gifts, *invalid on principle*, should be impliedly *confirmed* if the donee died *in matrimonio* without having manifested in his will the intention to revoke them.[3] This is the reverse of Art. 1096 of the Code civil which declares gifts between husband and wife *valid unless revoked* (while the Roman law declares them *invalid unless confirmed*).

[1] *Frag. Vat.* 298 (Paulus).
[2] *Dig.* 24, 1, 1 (Ulpian).
[3] *Dig.* 24, 1, 32 pr. and §§ 1, 2 (Ulpian).

CHAPTER II

PROVISIONS IN FAVOR OF MARRIAGE

SECTION I. — Dos

841. Of Dos: When the wife is married *cum manu*, all her property is absorbed in that of her husband's.[1] But, in "free" marriage, no merging of the property of husband and wife takes place; the wife preserves the administration, enjoyment, and control of her property. It is customary, in such case, that the wife bring to the husband certain property to aid him in meeting the household expenses. Property thus brought constitutes the dos. The other property of the wife is called *paraphernalia*.[2]

842. Different Kinds of Dos: The dos can be furnished either by the wife herself, or by the paterfamilias of the wife, or by a third person. The dos is called *profecticia*, if furnished by the paterfamilias, *adventicia* in all other cases.[3] The name of *dos recepticia* is applied to the dos, the restitution of which, in case of the wife dying first, was expressly stipulated for in the conditions which we will examine later.[4]

843. Modes of Constitution:[5] Dos is constituted by the transfer of property (*datio*) — by a *promise*, under the ordinary form of a stipulatio

---

[1] Cicero, *Topica*, 4, 23.†
[2] The wife preserves not only the right to dispose but also the enjoyment and administration.
[3] Ulpian, *Reg.* 6, § 3.
[4] *Ibid.* §§ 4 and 5.
[5] *Dos aut datur, aut dicitur aut promittitur. Ibid.* § 1.

(*spondes ne? spondeo*). — By *dictio dotis*, a verbal contract not well known, in which the promise does not seem to have been preceded by a question:

CHREMES. *Dos, Pamphile, est Decem talenta.* PAMPH. *Accipio.*[1]

and which can be employed only by the wife, her paterfamilias, or a debtor of the wife.[2]

844. **Powers of the Husband over the Dotal Property:** The husband, in Roman law, is *dominus dotis*. Must this expression be translated as owner? On principle, the affirmative is unquestionable: but from the end of the Republic, the powers of the husband over the dotal property admit of some restrictions which will become more perceptible under the Empire.

845. (1) There is a distinction between the *dos aestimata* given to the husband and *dos non aestimata*: the *dos aestimata* becomes the *absolute* property of the husband, who profits from its increase in value, bears the risks of its loss or deterioration, and is bound, if the marriage is dissolved, to return a sum equal to the valuation. As to *dos non aestimata*, the risks belong to the wife: that is, it is she who benefits from its increase in value, and who bears the consequences of loss or deterioration caused through accident. Lastly, the husband obtains only the fruits, and not the other products of the *dos non aestimata* (fruits which are acquired, moreover, by simple separation unless a taking be requisite). The title of *dominus dotis* is evi-

---

[1] Terent. *Andria*, act V, iv, 47.†
[2] Ulpian, *Reg.* 6, § 2.

PROVISIONS IN FAVOR OF MARRIAGE 295

dently less comprehensive when it defines the powers of the husband over the *dos non aestimata*.[1]

846. (2) Under Augustus, the powers of the husband are profoundly modified by the *lex Julia de fundo dotali*, by the terms of which the husband can no longer alienate the dotal immovables without the consent of the wife.[2]

847. (3) Under Claudius, the senatusconsultum Velleianum prohibits the wife from *intercessio*, that is, from binding herself or her property for the account of another;[3] it results from this that the wife cannot consent to the hypothecation by the husband of the 'fundus dotalis': hence this second restriction on the powers of the husband which is ordinarily attached, but wrongly, according to the most recent authorities, to the lex Julia: the husband cannot hypothecate the 'fundus dotalis' even with the consent of the wife. (This consent in effect constituted an intercessio prohibited by the SC. Velleianum.)

848. The consequence of the nullity of alienating the 'fundus dotalis' is that this 'fundus' can be vindicated against the purchaser or his assigns. By whom shall it be vindicated? By the wife or her representatives? or by the husband.

By the husband, who alone has the actions concerning dos: but upon dissolution of the marriage, the husband should *assign* this action to the wife or her heirs. Under Justinian the assignment operates *vi*

[1] There are even texts which go so far as to say that the dos belongs to the wife: *Quamvis in bonis mariti dos sit, mulieris tamen est.* Dig. 23, 3, 75 (Tryphoninus).
[2] Gaius, 2, § 63.
[3] *Dig.* 16, 1 pr. and § 1.

legis, and there is no longer any need of demanding it from the husband (who, moreover, at an early era, could not refuse it).[1]

849. Return of the Dos: *Praelegatum dotis.* In the first state of the law, the husband did not have to return the dos; but, in order to conform to a settled usage which could not be derogated without offending propriety, he always made to the wife a legacy of her dos or something equivalent. This is what was called the *praelegatum* or *relegatum dotis,* or *praelegatum pro dote.*[2]

850. *Cautio rei uxoriae:* The *praelegatum dotis* did not remedy all dangers: it especially did not provide for the cases of the dissolution of the marriage by the wife dying first, by a *repudium,* or by a divorce.

The interested parties themselves provided for their security by making agreements for restitution at the time of the marriage. The wife or a third person who gave her the dos used to stipulate for the return of the dos (cautio rei uxoriae).[3]

851. *Actio rei uxoriae:* The progress of ideas, perhaps also the increase of divorces, caused to be introduced into the law the obligation for the husband to return the dos, even in the absence of any agreement to return, and that this obligation was sanctioned by an action: the actio rei uxoriae. At what time did this take place? After the lex Aebutia, according to some; much earlier, according to others.[4]

[1] Cf. Girard, *Manuel*, p. 948.
[2] Esmein, *Mélanges*, p. 41 *et seq.*
[3] Aulus Gellius, 4, 3, 2.†
[4] Girard, *Manuel*, first opinion, p. 946 ; of the second opinion, Esmein, *Mélanges*, p. 165 *et seq.*

852. *Features of the ACTIONES REI UXORIAE and EX STIPULATU:* At any rate, at the end of the Republic the dos, when the marriage was dissolved by the death of one of the spouses or by a divorce, might be reclaimed either by the *actio ex stipulatu*, which assumed the existence of an agreement to restore, or by the *actio rei uxoriae*, which might be brought even in the absence of any agreement.

The first of these actions is an action *stricti juris*, the second an action *bonae fidei*. The first belongs to the heirs of the wife as well as to the wife herself, the second belongs only to the wife or to her paterfamilias when the dos is *profecticia*. In the *actio rei uxoriae*, which is *bonae fidei*, the husband can exercise various rights of retainer:[1] *propter res amotas* (on account of things taken away by the wife); *propter liberos* (right of retainer on account of the children whom the husband has to bring up, and which is a fixed sum for each child born from the marriage); *propter mores:* on account of the misdeeds of the wife: there was a distinction between *graviores mores* (adultery) and *leviores mores* (misdeeds of less importance).[2]

The husband held by the *actio rei uxoriae* can free himself from obligations *eiusdem generis*[3] by three annual installments (*annua, bima, trima die*);[4] lastly, the husband who is sued enjoys the *beneficium competentiae*,[5] that is, the advantage of being condemned

[1] *Retentiones.*
[2] Ulpian, *Reg.* 6, §§ 9, 14.
[3] Capital, money, *res fungibiles* (consumable things of same class), Sohm, *Institutes of Roman Law* (Ledlie's translation), § 59. — S.
[4] Ulpian, *Reg.* 6, 8.
[5] See Colquhoun, *A Summary of the Rom. Civ. Law*, § 1106.

only to the extent of his resources (*in id quod facere potest*).[1]

When, on the contrary, the husband is sued by the *actio ex stipulatu*, he is bound immediately to return in full the dos which he has received.

852. *Cont. Fusion of the two actions by Justinian:* Justinian merged the two actions into a single action to which he gives, with the name of *actio ex stipulatu*, nearly all the features of the *actio rei uxoriae* (an action *bonae fidei*), periods of time for the return [one year for movables], and *beneficium competentiae;* but this may be brought by the wife or her heirs, whatever the causes for the dissolution of the marriage.[2]

853. **Assurances for the Return of the Dos:** The return of the dos was first assured only by a *privilegium inter personales actiones*.[3] Justinian bestowed on the right to the dos, first, the benefit of an hypotheca taking effect on the date of the marriage,[4] then, by the famous *lex Assiduis*,[5] the excessive benefit of a privileged hypotheca which was superior to all others.

SECTION II. — **Donatio Propter Nuptias**

854. *Donatio propter nuptias* is an invention of the Later Empire: it first took the name of *donatio ante nuptias*, for, menaced by the prohibition of gifts between husband and wife, it could only take place before marriage. It is a gift from the husband to the wife made

[1] *Dig.* 42, 1, 20 (Modestinus).
[2] *Code*, 5, 13, 1 (Justinian).
[3] *Dig.* 42, 5, 17, § 1.
[4] *Code*, 5, 13, 1, 1b ; Girard, *Manuel*, p. 956, note 1.
[5] *Code*, 8, 17, 12 ; Girard, *Manuel*, p. 956, note 2.

by analogy and as an offset for dos. The property which composed it was, like the 'fundus dotalis,' removed from the pursuit of creditors. At the termination of the marriage it went to the wife as a sort of supplementary dos.

Justin permitted this gift to be increased, and Justinian even to be made during marriage. Then its name was changed from *donatio ante nuptias* to *donatio propter nuptias*.[1]

[1] *Inst.* 2, 7, § 3.

TITLE II

DONATIONES MORTIS CAUSA

CHAPTER I

GIFTS MORTIS CAUSA

855. **Definition:** A *gift mortis causa* is one which a person makes in anticipation of his own predecease. If this predecease does not occur, if it is the donee who dies first, the gift is null.

856. **Varieties:** Often a gift *mortis causa* is not made in a general manner with a view to the donor dying first, but with a view to an ascertained danger which threatens death. Thus Telemachus, on the point of attacking the suitors for the hand of Penelope, makes a gift of his property to Piraeus, conditioned that the latter restore it to him if he escapes the danger.[1]

857. **Suspensive and Resolutive Conditions:**[2] A gift *mortis causa* may be shown under two forms: it may be made under a suspensive condition: in this case the act of *donatio*, whatever it may be (transference of ownership, extinction or formation of an obligation), is considered never to become operative if the suspensive condition of predecease is not realized.[3]

---

[1] *Inst.* 2, 7, § 1 ; *Dig.* 39, 6, 13 (Julian).
[2] See Roby, *Rom. Priv. Law*, vol. i, p. 531.
[3] *Dig.* 39, 6, 2 (Ulpian).

DONATIONS MORTIS CAUSA

But there may also be gifts *mortis causa* under a resolutive condition in which the transference of ownership, the extinction or formation of an obligation, are produced at the very moment of the gift.[1] What happens if the gift becomes null by reason of the survival of the donor? The donee will be obliged to re-transfer the ownership, to revive the obligation extinguished, or to extinguish by an *acceptilatio* the obligation created for his benefit; and to do all this, he will be constrained by a *condictio*.

858. It is asked if the classical jurisconsults had not gone farther, and if at least some of them had not allowed of full right the vesting of ownership in the donee and the action of *vindicatio*. This question is the same as that presented as to *gifts sub modo*.[2] It will be examined in the second year course.[3]

859. **Revocability of Gifts Mortis Causa:** The characteristic difference existing between gifts *inter vivos* and gifts *mortis causa* is that gifts *mortis causa* are *essentially revocable*.[4]

860. **Resemblance to Legacies:** Gifts *mortis causa*, apart from the actual divestment which they may (sometimes but not always) entail, much resemble legacies: so Justinian states that he has assimilated legacies and gifts *mortis causa fere per omnia*. They are indeed subject to reduction by virtue of the lex Falcidia,[5] and are null if the beneficiaries are incapable

---

[1] *Dig.* 39, 6, 2 (Ulpian); *ibid.* 35, § 4 (Paulus).

[2] See § 837 *in fine, supra*.

[3] Bernard, *La deuxième année de droit romain*. See, also, Roby, *Rom. Priv. Law*, vol. i, p. 531. — S.

[4] *Dig.* 39, 6, 16 (Julian).

[5] Roby, *Rom. Priv. Law*, i, p. 352. — S.

of receiving by virtue of the leges Julia et Papia Poppae: but they noticeably differ from legacies in that their fortune is not tied to that of a will.[1]

CHAPTER II

LEGACIES AND FIDEICOMMISSA

SECTION I. — **Codicils**

861. It now remains to examine the last two varieties (the most common also) of *donationes mortis causa:* legacies and singular *fideicommissa*. These *donationes* may be made either by will or by *codicils*.

862. **Codicils**: Codicils are acts of last will destitute of form by which a testator bequeaths to those whom he wishes to favor either legacies or fideicommissa. These bequests appeared at the beginning of the empire, and as Augustus himself carried out the bequests with which he was charged by codicil, these *donationes* obtained favor and came into vogue.[2]

863. *Codicilli confirmati and non confirmati:* Two kinds of codicils were distinguished: codicilli confirmati and codicilli non confirmati. These are called *codicilli confirmati* which are validated by a subse-

---

[1] *Code*, 6, 50, 5 (Alexander Severus); *Dig.* 39, 6, 35 pr. — We mention by way of notice the great controversy on this subject, which would be out of place here: when the gift is made on the *suspensive* condition of the predecease of the donor, what is at the time of this death the nature of the right of the donee over the object of the gift, and by what action will it be enforced? There are on the question many theories, of Pellat., Glasson, Appleton, etc.

[2] *Inst.* 2, 25 pr.

quent will, or even by a clause inserted in an earlier will and by which the testator declares to be validated in advance all codicils which he shall subsequently make. This clause bears the name of *codicillary clause*.[1]

864. *Codicilli confirmati* can contain every kind of bequests: legacies or fideicommissa.

Codicilli non confirmati are those which have been made by a person dying intestate: they can contain only fideicommissa, for the validity of legacies strictly requires the existence and validity of a will.[2]

Section II. — Legacies

865. **What is a Legacy**: A legacy is styled by Justinian as a *donatio quaedam a defuncto relicta*, as gift left by a deceased person. This *donatio* may have for its object an aliquot share of the hereditas or a particular benefit.

866. **Legatum Partiarium**: The legacy of a *pars quota* of the hereditas is called a legatum partiarium.[3] It is necessary to guard against confusing it with the institution of an heir, for the same aliquot share. In French law, to appoint a person heir for a half or a quarter of the succession, or to bequeath him a half or a quarter of the succession is absolutely the same thing: in Roman law the situations of the heir for a part and the *legatarius partiarius* are separated by a veritable abyss. The heir for a part is a continuator of the persona and chargeable with the part of the debts going

---

[1] *Dig.* 29, 7, 2, § 2 (Julian); *ibid.* 14 (Scaevola); *si quos codicillos reliquero valere volo; Dig.* 40, 5, 56 (Marcellus).

[2] Paulus, *Sent.* 4, 1, § 10; Gaius, 2, § 273.

[3] See Roby, *Rom. Priv. Law*, vol. i, pp. 293, 325; Colquhoun, *A Summary of the Rom. Civ. Law*, § 1164. — S.

with his part of the gain: the legatarius partiarius is not a continuator of the *persona*, and is not liable in regard to creditors of the hereditas who have only to do with the heirs.[1]

867. But as "*bona non intelliguntur nisi deducto aere alieno*" the property is estimated only by making a deduction of the debts, and the heir liable for a *legatum partiarium* took security when turning over the legacy: to the assignment by means of which the delivery operated, he added a *stipulatio* in which the *legatarius partiarius* bound himself to reimburse to him, to the extent of a fraction corresponding to the aliquot share with which he was favored, the sum which he (the heir) would be obliged to pay to the creditors of the hereditas. This contract was called *stipulatio partis et pro parte*.[2]

868. **Forms of Legacies:** Legacies may be made under four forms: *per vindicationem, per damnationem, sinendi modo*, and *per praeceptionem*.[3]

869. (1) *A legacy per vindicationem* is thus framed: "*Titio do lego.*" It carries with it, as soon as the hereditas is accepted, direct transmission of ownership to the legatee who has, in order to reclaim the object of his legacy, the action of *vindicatio;* hence the name of legacy *per vindicationem*.[4]

870. (2) The form of *the legacy per damnationem* is: "*Heres meus, damnas esto dare*, let my heir be condemned to give to . . ." This legacy creates for the benefit of the legatee against the heir simply an ob-

---
[1] Example in the *Laudatio funebris Murdiae*, Girard, *Textes*, p. 781; Ulpian, *Reg.* 25, § 15; Girard, *Manuel*, pp. 922, 923.
[2] Ulpian, *Reg.* 25, § 15; Girard, *Manuel*, p. 923.
[3] Ulpian, *Reg.* 24, § 2.   [4] Gaius, 2, § 193.

ligatory right [1] which was sanctioned, in the time of the *legis actiones*, by *manus injectio*, and which after the disappearance of the *legis actiones* has for its sanction a condictio which carries with it the condemnation of the heir *in duplum* in case of unjustifiable resistance (*quae crescit in duplum adversus infitiantem*).[2]

871. (3) *The legacy sinendi modo* has for its form: "*Heres meus damnas esto sinere Titium sumere . . .*" The heir by this expression is condemned to allow the legatee to take the thing bequeathed. This legacy is productive of an obligatory right [3] against the heir like the preceding one.[4]

872. (4) *The legacy per praeceptionem*, that is, a preferred legacy: "this legacy was given to one of the heirs and authorized him to take first, before any division, the property bequeathed. There has been a controversy over the action which was produced, but the jurisconsults had finished by assimilating this to the legacy *per vindicationem* and by giving to the favored heir the *vindicatio*." [5]

873. **Effect of Legacies:** By the legacy *per vindicationem* the testator can dispose of only his own property, for, in order to transmit ownership, it is necessary to be an owner. Under the form *per damnationem* the testator can bequeath either an object belonging to him, or an object belonging to the heir, or even an object belonging to a third person, which the heir is obliged to procure in order to carry out the

---

[1] That is, an action *in personam* is given. See Colquhoun, *A Summary of the Rom. Civ. Law*, § 1152. — S.
[2] Gaius, 2, § 201.   [3] See § 870, note 1. — S.
[4] Gaius, 2, § 202.   [5] Gaius, 2, §§ 216–222.

legacy; if he cannot procure it, he should pay the value of it.

This legacy is therefore more comprehensive than the rest, and so the right which it confers is called "*optimum jus legatorum.*"[1]

As the heir can "let him (the legatee) take" only what belongs to him or to the hereditas, the legacy *sinendi modo* cannot have for its object something belonging to a third person.[2]

874. Senatusconsultum Neronianum: It was thus down to the reign of Nero: at this time a senatusconsultum (the SC. Neronianum) rendered this old division of no importance by declaring that all legacies would be considered to be made "*optimo jure,*" and that such a legacy as would not be valid as a legacy *per vindicationem* or *sinendi modo* should be valid as a legacy *per damnationem.*[3]

875. Legacy of Another's Property: In view of these conditions the legacy of another's property became possible under all forms: but the Romans allowed a distinction: did the testator bequeath another's property by mistake, believing it to be his? The legacy is void. Did he knowingly bequeath an object which he knew belonged to another? The legacy is valid.[4]

SECTION III. — **Singular Fideicommissa**

876. A bequest by will may take not only the form of a legacy, but also that of a singular fideicommissum.

[1] Gaius, 2, §§ 196–202.   [2] Gaius, 2, § 210.
[3] Gaius, 2, § 197; Ulpian, *Reg.* 24, § 11.
[4] *Inst.* 2, 20, § 4. Justinian attributes the distinction to Antoninus Pius.

LEGACIES AND FIDEICOMMISSA

The *fideicommissum particulare* differs from a *legatum*: (1) in that it can be contained in a *codicillus nonconfirmatus;* (2) in that it can be imposed on a legatee, while *a legatorio legari non potest;* (3) in that it is expressed in precatory and not in imperative terms; (4) in that originally it was not obligatory (but this difference is effaced from the reign of Augustus).[1]

877. System of Legacies and Fideicommissa under Justinian: Justinian was not content with unifying all legacies, which was, after all, a matter already completed; he assimilated also legacies and fideicommissa, and gave to every beneficiary of a legacy or a fideicommissum three actions: (1) a *vindicatio* when it is possible, for the nature of a legacy does not always so make it; (2) an action *in personam* against each heir; (3) an *actio hypothecaria:* by the terms of Justinian's constitution the legatee has a general *hypotheca* on all the immovables of the hereditas; but his *actio hypothecaria* can be exercised against each heir only to the extent of the portion for which he is liable on an action *in personam*.[2]

SECTION IV.—**Restriction of the Right to make Legacies. — The lex Falcidia**

878. Ancient Law: The right to make legacies was, on principle, unlimited. Nothing prevented the testator from consuming by legacies his entire hereditas. What was the result of this? The heir used to refuse a succession from which he had no gain to expect.[3]

879. Restrictive Laws: Three times the legis-

---

[1] See *supra*, §§ 813, 814.
[2] *Code*, 6, 43, 1, § 1. [3] Gaius, 2, § 224.

lator tried to remedy this disadvantage: the way was found only on the third. (1) The *lex Furia testamentaria* (date uncertain, but prior to 169 B. C.) prohibited the making of a legacy for more than 1000 *asses*, — a poor measure; several legacies of 1000 *asses* could reduce the rights of the heir to *nil*.[1]

(2) The *lex Voconia* (169 B. C.) prohibited the making of a legacy for more than the instituted heir would take: a large number of small legacies resulted, however, in rendering the right of the heir almost illusory.[2]

(3) Lastly the *lex Falcidia*, a plebiscitum of 40 B. C., prohibited testators from bequeathing to the detriment of the heir more than three fourths of the hereditas. We should say to-day that it reserved one fourth for the instituted heir. This fourth was called the Falcidian fourth, or by abbreviation "the Falcidian."[3]

880. Calculation of the Quarta Falcidia: In order to calculate the Falcidian fourth, first everything composing the estate is estimated according to their value at the time of the decease: in other words, the gross assets at the time of the decease are ascertained. From the gross assets the amount of the debts and the manumissions are deducted, and thus the net assets are obtained. The heir keeps a fourth of the net assets, and distributes the remaining three fourths to the legatees *pro rata* to their legacies, making each of them suffer a proportional reduction.[4]

881. Observation: We have already encountered in studying successions: (1) the *quarta legitima*

[1] Gaius 2, § 225 ; Ulpian, *Reg.* 1, § 2.
[2] Gaius, 2, § 226.
[3] Gaius, 2, § 227 ; *Dig.* 35, 2, 1 pr. (Paulus) ; *Inst.* 2, 22, § 2.
[4] *Inst.* 2, 22, § 2.

LEGACIES AND FIDEICOMMISSA 309

reserved to the disinherited *suus heres* against the instituted heir; (2) the *quarta Pegasiana* reserved to the heres fiduciarius against the *fideicommissarius*. We now encounter the *quarta Falcidia*, the *first one created*. The Roman writers made the name of "the Falcidian" a general term which they use at times to designate a *reserve* which may be the Pegasian reserve or even the statutory (reserve). It is well to be acquainted with this use in order not to become embarrassed in the interpretation of certain texts.[1]

SECTION V. — **Effects of Legacies and Fideicommissa**

882. **Dies Cedit and Dies Venit:** Two moments are to be considered in the acquisition of legacies and fideicommissa: when the right is opened (*dies cedit*), when it is definitely acquired (*dies venit*).

The expression *dies cedit*, which is not peculiar to the subject of legacies, signifies that the contingent right to the legacy is fixed for the benefit of the legatee, that its maturity *is on the way*. The expression *dies venit* means that maturity has arrived and that the legacy is demandable; *cedere diem significat incipere deberi pecuniam; venire diem significat eum diem venisse cum jam peti possit.*[2]

883. **Dies Cedens:** *Dies cedens* occurs: (1) for unconditional legacies or (legacies) after a certain time, at the day of the decease.[3]

884. The lex Papia Poppea had postponed the time

[1] See § 790, note 1, *supra*.
[2] *Dig.* 50, 16, 213 (Ulpian).
[3] Ulpian, *Reg.* 24, § 31.

of *dies cedens* to the opening of the will (*apertura tabularum*). Justinian came back to the original law.[1]

885. (2) For conditional legacies, upon the fulfillment of the condition.[2]

886. The effects of *dies cedens* are: (1) To render the right of the legatee transmissible to his heirs if he happened to die before the *aditio hereditatis* : *the right is acquired.*[3]

(2) If the legatee is *alieni juris*, of fixing the right to the legacy on the person who exercises the power at this time, so a legacy made to a slave benefits his master at the time of the *dies cedens*, — but not his master at the time of the *dies veniens* or even himself if he has been freed between the *dies cedens* and the *dies veniens.*[4]

(3) Of determining the extent of the legacy if the thing bequeathed is susceptible of being increased or diminished, like a herd or a peculium.[5]

887. By way of exception *dies cedens* occurs only on the *aditio hereditatis*. (1) When the legacy is made to the testator's own slave: (the application of the ordinary rules of *dies cedens* would here go against the legatee, for he becomes free and capable of receiving the legacy only at the time of the *aditio*);[6] (2) in legacies of *usufructus, usus,* and *habitatio.*[7]

888. **Dies Veniens:**[8] *Dies veniens* takes place:

[1] Ulpian, *Reg.* 24, § 31 ; *Code,* 6, 51, 1, § 1 (Justinian).
[2] *Ibid.*
[3] Ulpian, *Reg.* 24, § 30.
[4] *Dig.* 36, 2, 5, § 7 (Ulpian).
[5] *Inst.* 2, 20, § 20.
[6] *Dig.* 36, 2, 7, § 6 and fr. 8 (Ulpian).
[7] *Frag. Vat.* 60 (Ulpian).
[8] See on *dies veniens,* Colquhoun, *opus cit.* § 1179. — S.

(1) for an unconditional [1] legacy at the time of the *aditio hereditatis.*

(2) for a conditional legacy, on the realization of the condition *if it is produced subsequently to the aditio hereditatis.*

(3) for a legacy after a certain time, when the time has arrived (if, of course, it is subsequent to the *aditio*).

889. It is seen that *dies veniens* may occur, in certain cases, *after* the aditio hereditatis, but *never* before, which is easily explained, since until then the existence of the will is in question, and with the existence of the will, the existence of legacies.[2]

889. *Cont.*—*Cautio Muciana:* When the legacy is made under a *conditio potestiva negativa* [3] on the part of the legatee (*si in Capitolium non ascenderit*), a condition the fulfillment of which will be certain only at his death, the legacy is immediately freed, but the legatee is obliged to furnish security to restitute it, if he contravenes the condition imposed upon him. This security is called Cautio Muciana from the name of one of the two Mucius Scaevola (Quintus or Publius?) who invented it.

890. **Regula Catoniana:** The regula Catoniana invented by Cato the Censor or by his son is thus expressed: *quod si testamenti facti tempore decessisset testator inutile foret id legatum quandocunque decesserit non valere.*[4] It does not aim at the avoidance of legacies: it stands in the way of a person who is capable, of a

[1] *Pure et sine die relictum.* — S.
[2] *Dig.* 31, 32 pr. (Modestinus); *ibid.* 45, § 1 (Pomponius).
[3] Colquhoun, *opus cit.* §§ 1265, 1266. — S.
[4] *Dig.* 34, 7, 1 (Celsus).

legacy in due form, of a lawful object, and an essential impossibility of carrying out a legacy, — impossibility which will exist no longer at the time of the decease, — and this impossibility it prolongs, so to speak, until the decease.

I bequeath to Primus the slave Eros, who belongs to him: certainly, if I should die at the same instant, my gift would be but a bad jest; but if Eros, at the time of my decease, no longer belongs to the legatee, my legacy will become quite serious and possible of execution. Will it be valid? No.

The regula Catoniana stands in the way.[1] Why? The Roman jurisconsults have not told us. Should not they have seen something derisive in a bequest which is not performable and which will become so only by reason of events which cannot be provided for at the time the will is made?[2]

891. The regula Catoniana did not apply to conditional legacies. Indeed, if the testator should die at the time when he makes the bequest, the *dies cedens* would not immediately occur; it would be postponed to the time of the realization of the condition, and until then it is not to be said that the execution of the legacy will become possible.

Thus: I bequeath to Primus the slave Eros, who belongs to him: this is of no effect. — I bequeath to Primus the slave Eros, who belongs to him, *on condition that he shall not belong any longer to him after my decease:* will the expression of this condition which would be taken to be understood in the first bequest render the legacy valid? Is there not something in

---

[1] *Inst.* 2, 20, § 10.
[2] *An cavillamur?* says Celsus, in *Dig.* 34, 7, 1.

to justify the epithet "arbitrary" which has been that applied to the regula Catoniana? [1]

892. Lapsed Legacies: What becomes of legacies which, for any reason, cannot be obtained or are not accepted by the legatee? They fall back into the mass of the hereditas, and the heir profits by their lapse or *repudiatio*.[2]

893. Plurality of Legatees: But this rule is defeated when there are, as to the same legacy, *several legatees*. The disposal of the lapsed shares, in the different cases which are reported in regard to this class of principles, has been subjected to successive legislation.

894. First Period — jus adcrescendi: The right of accretion [3] (*jus adcrescendi*) is the right belonging to legatees who are given the same property by the testator which they are obliged to share by reason of their conjunction, of keeping the share of those among them who happen not to take.

895. The 'jus adcrescendi' does not arise as to legacies productive of obligatory rights (legacies *per damnationem* or *sinendi modo*), for several persons jointly given the same legacy *per damnationem* never have

---

[1] Moreover the texts do not show very fixed decisions: "I bequeath you a slave who belongs to you at the time of the making of the will: that amounts to nothing (*Inst.* 2, 20, § 10) even though you should have sold the slave on the day the succession vests; I bequeath you a piece of land (fundus) which belonged to you; you have sold the land at the time of the vesting of the succession: the legacy is good (*Dig.* 34, 7, 1)."

[2] Colquhoun, *A Summary of the Rom. Civ. Law*, § 1178.

[3] Or "*right of survivorship*," Colquhoun, *A Summary of the Civ. Rom. Law*, § 1177. — S.

any right except to their own share (*damnatio partes facit*).[1]

896. It is in the domain of legacies which transfer ownership that we encounter the 'jus adcrescendi,' the applications of which vary according as the legacy is made *conjunctim* (without designation of shares), or *disjunctim* (with designation of shares).

897. (*a*) A legacy is made *conjunctim*, that is to say, there the same thing is given to two or more persons, either by a single bequest: "I bequeath the fundus Cornelianus to Primus and Secundus" (*conjunctio re et verbis*), or by distinct bequests: "I bequeath to Primus the fundus Cornelianus." "I bequeath to Secundus the fundus Cornelianus" (*conjunctio re tantum*): in case one of the legatees does not take, *each of them having been named for the whole*, the share of the one not taking will be obtained by the rest.[2]

898. (*b*) A legacy is made *disjunctim*: that is to say, the same thing is bequeathed to two or more persons with their shares designated, either by separate bequests: "I bequeath to Primus the *half* of the fundus Cornelianus" — "I bequeath to Secundus the other half of the fundus Cornelianus," — or by a single bequest: "I bequeath to Primus and Secundus the fundus Cornelianus each *a half*" (*conjunctio verbis tantum*): in this case if there is a failure of one of the legatees to take, the 'jus adcrescendi' will not arise for the benefit of the other or others, because each legatee was never named except for his own share.[3]

---

[1] Gaius, 2, § 205.   [2] *Ibid.* § 199.
[3] This doctrine results *a contrario* from the texts establishing the right of accretion (survivorship) in case of *conjunctio*.

899. Second Period: Jus caduca vindicandi: The leges Julia and Papia Poppea substituted for the doctrine of accretion that of the 'jus caduca vindicandi.' The lapsed shares, — and they become much more numerous by reason of the incapacities created by the new leges, — accrue no longer to the co-legatees jointly, but to the co-legatees *patres conjuncti re et verbis, re tantum,* and even *conjuncti verbis tantum* (in reality *disjuncti*, but connected by putting together of their names in a single bequest).[1]

900. **Third Period: Reëstablishment of the jus adcrescendi:** Justinian abolished the last vestiges of the *leges caduciariae* and reëstablished the old law of accretion, but, by an inexplicable provision, — at all events criticised by all the commentators, — the existence of which is called into question by the most recent authorities, he would have allowed the 'jus adcrescendi' not only for *conjuncti* either *re et verbis*, or *re tantum*, but even *conjuncti verbis tantum*. It is possible that the texts in which this solution is indicated, texts which before their alteration necessarily referred to the 'jus caduca vindicandi,' were inadvertently inserted in the Digest.[2]

[1] Ulpian, *Reg.* 17, 1; *ibid.* 18, 1; *Dig.* 50, 16, 142 (Paulus); Gaius, 2, § 206. — The provisions of the *leges caducariae* do not affect ascendants and descendants to the third degree: they have the *jus antiquum*.

[2] *Code*, 6, 51, 1.

INDEX

The references are to sections, not to pages.

Abandonment, 674.
Accarias, 90.
Acceptilatio, 374, 459, 827, 857.
Accessio, 666, 671, 672.
Accretion, right of, 753, 754, 894–898, 900.
Acquisition, see Ownership, Possession, Usucapio.
    lege, 663.
Actio, 384, 464.
    ad exhibendum, 626, 671, 672.
        supplendum, 790.
    arbitraria, 524, 672, 730.
    bonae fidei, 529, 534, 852.
    contraria tutelae, 386.
    de inofficioso testamento, see Querela inofficiosi testamenti.
    peculio, 314.
    tigno juncto, 672.
    directa, 520, 521.
        tutelae, 386.
    ficticia, 518, 519, 621, 823.
    hypothecaria, 744, 877.
    in factum, 518, 520.
    jus, 518.
    judicati, 560.
    legis, see Legis actio.
    negatoria, 728, 729, 730.
    publica, 385, 658.
    Publiciana, 620–623, 639.
    quasi Serviana, 744, 745.
    rei uxoriae, 851, 852.
    rescissoria, 625.
    Serviana, 743.
    stricti juris, 529, 534, 852.
    subsidiaria, 388, 423.
    utilis Aquiliae, 521.
Actions, classification of, 543–548.
    in personam, 544.
        rem, 544.

Actions, limitation of, 535–542.
    mixtae, 545.
    perpetuae, 537.
    poenales, 385, 545.
    prosecutoriae, 545.
    temporales, 537.
Actor, 504.
Actus, 370.
Aditio hereditatis, 372, 777, 804–810.
Adjudicatio, 507, 632–634, 695.
Adjunctio, 668.
Adoption, 292–323.
Affinitas, 256, 266.
Africanus, 81.
Agnates and agnation, 209, 211, 216, 264, 265, 360, 793.
Agrarian laws, 56.
Album of the praetor, 48, 478, 503.
Alluvio, 666.
Anastasius, 333.
Antoninus Pius, 303.
Apertura tabularum, 884.
Arbiter, 478.
Arbitrium liti aestumandae, 607, 615, 616.
Arrogatio, 299–314.
Ascendants, inheritance by, see Agnates, Succession.
Assembly of the plebs, see Concilium plebis.
Auctoritas, 367, 369, 377, 393, 418.
Augustus, 68, 69, 77, 309, 755, 814, 862.

Basil, 101.
Basilica, 101.
Beneficium inventarii, 807, 808.
Bona adventicia, 338, 350.
    fides, 649, 652, 658, 821.
Bonitary ownership, 599–602, 639.

318   INDEX

Bonorum collatio, 796.
    distractio, 563.
    emptor, 561.
    possessio, 372, 519, 794, 795, 809, 823.
    publicatio, 561, 800.
    separatio, see Separatio bonorum
    venditio, see Venditio bonorum.
Byzantine law, 101, 336, 351.
    nobility, 87.

Caduca, 663, 755, 899.
Capitis, deminutio, 279–281, 313, 331, 341–354, 381, 382, 715, 721, 780.
Capito, 79.
Caput, 101–105.
Caracalla, 182, 183.
Causae probatio, 165.
Celsus, 821.
Censor, 317.
Census, 17, 144, 342.
Centumviri, 482, 483, 502, 789.
Centuriae, 18–20.
Cessio bonorum, 827.
    in jure, 318, 331, 631, 694.
Cicero, 65, 213, 248, 295, 485, 518.
Citations, law of, 89.
Citizenship, extension of, 182, 183.
Civitas, 176–190.
Clergy, 335.
Clientes, 8, 9.
Codex accepti et expensi, 448.
    Gregorianus et Hermogenianus, 88.
    Justinianus, 94.
    Theodosianus, 88.
Codicillary clause, 863.
Codicils, 861–864.
Coëmptio, 245, 249.
Cognates and cognation, 210, 211, 264, 794.
Cognitor, 553.
Collaterals, inheritance by, see Cognates, Succession.
Collegia, 103.
Coloni, 137–139, 175.
Colonies, 190, 199, 204.
Comitia Centuriata, 17–21, 54, 59.

Comitia Curiata, 12–15, 17, 301, 302, 761.
    Tributa, 32, 33, 59.
Comitiatus maximus, 33.
    minor, 33.
Commixtio, 669.
Concilium plebis, 29, 30, 32, 33, 59.
Condemnatio, 506, 523, 529, 533, 566.
Condictio, 498–500.
Confarreatio, 244.
Confusio, 670.
Connubium, 256, 260.
Consensual contracts, 462.
Consensus, 258, 406, 418, 445.
Constantine, 87, 375, 423.
Constitutions, imperial, 74–76.
Consuls, 22, 44, 45, 468.
Contracts, essential features of, 445.
    made consensu, 462.
    literis, 448, 451, 458.
    re, 454.
    verbis, 449, 452, 459.
Contubernium, 261.
Conventio in manum, see Manus.
Conveyance per aes et libram, see Mancipatio.
Corporations, 103.
Corpus juris civilis, 93–99, 100.
Coruncanius, 65.
Courts, 464–483.
    representation in, 551–554.
Cretio, 805, 806.
Crimen, 423, 658; see Quaestiones perpetuae.
Cuq, 8, 15, 500.
Curatela, 398–423.
Curators, see Curatela.
Curiae, 3, 5, 13, 217, 329.

Decemvirs, 35–37.
Decisions, the fifty, 99.
Decreta, 76.
Decuriae, 3.
Dedititii, 156, 773.
Delict, Roman idea of, 441.
Derelictio, 674.

INDEX

Descendants, inheritance by, see Agnates, Cognates, Succession.
Detentio, 574.
Dictatorship, 23.
Dies cedit, 882–887.
    fasti, 485.
    nefasti, 536.
    venit, 888, 889.
Diffareatio, 282.
Digest or Pandects, 95–97.
Diocletian, 85.
Disinherison, 785–790.
Distractio bonorum, see Bonorum distractio.
Divorce, 282–288.
Dominium, 6.
Donationes, 824, 825.
    ante nuptias, 854.
    between husband and wife, 838–840.
    causa mortis, 855–900.
    in favor of marriage, 841–853.
    insinuatio of, 834, 835.
    inter vivos, 462, 826–854.
    propter nuptias, 854.
Dos, 841–853.
Duplicatio, 512.

Edict, of Caracalla, 182, 183.
Edicts, imperial, 76.
    of magistrates, 64.
    praetorian, 48, 83.
Edictum novum, 83.
    perpetuum, 48, 83.
    repentinum, 48.
    tralatitium, 83.
Edilecurule, 45, 50, 472.
Emancipati, succession of, 339, 788, 794, 796.
Emancipatio, 331–335, 337, 361; see Mancipatio, Manumissio.
Emperor, position of, 68, 69.
Emphyteusis, 737, 738.
Emphyteuta, 462.
Emptor bonorum, see Bonorum emptor.
Epistolae, 76.
Equites, 19, 20, 57.
Ergastulum, 560.

Esmein, 657.
Exceptio, 510, 511.
    justi dominii, 512, 622.
    longi temporis, 517.
    pacti conventi, 511.
    rei in judicium deductae, 513, 526, 542, 553.
    venditae et traditae, 623.
Excusationes, 391.
Execution, 558, 561, 566; see Manus injectio.
Exheredatio, see Disinherison.
Existimatio, 341, 351.
Expensilatio, 448, 456.
Expiratio judicii, see actions, limitation of.
Extraordinary procedure, 564–566.

Factio testamenti, see Testamenti factio.
Falcidian portion, 880.
Familiae emptor, 762, 763.
Family, 4, 6, 206–423.
Fideicommissa, 471.
    hereditatis, 760, 813–818.
    singular, 876, 877.
Fides, see Bona fides.
Fiducia, 332, 358, 361, 740.
Fifty decisions, the, 99.
Fiscus, 69, 660, 755.
Flamines diales, 244.
Flavius, 485.
Foreigners, status of, see Peregrini.
Formula arbitraria, 610.
Formulae, 65, 504, 506–521.
Formulary system, 503–563.
Freedmen, status of, 140–175.
French law, 277, 379, 406, 445, 747, 750, 760.
Fructus, or fruits, 617–619, 710–714, 718, 719, 821.
Fundus, 429.
Furiosus, 400–404, 772.

Gaius, 81, 83, 500.
Gens, its early organization, 3, 4, 17.

320 INDEX

Gens, defined, 3, 212-218.
Gentiles, 212, 213, 218, 793.
Gifts, see Donationes.
Girard, 14, 91, 183, 497, 505, 553, 590.
Gregorianus, 88.
Guardianship, see Tutela.

Habitatio, 724, 725.
Heirs, or heredes, 748, 760, 768, 819, 823; see Fideicommissa.
    defined 799-805.
    extranei, 803.
    institution of, 748-760, 768, 774-777.
    necessarii, 800, 801.
    postumi, 786.
    praetorian, 809, 822.
    substitution of, 756-760.
    sui, 258, 570, 785-790, 793, 802.
Hereditatis aditio, see Aditio hereditatis.
    petitio, 819, 820.
Hereditatum vicesima, 182.
Hermogenianus, 88.
Honores, 50, 161.
Husband and wife, see Donationes, Dos, Marriage, Possessio.
Hypotheca, 700, 739-746, 853.

Ihering, 571, 588, 590.
Incapacities of fact, 106.
    law, 106.
Incensus, 128.
Incertae personae, 774.
Infamia, 352.
Ingenui, 109.
Inheritance, its nature, 747, 748.
In jure and in judicio, see Jus and judicium.
In jure cessio, see Cessio in jure.
In jus vocatio, see Vocatio in jus.
Insinuation, 834, 835.
Institutes of Gaius, 81.
    Justinian, 98.
    Theophilus, 98.
Institution of heirs, 748-760, 768, 774-777.

Intentio, 506, 508, 509, 518, 529-534.
Intercessio, 847, 848.
Interdicta, 548.
    as to servitudes, 731-734.
    causa retinendae et recuperandae possessionis, 592, 594.
    de precario, 595.
    quem fundum, 612.
    quorum bonorum, 822.
    Salvianum, 743.
    unde vi, 596.
    uti possidetis, 592, 596.
    utrubi, 592.
Interrex, 10.
Intestabilis, 353; see Wills.
Intestate succession, see Succession.
Inventory, see Beneficium inventarii.
Italy, 52.
Iteratio, 164.

Javolenus, 81.
Judex, in the formulary system, 503, 518, 522-534, 540, 541; see Judices.
Judices, 154, 475-481, 566, 695.
    pedanei, 565.
    privati, 466.
Judicis postulatio, 488, 489.
Julian law, see Lex Julia.
Julianus, 81, 83.
Jura condendi permissio, 77.
Jurisconsults, 64-67, 77-82, 88, 91, 703.
    their schools, 79.
Jus abutendi, 567.
    accrescendi, 753, 754, 894-898, 900.
    Aelianum, 66.
    aureorum annulorum, 161.
    caduca vindicandi, 755, 899.
    civile, 50, 444, 627.
    commercii, 185, 193.
    connubii, 185, 193.
    deliberandi, 806-808.
    distrahendi, 746.
    edicere, 47, 50, 74.

Jus Flavianum, 485.
　fruendi, 567, 572.
　gentium, 193.
　honorarium, 50, 339, 444, 644.
　honorum, 161, 186, 193.
　in re, 433.
　　aliena, 433.
　　rem, in personam, 431-438.
　Italicum, 205.
　liberorum, 396.
　Papirianum, 13.
　possidendi, 746.
　postliminii, 121, 124, 344.
　Quiritium, 15.
　respondendi, 77.
　suffragii, 185, 193, 198.
　utendi, 567, 572.
Jus and judicium, 466, 467, 503, 564.
Jussus judicis, 524.
Justa causa, 636, 637.
Justae nuptiae, 117, 177, 235-291.
Justin, 255, 263, 284, 854.
Justinian, his legislation, 92, 96, 169, 279, 284, 334, 335, 338, 392, 661, 807, 818, 828, 852, 854, 860, 877, 899.
Justus titulus, 649, 651, 653, 658.

Labeo, 79, 80.
Latini Juniani, 148, 149, 156, 160, 163, 197, 773.
Latinitas, 176.
Latins, 148, 190, 195-205.
Law of citations, 89-91.
Legacy, 493, 663, 860, 865-875, 877-881, 882-900.
　lapsed, 892.
　per damnationem, 870.
　　praeceptionem, 872.
　per vindicationem, 869, 873.
　Regula Catoniana, 890, 891.
　restrictions on, 878-881.
　sinendi modo, 871.
Leges, 59-62, 70.
　caducariae, 291.
　datae, 60.
　judiciariae, 57, 477.
　regiae, 13.

Leges rogatae, 60.
　Valeriae, 54.
Legis actiones, 371, 484-502, 505, 551, 604, 819.
Legitimation, 324, 329.
Leo the Philosopher, 101.
Letting and hiring, 462.
Lex, see Leges.
　Aebutia, 386, 410, 501.
　Aelia Sentia, 153-157.
　Aquilia, 61.
　Assiduis, 853.
　Atilia, 364.
　Atinia, 656.
　Aurelia, 477.
　Calpurnia, 55.
　Cincia, 61, 829-833, 838.
　Cornelia, 123, 124, 344.
　Falcidia, 61, 860, 878-881.
　Fufia Caninia, 150-152.
　Furia de sponsu, 491.
　　testamentaria, 879.
　Hortensia, 42, 43.
　Julia de adulteriis, 288.
　　civitate, 203.
　　fundo dotale, 846.
　　maritandis, 259, 289.
　　et Papia Poppaea, 70, 291, 663, 755, 860, 884.
　　Plautia, 656.
　　Titia, 365.
　Junia Norbana, 148, 149.
　Licinia, 45.
　Marcia, 493.
　Plaetoria, 409.
　Poetelia Papiria, 51, 431, 561.
　Publilia, 42, 491.
　regia, 75.
　Sempronia, 477.
　Servilia, 477.
　Thoria, 56.
　Valeria Horatia, 31, 42.
　Vallia, 496.
　Velleia, 786.
　Voconia, 774, 879.
Libellus conventionis, 566.
　repudii, 288.
Libertus, 109, 158-175.
Libripens, 25, 245, 429, 450, 629.

INDEX

Literal contracts, 448, 451.
Litiscontestatio, 525-528.
Locatio et conductio, 462.

Magistrates, 468-475, 555-557.
Mancipatio, 175, 245, 317, 373, 429, 629, 692, 693, 707, 762, 827.
Mancipia, 108, 136, 137; see Slavery.
Mancipium, 429.
Mandata, 76.
Manumissio, 140-157, 218.
Manus, 6, 241, 243, 248, 235, 254, 269-275, 285.
    injectio, 436, 490-497, 559, 560, 607.
Marcus Aurelius, 285, 365, 408, 415, 814.
Marriage, 41, 235-291.
Modestinus, 82, 415.
Mortgage, see Hypotheca.
Municipium, 204.

Natalium restitutio, 162.
Natural Law, 628.
Negotiorum gestio, 368.
Neratius, 81.
Nero, 69.
Nerva, 80.
Nexum, 24, 25, 51, 133, 436, 447, 493.
Niebuhr, 81, 217.
Nobility, Byzantine, 87.
Non-user, 702-704, 721.
Novels (novellae constitutiones), 100.
Noxae datio, 221, 224, 226.
Nuptiae justae, 117, 177, 235-291.

Obligations, 435, 439-463.
    character of, 439.
    ex contractu, 441, 445-463.
    delicto, 441-444.
Obsequium, 171.
Occupatio, 665.
Oratio principis, 73.
Ordo judiciorum, 466, 503.
Ortolan, 183.
Ownership, 432-438.

Ownership, attributes and evolution of, 567-570.
    bonitary, 599-603, 639.
    dismemberments of, 675-746.
    extinction of, 673, 674.
    how sanctioned, 603-626.
    kinds of, 597-662.
    modes of acquiring, 627-674.
    quiritary, 597, 598, 602.

Pactum, donationis, 828.
Papinian, 82, 812.
Pars Falcidia, 880.
    legitimia, 790.
Pegasiana, 817, 880.
Partnership, 462.
Paterfamilias, 6, 7, 206; see Marriage, Patria potestas, Wills.
Patientia, 697, 700.
Patres, 3, 6.
Patria potestas, 6, 206, 219-234, 258, 276, 285, 307, 315-320, 323, 330, 340.
    in the early law, 221.
    melioration of, 222, 223.
Patricii, 3-5, 17, 87.
    struggle between patricians and plebeians, 39-45.
Patronus, 9, 360.
Paulus, 82, 286.
Peculium, 115, 227, 232.
    adventitium, 230.
    castrense, 228, 229, 338.
    profectitium, 231, 338.
Pegasus, 80.
Peregrini, 157, 176, 178, 183, 191-194, 279, 479, 699, 770.
Permissio jura condendi, 77.
Persona, legal idea of, 102-105.
Personae incertae, 774.
Personality, its elements, 105.
Personal servitudes, see Servitudes.
Petitio, plus, see Plus petitio.

INDEX 323

Pignoris capio, 497.
Pignus or pledge, 741.
Plebiscita, 30, 31, 42, 43, 59, 61, 62, 70.
Plebs, 16, 35.
    struggle between patricians and plebeians, 39–45.
Plus petitio, 531, 532, 533, 566.
Poena, 130, 188, 384.
Pomponius, 13, 77, 81.
Pontifices, 65, 485.
Populus Romanus, 33, 54.
Populi fundi, 194.
Possessio ad interdicta, 575.
    usucapionem, 576.
    bonae fidei, 617–619.
    bonorum, see Bonorum possessio.
    cum re or sine re, 795.
    unde cognati, 794.
        legitimi, 794.
        liberi, 794.
        vir et uxor, 794.
Possession, 571–596, 643.
    its acquisition, 578–580.
    elements, 577.
    quasi, 698.
    its loss, 581–584.
    protection, 585–596.
    relation to ownership, 571, 572, 587.
Postumus, 774, 786.
Postulatio judicis, see Judicis postulatio.
Praedes litis ac vindiciarum, 605.
Praedia, 375.
Praedial servitudes, see Servitudes.
Praefectures, 86, 204.
Praefectus annonae, urbi, praetorio, 86, 473.
Praescriptio, 513–517.
Prescription, 175, 642–648, 661, 662, 697, 709.
Praesides, 50, 86, 474, 564.
Praetor, 45, 46–50, 314, 349, 469–472, 505, 518–521, 524, 565.

Praetor, fideicommissarius, 471, 814.
    hastarius, 483.
    peregrinus, 470, 505, 565.
    urbanus, 198, 470, 565.
Praetorian edicts, 48, 50, 83.
    jurisdiction, 470, 471.
    prefect, 86.
Princeps, see Emperor.
Privilegia, 389, 390, 423, 853.
Procedure, 465.
    legis actiones, 482–502.
    formulary, 503–563.
    extraordinary, 564–566.
    per formulam arbitrariam, 610.
    sponsionem, 609.
Proculus, 79, 80.
Proculeians and Sabinians, 79, 80, 674.
Procurator, 554.
Prodigus, 404–408, 772.
Pronuntiatio, 524, 611, 647.
Property, 438; see Res.
Proprietas, see Ownership.
Provinces, 60, 69.
Prudentes, see Jurisconsults.
Publicatio bonorum, see Bonorum publicatio.
Publiciana actio, 620–623.
Publicius, 620.

Quarta, Antonina, 311.
    Falcidia, 880.
    Pegasiana, 817, 880.
Querela inofficiosi testamenti, 789.
Quaestio, 54, 55.
Quaestiones perpetuae, 54, 55, 471.
Quaestor sacri palatii, 87.
Quinquaginta decisiones, 99.
Quiritary ownership, 597, 598, 602.
Quirites, 5, 184.

Real contracts, 454.
Rector, 86.
Recuperatores, 154, 479–481.

324 INDEX

Regula Catoniana, 890, 891.
Rei vindicatio, 318, 587, 604–619, 645, 647, 671, 858.
Remancipatio, see Mancipatio.
Replicatio, 512, 623.
Representation in court, see Courts.
Repudium, see Divorce.
Res, 424–463.
    corporeal and incorporeal, 430.
    definition of, 424.
    divini juris, 426.
    division of, 425–427.
    humani juris, 426, 427.
    mancipi, nec mancipi, 429, 629, 635.
    nullius, 425, 674.
Rescripts, 74.
Responsa prudentum, 65-67, 77, 78.
Restitutio in integrum, 314, 349, 376, 410, 416, 418.
    natalium, 162.
Reus, 504.
Rex, 10, 11.
Rights, 430.
    division of, 430.
    in rem, in personam, 431–438.
Rogatio, 60.
Rome, 2–5, 52, 86, 204.
Romulus, 2, 4.
Rural servitudes, see Servitudes.

Sabinus, 79, 80.
    Coelius, 80.
Sacramentum, 487, 604, 819.
Sacra privata, 252.
Sacrificia, 216.
Sale, 462.
Salvius Julianus, 81, 83.
Savigny, 588, 591.
Scaevola, 213.
Secession of the plebs, 26, 27.
Senate, early Roman, 3, 10, 11.
    in relation to the Emperor, 68, 69, 71, 84, 85.
    under the Republic, 22, 30, 43, 55.
Senatusconsulta, 63, 71–73.

Senatusconsultum, Juventianum, 821.
    Macedonianum, 71.
    Neronianum, 71, 72, 874.
    Orphitianum, 275.
    Pegasianum, 71, 817.
    Plancianum, 290.
    Tertullianum, 275.
    Trebellianum, 71, 72, 816.
    Velleianum, 71, 847.
Separatio bonorum, 801, 811, 812.
Servitudes, effects of, 688, 689.
    indivisibility of, 690.
    interdicts as to, 731–734.
    negative, 680–683, 703.
    pactis et stipulationibus, 699, 700.
    personal, 705–746.
    positive, 680–685, 698, 703.
    praedial, 676–704.
        special cases of, 687.
    rural, 678, 679, 683, 703.
    urban, 678, 679, 683, 703.
Servus publicus, see Slavery.
Servius Tullius, 17, 18, 24.
Slavery, 6, 16, 107, 139, 770, 775, 777.
    its mitigation, 112.
    penal, 130.
    public slaves, 114, 770, 775.
    quasi, 131–139.
Specificatio, 667.
Spendthrift, see Prodigus.
Sponsio, 609, 819.
Statuliberi, 147.
Status, 104, 105.
Stipulatio, 387, 449, 457, 461, 815.
    aquiliana, 461.
Stoic philosophy, 111.
Substitution of heirs, 756–760.
Succession, 747–823.
    acceptance and disclaimer, 799–812.

INDEX

Succession, actions as to, 819–823.
    civil law of, 793.
    defined, 747.
    fideicommissa of, 813–818.
    imperial law of, 797.
    interstate, 791–798.
    law of Justinian, 798.
    praetorian, 794.
    tax on, 182.
    testate, 747–790.
    to Empire established by Diocletian, 85.
Sui heredes, 258, 570, 785–790, 793, 802.
Summons, see Vocatio in jure.
Superficies, 735, 736.
Suspecti crimen, see Crimen suspecti.

Tax on successions, see Successions.
Testament, see Wills.
Testamenti factio, 185, 769–777.
Testamentum calatis comitiis, 761, 771.
    destitutum, 782, 800.
    inofficiosum, 781, 789.
    in procinctu, 764.
    irritum, 780.
    per aes et libram, 762.
    praetorium, 766.
    ruptum, 777, 796.
Theodosius I, 92.
    II, 88, 89, 662.
Theophilus, 43, 98.
Things, see Res.
Tiberius, 43.
Titulus justus, see Justus titulus.
Traditio, 635–639, 827.
    quasi, 700.
Trial, see Procedure.
Tribes of Rome, 2, 3, 217.
Tribonian, 96.
Tribus (quarters of Rome) 2, 32, 161.
Tribunes, 28–30, 44.
Tripertita, 66.

Turpitudo, 354.
Tutela, 356–397.
    of minors, 357–392.
        women, 260, 251, 393–397.
Tutors, see Tutela.
Twelve Tables, 13, 15, 34–38, 385, 444, 490, 498, 570, 626, 640, 644, 656, 657, 783.

Ulpian, 82, 839.
Universitas, see Corporations.
Urban servitudes, see Servitudes.
User, non, see Non-user.
Usucapio, 640, 641, 644–659, 661, 662, 696, 700.
    libertatis, 702–704.
Usufructus, 706–722.
Usureceptio, 659–661.
Usurpatio, 247.
Usus, 245–248, 697, 698, 723.

Valentinian III, 89.
Varro, 5.
Venditio bonorum, 561, 562, 800.
Venia aetatis, 420, 421.
Verbal contracts, 449, 452, 459.
Vicarius, 86.
Vicesima hereditatum, 182.
Vindex, 494, 495.
Vindicatio, 318, 820, 858; see Rei vindicatio.
    utilis, 624.
Vindicta, 143.
Vocatio in jure, 499, 550, 566.

Wills, 145, 748, 761–790; see Fideicommissa.
    calatis comitiis, 761, 771.
    codicils, 861–864.
    freedom to make a will, 783–790.
    how invalidated, 778–782.
    in procinctu, 764.
    nuncupative, 765, 766.
    opening of, 884.
    per aes et libram, 762.
    praetorian, 766.
    Later Empire, 767.
    legacies, 865–875, 877–881, 882–900.

Wills, nomination of heir, 768.
   testamenti factio, 769–777.
   tripartite, 767.
   women, 771, 774, 776.

Witnesses, in wills, 353.
Women, see Donationes, Dos, Marriage, Patria potestas, Wills.
Written and unwritten law, 13, 15, 35, 37.

www.ingramcontent.com/pod-product-compliance
Lightning Source LLC
Chambersburg PA
CBHW022103150426
43195CB00008B/241